Banking On It

THE TEN MOST COMMON CLAIMS INVOLVING BANKS

EDITED BY
Brett D. Watson

AMERICAN BAR ASSOCIATION
Litigation Section

Cover design by Carolina Martinez/ABA Design

Printed in the United States of America.

28 27 26 25 24 5 4 3 2 1

Library of Congress Cataloging-in-Publication Data

Names: Watson, Brett D., author. | American Bar Association. Section of Litigation, issuing body.
Title: Banking on it : the ten most common claims involving banks / Brett D. Watson.
Description: 1st edition. | Chicago, IL. : American Bar Association, Section Litigation, 2024. | Includes index. | Summary: "Banks provide many different products and services, so there are myriad of ways that litigation can result. This book addresses ten of the most common areas in which banks, lenders, and other financial institutions face litigation, with one chapter dedicated to each area. Our goal with each chapter is to provide an overview of the relevant area of the law as well as practical advice on the issues that usually arise. Each chapter also includes a discussion of the strategies that practitioners usually employ when faced with a case in that area. Because each chapter essentially stands alone as a primer on litigation in a particular area, a practitioner can consult each chapter independently as issues arise. Alternatively, a "front to back" reading of this book will orient a practitioner to the issues that are most likely to arise in this area over time and will give guidance on issues to look for when counseling clients"-- Provided by publisher.
Identifiers: LCCN 2024013256 (print) | LCCN 2024013257 (ebook) | ISBN 9781639054893 (paperback) | ISBN 9781639054909 (epub)
Subjects: LCSH: Banking law--United States. | Banks and banking--State supervision--United States. | Foreclosure--United States. | Mortgages--United States
Classification: LCC KF974 .W38 2024 (print) | LCC KF974 (ebook) | DDC 346.73/082--dc23/eng/20240326

LC record available at https://lccn.loc.gov/2024013256
LC ebook record available at https://lccn.loc.gov/2024013257

Contents

Acknowledgments

I wish to acknowledge the individual chapter authors and the American Bar Association Litigation Section editors, without whose hard work and dedication this book would not exist, as well as Aaron Krauss, who not only authored a chapter himself but also encouraged me to write the book in the first instance and provided invaluable guidance on how to do so.

Brett D. Watson
—Editor

Introduction

Banks provide many different products and services, so there are a myriad of ways that litigation can result. This book addresses ten of the most common areas in which banks, lenders, and other financial institutions face litigation, with one chapter dedicated to each area. Our goal with each chapter is to provide an overview of the relevant area of the law as well as practical advice on the issues that usually arise. Each chapter also includes a discussion of the strategies that practitioners usually employ when faced with a case in that area. Because each chapter essentially stands alone as a primer on litigation in a particular area, a practitioner can consult each chapter independently as issues arise. Alternatively, a "front to back" reading of this book will orient a practitioner to the issues that are most likely to arise in this area over time and will give guidance on issues to look for when counseling clients.

Chapter 1 addresses check claims. The chapter begins by addressing the contractual relationship between a bank and its customers, along with the general duties regarding authorized versus unauthorized checks, and then discusses the forged check claim procedure and the Uniform Commercial Code provisions that govern the liability analysis. This discussion includes the duties borne by both customers and banks, as well as the balancing of fault. Finally, the chapter concludes with a discussion of tort-based claims, typically sounding in negligence, and claims brought by noncustomers.

Chapter 2 addresses wire fraud. A general discussion of the relevant provisions of the Uniform Commercial Code is provided, including remittance procedures and authorized versus unauthorized payment orders. The bulk of the chapter focuses on security procedures and how to analyze whether those procedures are commercially reasonable and/or executed in good faith. The chapter concludes with a discussion of the liability of beneficiary banks and common law claims.

Chapter 3 addresses credit and debit card claims. The chapter begins with a description of the typical claim involving credit or debit card fraud and how claims are analyzed under the Electronic Funds Transfer Act, the Truth in Lending Act, the Fair Credit Billing Act, and Regulation Z. It also discusses claims brought under the Fair Debt Collection Practices Act and the Equal Credit Opportunities Act.

Chapter 4 addresses lender claims. The chapter separately discusses claims arising out of the loan application process and claims arising during the life of the loan. During the application process, claims can arise regarding the formation of the contract itself, sounding in negligence, negligent misrepresentation, fraud or fraudulent inducement, breach of fiduciary duty, or redlining claims. During the life of the loan, claims can arise related to loan modification, promissory estoppel, or breach of contract. The chapter concludes with a discussion of workout issues and claims arising out of loan default.

Chapter 5 discusses commercial real estate loan defaults. A discussion of loan classification leads into collection issues (including election of remedies) followed by judicial and nonjudicial foreclosure issues. The chapter closes with a discussion of the one-action rule and anti-deficiency statutes.

Chapter 6 discusses employment claims. After summarizing how banks are different than other defendants in the context of employment claims, including the fact that banks have cameras everywhere, have written policies on almost everything, and are heavily regulated, the chapter discusses discrimination claims, including direct versus retaliation claims, Title VII, Section 1981, the ADEA, the FMLA, and the ADA. The chapter concludes with a discussion of state law claims and wage and hour claims.

Chapter 7 discusses safe deposit box claims. Although safe deposit boxes are not as common today as they were in years past, they do remain in use, and claims do arise from time to time. The chapter opens with a general discussion regarding what safe deposit boxes are and who has access to them. The chapter then discusses duties owed by banks and potential liability to safe deposit box customers, followed by a discussion about accessing a safe deposit box after the death of the customer. The chapter ends with a discussion of the limited bank duty associated with monitoring the contents of a safe deposit box.

Chapter 8 addresses fiduciary claims against banks. Specifically, it discusses the fiduciary duty claims that can arise out of the many roles often assumed by banks: banks as investment advisers, banks as lenders/creditors, banks as trustees, banks as ERISA trustees, and banks as transfer agents, registrars, or executors.

Chapter 9 addresses the issue of third-party discovery of banks. The chapter lays the foundation for why a bank typically will not respond to discovery requests/demands absent a legal obligation to do so, and why the responses will typically be narrowly tailored. Next is a discussion of service of process requirements, the methods by which banks will accept service of process, and the different standards that may apply to various discovery methods. Finally, the chapter provides valuable insight into the pitfalls that many lawyers face when drafting third-party discovery requests.

Finally, Chapter 10 addresses class actions. The chapter methodically walks the reader through the entire process, beginning with initiating a class action lawsuit and the requirements of numerosity, commonality, typicality, and adequacy of representation, along with the consideration of whether to file in state or federal court. Guidance on whether to answer or seek to dismiss a class action complaint is provided, including issues regarding litigation holds and early settlement discussions, which leads into a discussion of damages. The chapter ends with a discussion of alternative dispute resolution procedures and settlement strategy.

Brett D. Watson†

† Brett D. Watson is a commercial litigator who practices in Cozen O'Connor's Santa Monica office, where he also serves as chair of the firm's Retail Banking Practice. For more than two decades, top banks, credit card issuers, and financial institutions across the United States have called upon him to litigate issues relating to the full spectrum of their retail financial products. In his spare time, Brett enjoys going on hikes or to the beach with his wife and daughter, and he considers himself a stand-up comedy aficionado. This chapter should not be construed as giving legal advice. If you would like to receive legal advice, contact Brett directly. Brett can be reached at (213) 892-7938 or bwatson@cozen.com. The views expressed are Brett's alone and are not necessarily the views of Cozen O'Connor.

Check Claims

1

Brett D. Watson[†]

Bob Bookkeeper worked for ABC Widgets, Inc., a relatively small company that manufactured widgets. It was a dream job for Bob Bookkeeper because his boss trusted him to manage the company's books and finances with little supervision, giving Bob Bookkeeper a real sense of autonomy and accomplishment.

Bob Bookkeeper did it all. He managed all of ABC's deposit accounts and reconciliations, handled all accounts payable and receivable, and handled ABC's corporate credit card accounts. He kept ABC's finances running smoothly so that management could focus its time on developing more and better widgets.

† Brett D. Watson is a commercial litigator who practices in Cozen O'Connor's Santa Monica office, where he also serves as chair of the firm's Retail Banking Practice. For more than two decades, top banks, credit card issuers, and financial institutions across the United States have called upon him to litigate issues relating to the full spectrum of their retail financial products. In his spare time, Brett enjoys going on hikes or to the beach with his wife and daughter, and he considers himself a stand-up comedy aficionado. This chapter should not be construed as giving legal advice. If you would like to receive legal advice, contact Brett directly. Brett can be reached at (213) 892-7938 or bwatson@cozen.com. The views expressed in this chapter are Brett's alone and are not necessarily the views of Cozen O'Connor.

One day, Bob Bookkeeper found himself in an unexpected and difficult situation. He was a bit short on funds for the month and needed an extra $200 to pay his rent. Unable to borrow money from friends or family, Bob Bookkeeper started to panic. He tried to calm his nerves by placing deeper focus on his job, and he started to review the pile of accounts receivable on his desk:

$148 from Charlie Customer
$396 refund from Victor Vendor
$200 from Kevin Kustomer

$200? $200! Ugh, the exact amount of money needed to pay his rent.

Bob Bookkeeper went to his bank and sat down with a business banker. Bob explained that he wanted to open a business checking account in the name of ABC Widgets, LLC. After the bank obtained the necessary paperwork to ensure it had complied with its Know Your Customer protocols[1] (for more on this, see "Forged Payee Checks" in this chapter), Bob walked out of the bank with a shiny new checking account in the name of ABC Widgets, LLC.

Bob Bookkeeper took the $200 check from Kevin Kustomer, conveniently payable only to "ABC Widgets" instead of "ABC Widgets, Inc." and deposited it into his new ABC Widgets, LLC account. One day later, Bob transferred the money to his personal checking account and successfully paid his rent. Crisis averted.

Despite feeling some guilt, Bob Bookkeeper took comfort in knowing that it was highly unlikely he would ever get caught. After all, it is *just* $200, and he handled all of ABC's finances. Some time passed, and when Bob's car broke down, he needed an extra $800 for the repairs. He got away with taking $200. Could he get away with $800 as well? Bob devised another plan. He told his boss that ABC had a rodent problem in one of its warehouses, and he needed a check for $800 to pay the exterminator. Bob's boss presented Bob with a signed check for $800 with the payee line left blank. Bob returned to his office, wrote his own name on the payee line, deposited the check, and paid for the repairs to his vehicle with the funds.

---

1. The paperwork includes, but is not necessarily limited to, the LLC's formation documents and ownership agreements, any necessary business license, and the Employer Identification Number (EIN).

But what happens when ABC's bank issues a monthly account statement? Wouldn't a copy of the $800 check payable to Bob be included? Not to worry. Bob got the mail and had exclusive control over reconciling the accounts. Bob would simply dispose of the check, and ABC would be none the wiser.

Additional time passed, and Bob started to dwell on how easy it was to take the money, and the fact that he had gotten away with taking $1,000 from his employer. He developed other schemes and created fake vendors. More boldly, Bob began to forge his boss's signature on certain checks made payable to himself. Bob engaged in each of these scams each month, and with each passing month of not getting caught, his confidence grew, and eventually he was siphoning thousands of dollars away from ABC Widgets each month . . . for years.

One day, Oliver Owner, the owner of ABC Widgets, read on his favorite local news website that Evan Exterminator passed away. But wait, Oliver remembered signing a check yesterday that Bob Bookkeeper said was intended for Evan Exterminator. How could that be if Evan passed away a few days ago? Oliver went to speak with Bob, and Bob's entire scheme fell apart. Oliver hired a forensic accountant to examine their books, and Oliver learned that Bob had stolen over $500,000 from ABC Widgets over the course of more than two years.

Oliver is furious and wants Bob to be imprisoned. Oliver wants to sue anyone and everyone under the sun: Bob, Bob's bank, and even ABC's own bank. How could this happen? Oliver trusted Bob, and now his business has suffered this enormous loss. This loss certainly wasn't his fault—after all, he hired Bob to handle his company's finances. What else could he have done? Or was it his fault? Should he have supervised Bob Bookkeeper and placed tighter controls over his company's finances? It is time to go see Lisa Lawyer.

Lisa Lawyer is sitting at her desk when Oliver Owner walks in. Lisa has been representing Oliver for a long time and considers Oliver to be one of her favorite clients. She is eager to help. Oliver explains everything—how he did a full criminal background check on Bob Bookkeeper that came back clean, how he hired Bob to take care of ABC's finances, and that he trusted that Bob was an honest person who would handle ABC's finances responsibly. How could Bob do this and get away with it? Why didn't ABC's bank notify Oliver of potentially suspicious activity? Lisa Lawyer dug in.

I. CLAIMS AGAINST ABC'S BANK: THE GENERAL RULE

Lisa Lawyer explains to Oliver Owner the general rule that a customer is not liable for a check drawn on his account if he did not sign the check or otherwise benefit from its proceeds, a rule that dates back centuries.[2] Perfect, Oliver exclaims! He did not sign any of these checks, and ABC certainly did not benefit from any of the proceeds. Will ABC's bank reimburse ABC for its losses?

Well, not so fast, cautions Lisa Lawyer. It is not quite that easy. Oliver cannot simply walk into ABC's bank, inform a banker that he did not personally sign or benefit from $500,000 in checks, and expect the bank to reimburse him. Lisa Lawyer explains there are many considerations and defenses.[3]

A. The Account Agreement

Lisa Lawyer explains to Oliver Owner that his relationship with ABC's bank is founded on contract, and that the contract will, at least in part, determine the extent to which, if any, he can recover against ABC's bank. The contractual relationship between a bank and its depositors (i.e., customers) is memorialized by a signature card that the depositor signs upon opening an account.[4] The signature card identifies all of the authorized signers (owners) of the account and is provided by the bank to the depositor concurrent with a standard deposit account agreement (typically referred to as the DAA). Although the specific language varies from bank to bank, the signature card will include language to the effect that by signing the signature card and/or by utilizing the account, the customer agrees to be bound by the terms of the DAA. The DAA outlines the rights and responsibilities of the bank and the depositor.

B. Forged Check Claim Procedure

Anxious to get started, Oliver Owner asks Lisa Lawyer how he should commence a claim against ABC's bank for payment on the forged checks. The

2. Price v. Neal, 97 Eng. Rep. 871 (K.B. 1762).

3. The claims and defenses discussed in this chapter are not in any way meant to be exhaustive. Rather, this chapter is meant to be explorative and touches upon many of the most common issues presented in a typical check claim case.

4. *See, e.g.*, Chazen v. Centennial Bank, 61 Cal. App. 4th 532, 543 (1998).

first step in the process is typically to obtain, fill out, and sign an Affidavit of Forgery, as will be explained in the customer's DAA. A typical Affidavit of Forgery will identify the customer, the account number, and provide detailed descriptions of the allegedly forged checks. The customer must provide a declaration affirming that the checks are forged, and the forms will typically include a space for the customer to highlight if there are any persons suspected of the wrongdoing.

Lisa Lawyer advises that Oliver Owner should immediately obtain original copies, both front and back, of all forged checks (if available). Oliver Owner must identify the time period over which the loss occurred—i.e., the date of the first allegedly forged check and the date of the most recent allegedly forged check.

It is a relatively painless procedure, after which the bank will begin its investigation into the customer's forgery claim. It is possible, although not required, that the bank will issue the customer a provisional credit during its investigation. If the bank concludes that the customer is a victim of fraudulent activity, the bank may elect (with or without notice to the customer) to close or suspend the account to prevent further fraudulent activity. Under certain circumstances, the bank may simply give the customer the *option* of closing the account to prevent future fraudulent activity. It should be noted that if the customer refuses to close the account for whatever reason (e.g., if the customer insists that changing account numbers would be too big of a burden), then the bank will likely refuse to honor any potential future fraud claims, arguing that such losses were preventable if the customer had elected to close the account. Lisa Lawyer explains that the bank will look to the DAA and the applicable provisions of the Uniform Commercial Code as defenses to the claim.

C. Duty to Review Monthly Account Statements

One of the most routine duties placed upon depositors in *every* DAA is the duty to timely review monthly account statements. Lisa Lawyer asks Oliver to provide her with a copy of the DAA governing ABC's business checking account. Sure enough, there is a provision that customers are required to review their monthly account statements and report any abnormalities to the bank within thirty days of the date the account statement is made available. The "made available" language is particularly important in the internet age, because a depositor may no longer receive actual paper copies of its monthly account statements by mail. Instead, the customer may simply receive an email or other notification that the monthly account statement is available for viewing online. This notification is enough to trigger the commencement of the customer's thirty-day time period within which to review its statements and report abnormalities to the bank.

In addition to the contractual requirement in the customer's DAA, this duty has also been codified in the Uniform Commercial Code, which has been largely adopted (subject to, in most cases, relatively minor revisions) in all states.[5] Section 4-406 of the Uniform Commercial Code provides that if a bank "sends or makes available a statement of account or items" the

> customer must exercise reasonable promptness in examining the statement or the items to determine whether any payment was not authorized because of an alteration of an item or because a purported signature by or on behalf of the customer was not authorized. If, based on the statement or items provided, the customer should reasonably have discovered the unauthorized payment, the customer must promptly notify the bank of the relevant facts.[6]

Lisa Lawyer looks cautiously at Oliver Owner and asks, "Did you review your monthly account statements provided by ABC's bank?" Upset, Oliver explains that he has never looked at a single monthly account statement issued by ABC's bank. After all, he hired Bob Bookkeeper to take care of that responsibility.

Bookkeeper Knowledge Is Imputed to Account Holder

Lisa Lawyer explains that this is a common position taken by most business owners—i.e., that they hired an otherwise qualified bookkeeper who they trusted to take care of the company's finances. Unfortunately for Oliver, this argument will get him nowhere. It has long been settled that where the wrongdoer (in this case, Bob Bookkeeper) has been vested with authority concerning the bank account, any knowledge that a faithful employee would have gleaned from the information available to

5. *See Uniform Commercial Code Adoption*, Wikipedia, https://en.wikipedia.org/wiki/Uniform_Commercial_Code_adoption.

6. *See* Uniform Commercial Code § 4-406(c). Depending on the state, there may be some slight variations in a state's references to sections of the Uniform Commercial Code. For example, California does not utilize dashes in statutory section numbers. Therefore, Section 4-406 is referred to as Section 4406 in the California Commercial Code.

the wrongdoer is imputed to their principal.[7] This has been plainly and unequivocally stated by many courts:

> When the agent to whom the duty of examination is intrusted [*sic*] is a dishonest employee who by forgery has obtained funds of his employer from the bank, and whose consequent adverse interest causes him to conceal from his employer the circumstances which would naturally have been disclosed in the course of a proper verification, the employer, though not imputed with knowledge of the fraud of his faithless agent, is, as principal, chargeable with such information as an honest employee, unaware of the wrongdoing, would have acquired from an examination of the cancelled checks and bank statements.[8]

Accordingly, even though Oliver Owner hired Bob Bookkeeper to handle ABC's finances, Oliver Owner, as the principal of ABC, is imputed with the knowledge that a *faithful* employee would have obtained from an examination of the monthly account statements issued by ABC's bank.[9] Oliver Owner's argument that he personally failed to review his monthly account statements because he had hired Bob Bookkeeper to handle that function is a losing argument.

Balance of Duties

Recognizing that Oliver Owner is starting to squirm at the thought of losing $500,000 due to Bob Bookkeeper's conduct, Lisa Lawyer quickly moves on to a discussion regarding the impact of Section 4-406(c). Uniform Commercial Code § 4-406(d) provides that if the bank can prove that the customer failed to comply with the requirements of Section 4-406(c) by failing to timely review its monthly account statements and report any abnormalities to the bank, the customer is precluded from asserting a claim against the bank for that item.[10] However, if the customer can establish that the bank failed to exercise ordinary care in paying the item *and* that

7. *See, e.g.*, Kiernan v. Union Bank, 55 Cal. App. 3d 111 (1976).

8. *See, e.g.*, Basch v. Bank of America, 22 Cal. 2d 316, 327 (1943).

9. Note that, unlike California, certain jurisdictions carve out an exception if the employee was acting solely in their own interest, so be sure to check how strictly this rule is applied in your state.

10. *See* UNIFORM COMMERCIAL CODE § 4-406(d)(1).

the failure substantially contributed to the loss, the loss may be allocated between the customer and the bank according to the extent to which each contributed to the loss.[11] Oliver Owner starts to perk up a bit.

Oliver Owner reaches into his briefcase and pulls out a handful of checks forged by Bob Bookkeeper and lays them out on Lisa Lawyer's desk. He then shows Lisa Lawyer an exemplar of his own signature. Oliver believes that Bob Bookkeeper did a pretty poor job of forging his signature and believes ABC's bank should have been able to determine that the signatures were forgeries. "Ordinary care" is defined at Uniform Commercial Code § 1201(b)(2) as the observance of reasonable commercial standards prevailing in the area. In the case of a bank that takes checks for processing via automated means (such as acceptance via an Automatic Teller Machine [ATM]), reasonable commercial standards *do not* require the bank to examine each check so long as the bank's failure to do so does not violate the bank's internal policies and procedures and the bank's procedures do not vary unreasonably from general banking usage.[12] Because most banks accept checks via automated means, and because most banks accept at least several thousand checks per day via such means, it is generally accepted that most banks are not required to examine each check.[13] As such, the notion that the signatures may be obvious forgeries does not equate with a finding that the bank failed to exercise reasonable commercial standards in processing the check. Lisa Lawyer therefore advises Oliver Owner that it will be vitally important to determine the manner in which each check was deposited, whether electronically or over the counter.

The Repeater Rule

Lisa Lawyer then delivers information on the next hurdle—the Repeater Rule. Building on the rule set forth at Uniform Commercial Code § 4-406(d)(1) that a customer cannot recover against a bank if the customer failed to timely review the monthly account statements, Uniform Commercial Code § 4-406(d)(2) provides that if the same wrongdoer forges a series of checks over a period of time, and the customer fails to identify and report the first of such checks to the bank within a reasonable amount

11. *See id.* § 4-406(e). Further, depending on the state, this analysis can be one of contributory negligence, comparative negligence, or a straight bar to recovery.

12. *See, e.g.*, Story Road Flea Market, Inc. v. Wells Fargo Bank, N.A., 42 Cal. App. 4th 1733 (1996).

13. *Id.*

of time, not exceeding thirty days following the provision of the first statement reflecting the forgery, the customer is precluded from recovering as to any of the subsequent checks.[14]

Bob Bookkeeper was forging Oliver Owner's signature on checks for more than two years, and Oliver Owner's ability to recover will be substantially limited by the fact that Oliver Owner failed to identify and report the first of such checks to ABC's bank. Lisa Lawyer explains that the logic behind this rule is quite simple: if Oliver Owner had properly examined his monthly account statements in a timely manner, he would have learned of Bob Bookkeeper's forgeries after a very short amount of time had passed—at a time when the total loss was minimal. Instead, Oliver Owner's failure to review his monthly account statements allowed Bob Bookkeeper to continue his forgery scheme for more than two years. Hence, what could have been a *de minimus* loss has ballooned into a $500,000 loss.[15]

Issue Preclusion

Oliver Owner is growing tired of hearing bad news and asks Lisa Lawyer to shift back to the discussion about apportionment of losses. Oliver wonders if he can recover against ABC's bank if they can demonstrate that ABC's bank did fail to follow reasonable commercial standards. Uniform Commercial Code § 4406(f) provides that

> [w]ithout regard to care or lack of care of either the customer or the bank, a customer who does not within one year after the statement or items are made available to the customer (subsection (a)) discover and report the customer's unauthorized signature on or any alteration on the item is precluded from asserting against the bank the unauthorized signature or alteration.[16]

---

14. *See* Uniform Commercial Code § 4-406(d)(2). This thirty-day period can be reduced by the bank's account agreement with its customers. For example, in New York many banks use a fourteen-day period. If a bank lists a period of less than fourteen days, such a restriction may be difficult to enforce.

15. *See, e.g.*, Espresso Roma Corp. v. Bank of America, 100 Cal. App. 4th 525 (2002).

16. *See* Uniform Commercial Code § 4-406(f). Practitioners should note that Section 4-406(f) is not a statute of limitations; it is an issue-preclusion statute. As such, equitable tolling does not apply. Further, it is a separate affirmative defense and must be pled separately from the statute of limitations. If the bank fails to plead it as a separate affirmative defense, it is possible that a court will deem it waived. *See, e.g.*, Pinigis v.

Here, because Oliver Owner failed to detect Bob Bookkeeper's forgeries and report the unauthorized transactions to ABC's bank for more than two years, Oliver Owner will be precluded from recovering against ABC's bank regardless of ABC's bank's alleged lack of care.

Statute of Limitations

Another timing defense is a traditional statute of limitations defense. California, for example, added forged check claims to its broader one-year statute of limitations statute: "[w]ithin one year . . . [a]n action . . . by a depositor against a bank for the payment of a forged or raised check, or a check that bears a forged or unauthorized endorsement . . ."[17] While many statutes of limitations can be tolled or otherwise extended by, for example, a delayed discovery rule, California courts have consistently interpreted Section 340 to mean exactly what it says: the statute of limitations is one year, without exception.[18]

At this point, Lisa Lawyer must deliver the unfortunate news that, absent some other extraordinary facts, Oliver Owner has no viable claims against ABC's bank for the forged maker checks.

II. CLAIMS AGAINST BOB BOOKKEEPER'S BANK

Convinced that his claims against his own bank likely lack merit, Oliver Owner now shifts the discussion to Bob Bookkeeper's bank. Can Oliver Owner pursue any claims against Bob Bookkeeper's bank?

Lisa Lawyer dives in. She explains that claims by Oliver Owner against the depositary bank (the term used to describe Bob Bookkeeper's bank, as the bank of first deposit) are governed by an entirely different set of rules, and for obvious reasons. Bob Bookkeeper's bank does not provide account statements to Oliver Owner, so Oliver Owner is not obligated (or able) to

---

Regions Bank, 977 So. 2d 466 (Ala. 2007). Practitioners should also note that this one-year time period can be reduced by the bank in the applicable DAA, as permitted by Uniform Commercial Code § 4-103(a). Such reductions have been upheld by numerous courts throughout the country. *See, e.g.*, American Airlines Employees Fed. Credit Union v. Martin, 29 S.W.3d 86 (Tex. 2000).

17. *See* California Civil Code § 340(c).

18. *See, e.g.*, Roy Supply, Inc. v. Wells Fargo Bank, N.A., 39 Cal. App. 4th 1051 (1995); *Kiernan*, 55 Cal. App. 3d 111.

review any set of documents to determine if Bob Bookkeeper is engaged in wrongdoing. And certain types of fraud committed by bookkeepers would never be disclosed in an account statement. Remember that Bob Bookkeeper took a $200 check from Kevin Kustomer payable to ABC Widgets and deposited that check into an account he opened in the name of ABC Widgets, LLC. It is possible (although unlikely) that Karl Kustomer might discover this fraud, but Oliver Owner will be unable to discover this fraud because such a check would never be presented to Oliver Owner for review—the negotiated check did not flow through ABC's account. Because of this and other such facts, claimants will frequently attempt to shift a loss from themselves to the depositary bank.

A. Forged Payee Checks

Bob's forgery represents the classic example of a forged payee check. Kevin Kustomer issued a check payable to ABC Widgets. He, of course, intended the check to be payable to ABC Widgets, Inc., but only wrote ABC Widgets on the check itself. Bob Bookkeeper capitalized on that limitation by opening a business checking account in the name of ABC Widgets, LLC and deposited the check into that account for his own use. Kevin Kustomer's bank would not be liable for such a loss because the payor bank does not have a duty to check payee endorsements.[19] And Oliver Owner's bank would not be liable for that loss because that check was never presented to Oliver Owner's bank. But what about Bob Bookkeeper's bank?

If Bob Bookkeeper's bank accepted the check presented by Bob Bookkeeper into Bob's ABC Widgets, LLC, account in good faith and in accordance with reasonable commercial standards, recovery may be precluded. The primary issue here is whether Bob Bookkeeper's bank followed reasonable commercial procedures in allowing Bob to open an account in the name of ABC Widgets, LLC. Did Bob have the proper and necessary documents to establish his ownership or control of an entity by that name? Did Bob provide the bank with the LLC's formation documents and ownership agreements? Did Bob provide a copy of any necessary business license? What about the necessary Employer Identification Number (EIN)? If all the paperwork was in order, Bob Bookkeeper's bank likely acted in accordance with reasonable commercial standards in allowing the account to be opened, and recovery is precluded. However, if any of these items were

19. *See, e.g.*, Guardian Life Ins. Co. of America v. Weisman, 223 F.3d 229 (3d Cir. 2000).

missing and/or if any of these items contained obvious defects, recovery becomes a possibility.

Lisa Lawyer further explains to Oliver Owner that Bob Bookkeeper's bank may not be liable for accepting the checks payable to ABC Widgets into Bob Bookkeeper's ABC Widgets, LLC, account if the payor bank (in the above example, Kevin Kustomer's bank) is not liable to its customer. Accordingly, all the issues discussed above regarding the duty to examine monthly account statements, the duty to timely report unauthorized activity, and potential statutes of limitations come into play here as well.

B. Checks Payable to a Fictitious Payee

Another common scheme by bookkeepers is inducing the employer to properly endorse a check payable to a fictitious payee. The scheme operates like this: Bob Bookkeeper tells Oliver Owner that ABC Widgets needs to retain the use of Vivian Vendor for a specific purpose. Vivian Vendor does not exist; however, trusting Bob's representation, Oliver Owner actually signs a check payable to Vivian Vendor in the amount of $10,000. Bob Bookkeeper now opens a business checking account in the name of Vivian Vendor and deposits the check into that account for his own use.

Fictitious payee claims are governed by Uniform Commercial Code § 3-404. In this situation, no bank is liable in most circumstances because Oliver Owner's signature on the check is legitimate, and because he intended to issue a check payable to Vivian Vendor. The fact that Vivian Vendor does not exist does not translate to liability as against any bank unless, again, it can be established that Bob Bookkeeper's bank did not follow reasonable commercial standards in allowing an account to be opened in the name of Vivian Vendor.[20]

C. Claims Sounding in Negligence

The broader category of claims against Bob Bookkeeper's bank will sound in negligence based on the theory that Bob Bookkeeper's bank failed to follow reasonable commercial standards in processing the items. In addition to facing the same types of issues detailed above, claims sounding in negligence face a host of issues pertaining to the establishment of a duty.

20. *See* Uniform Commercial Code § 3-404.

Banks Owe a Duty of Care Only to Their Depositors

A bank owes a duty to use ordinary care in its transactions with depositors.[21] The duty is created by implication in the contract (the DAA) between the bank and its depositors.[22] Notably, "[t]his contractual relationship does not involve any implied duty 'to supervise account activity' or 'to inquire into the purpose for which the funds are being used.'"[23] Although a bank owes a duty to use ordinary care in its transactions with depositors, the California Court of Appeal also recently clarified that such duty extends only to utilizing care in transactions with the depositor's own account(s)—i.e., a bank does not owe a duty of care to a customer to monitor other depositors' accounts.[24]

In the context of check claims cases, Oliver Owner might wonder why Bob Bookkeeper's bank did not monitor Bob Bookkeeper's account usage or notice that Bob Bookkeeper would deposit money into his ABC Widgets, LLC, account only to then subsequently transfer the funds to his personal checking account. While there might be reasons why Bob Bookkeeper's bank was monitoring Bob Bookkeeper's account (e.g., for anti-money laundering purposes), such monitoring would be for the bank's own benefit, as required by the vast number of regulations imposed upon bank activity. There is no argument that Bob Bookkeeper's bank should have been monitoring Bob Bookkeeper's account for suspicious activity for the benefit of Oliver Owner or for any third party.

Banks Do Not Owe a Duty of Care to Noncustomers

Another general principle, sort of a corollary to the principle that banks owe duties only to depositors, is that banks do not owe a duty of care to noncustomers.[25] Banks do not even owe a duty of care to the officers or shareholders of a corporation that holds an account.[26] Taking this concept further, courts have likewise held that "a bank owes no duty to non-depositors to investigate or disclose suspicious activities on the part of an

---

21. *See, e.g.*, Chazen v. Centennial Bank, 61 Cal. App. 4th 532, 543 (1998).

22. *Id.*

23. *See, e.g.*, Barclay Kitchen, Inc. v. California Bank, 208 Cal. App. 2d 347 (1962).

24. Kurtz-Ahlers, LLC v. Bank of America, N.A., 48 Cal. App. 5th 952 (2020).

25. *See, e.g.*, Karen Kane, Inc. v. Bank of America Nat'l Trust and Savings Assoc., Inc., 67 Cal. App. 4th 1192 (1998).

26. *See, e.g.*, *Roy Supply*, 39 Cal. App. 4th 1051.

account holder."[27] The reasoning behind the refusal to recognize a duty by banks to inform on suspicious customers is the public policy of "avoid[ing] the loss of privacy, expense and commercial havoc that would result from such a holding."[28]

These concepts can often apply to check claims as well. For example, imagine that during the discovery phase it was revealed that Bob Bookkeeper's bank did suspect Bob Bookkeeper of fraud, and had, even temporarily, placed a freeze on Bob Bookkeeper's ABC Widgets, LLC, account. Neither that suspicion nor the account freeze would result in any *obligation* being imposed upon Bob Bookkeeper's bank to notify Oliver Owner of the suspected fraud.

Banks Do Not Owe Common Law Duty of Care to Protect Against Purely Economic Losses

In check fraud cases, it is relatively common to see a plaintiff attempt to assert a common law negligence claim against the depositary bank—i.e., a claim not based on the Uniform Commercial Code. However, courts have established a bar to the creation of a tort duty of care to protect against purely economic losses, otherwise known as the Economic Loss Rule.[29]

Outside the realm of contractual duties of care, in certain circumstances a defendant may owe a plaintiff a tort duty of care. However, the California Supreme Court has definitively held as a matter of law that a defendant does not owe a plaintiff a tort duty of care to protect against purely economic losses. "Purely economic loss" is shorthand for

> "pecuniary or commercial loss that does not arise from actionable physical, emotional or reputational injury to persons or physical injury to property." And although [defendant] of course had a duty to guard against the latter kinds of injury, we conclude it had no tort duty to guard against purely economic losses.[30]

---

27. *See, e.g.*, Casey v. U.S. Bank Nat'l Ass'n, 127 Cal. App. 4th 1138, 1149 (2005). Indeed, this goes beyond the issue of duty because a vast universe of bank regulations and privacy laws actually prevents a bank from disclosing activity to third parties, even if the bank wanted to make such a disclosure.

28. *Id.*

29. *See, e.g.*, Southern California Gas Leak Cases, 7 Cal. 5th 391 (2019).

30. *Id.*

Because Oliver Owner's losses are purely economic—i.e., neither he nor his company suffered any sort of physical, emotional, or reputational injury—it will be challenging to establish that Bob Bookkeeper's bank, or any bank, owed Oliver Owner a tort duty of care.

Banks Do Not Owe Fiduciary Duty to Customers or Noncustomers

In check claims cases, a plaintiff will frequently assert that the bank owed them some sort of fiduciary duty to protect against embezzlement and other financial crimes. It is black letter law that a bank does not even owe a fiduciary duty to its own depositors.[31] If a bank does not owe a fiduciary duty to its own depositors, there can be no colorable argument that it owes such a duty to a third party.

The Limited Duty of Care Owed to Third Parties

Perhaps the most popular case cited by plaintiffs in check claims cases, at least in California, is *Sun 'n Sand, Inc. v. United California Bank.*[32] Due to the case's prevalence, it is worth discussing in some detail. As an initial matter, it should be noted that the *Sun 'n Sand* decision is not considered precedential authority. The dispute in *Sun 'n Sand* was determined by only five justices (instead of the standard seven justices), and the lead opinion had the support of only two.[33] As such, courts have rejected the idea that *Sun 'n Sand* is precedential authority.[34]

Despite this fact, it is still heavily relied upon by plaintiffs and is still considered persuasive, if not binding, by many courts. The facts in *Sun 'n Sand* are similar to those involving Bob Bookkeeper. The plaintiffs were sister corporations that had the same shareholders and operated from the same premises. They hired an employee, Eloise Morales, whose duties involved preparing checks for signature by a corporate officer. Over a three-year period, Morales prepared nine checks payable to United California Bank. Each check was for a different, but relatively small, dollar amount. She obtained authorized signatures for each of the nine checks by representing that these small sums of money were actually owed by the corporation to United California Bank. After obtaining the authorized

---

31. *See, e.g.,* Price v. Wells Fargo Bank, 213 Cal. App. 3d 465 (1989).

32. Sun 'n Sand, Inc. v. United California Bank, 21 Cal. 3d 671 (1978).

33. *Id.*

34. *See, e.g., Roy Supply,* 39 Cal. App. 4th 1051.

signatures, Morales altered the checks by increasing the dollar amounts represented, and then deposited the checks into her own personal account at United California Bank. Although United California Bank remained the named payee on the checks, the bank "caused or permitted" the proceeds of the checks to be deposited into Eloise Morales's personal account.[35]

Following a detailed analysis of the facts, the two California Supreme Court justices that prepared the lead opinion articulated a "minimal" and "narrowly circumscribed rule": "it is activated only when checks, not insignificant in amount, are drawn payable to the order of a bank and presented to the payee bank by a third party seeking to negotiate checks for his own benefit."[36] Although originally limited to checks drawn payable to a bank—i.e., United California Bank—subsequent decisions have followed *Sun 'n Sand* and extended the rule to apply to any third party.[37] Courts have articulated the resulting minimal rule as follows: a bank may be liable for "allowing a person to deposit a check, payable to someone else, into a personal account, under circumstances that should have alerted the bank to the possibility of fraud."[38]

Oliver Owner wonders if Lisa Lawyer has finally articulated a possible basis for recovery against Bob Bookkeeper's bank. To make this determination, it is necessary to examine each of the forged checks in detail. If Bob Bookkeeper had asked Oliver Owner to sign checks payable to Fake Factory, Inc., by representing that ABC Widgets owed money to Fake Factory, Inc., and then was able to deposit those checks—again, payable to Fake Factory, Inc.—into his personal account at Bob Bookkeeper's bank (i.e., an account in the name of Bob Bookkeeper), then *Sun 'n Sand* and its progeny would provide some potential support for recovery against Bob Bookkeeper's bank. And because *Sun 'n Sand* provides for a three-year statute of limitations on the negligence claim and Bob Bookkeeper's fraud was discovered within less than three years, Oliver Owner would have a basis for recovery.[39] If, on the other hand, Bob Bookkeeper deposited checks into business accounts with names that closely resembled the named payees—for example, the checks he deposited into the ABC

35. *Sun 'n Sand*, 21 Cal. 3d 671.

36. *id.* at 695 (emphasis added).

37. *See* Joffe v. United California Bank, 141 Cal. App. 3d 541 (1983); E. F. Hutton & Co. v. City Nat'l Bank, 149 Cal. App. 3d 60 (1983); Sehremelis v. Farmers & Merchants Bank, 6 Cal. App. 4th 767 (1992).

38. *See, e.g.*, *Chazen*, 61 Cal. App. 4th at 543.

39. *Sun 'n Sand*, 21 Cal. 3d at 698.

Widgets, LLC, account—then the analysis reverts to that detailed earlier in this chapter. Bob also tricked Oliver into signing checks allegedly payable to Evan Exterminator, but the payee line was blank at the time Oliver signed the checks, and Bob subsequently added his own name. Neither of these scenarios are those envisioned by *Sun 'n Sand* and would not provide Oliver Owner a basis for pursuing a common law negligence claim against Bob Bookkeeper's bank.

III. WHAT DOES LISA LAWYER RECOMMEND?

Lisa Lawyer realizes that due diligence will require that she sit down with Oliver Owner and carefully analyze each and every check that was in any way forged or altered by Bob Bookkeeper before she can determine definitively if any claims can be properly stated against anyone other than Bob Bookkeeper himself. For now, Lisa Lawyer shifts from litigation mode into counseling mode. She suggests that if ABC Widgets, Inc., intends to proceed with hiring a new bookkeeper, then Oliver Owner, or another officer, should review and approve all check requisitions (and require the presentation of documentation supporting both the payee and the dollar amount). Oliver should directly receive monthly bank account statements and should consider retaining an outside accountant to conduct bank reconciliations. And, most importantly, no employee should ever be given complete authority over a company's entire business account apparatus.

Wire Fraud

2

Alicia Hou, Catherine Bentley Harris, and Jonathan Turner†

I. BACKGROUND

Biff Banker had been working at Bank for five years and was proud of his job. Biff had a good relationship with all his clients and prided himself on always going above and beyond to meet their needs.

So when Biff received an email marked "URGENT" from Customer, a high-value client, he quickly sprang into action. The email was professionally drafted and contained Customer's usual email signature, company logo, and was sent from a recognized email address. It requested that Biff transfer $10,000 from Customer's account to an offshore account as part of an ongoing investment deal that was due

† Alicia Hou is a partner in Akerman LLP's Los Angeles office. She can be reached at (212) 533-5907 or alicia.hou@akerman.com. Catherine Bentley Harris is a partner in Akerman LLP's Austin office. She can be reached at (737) 999-7107 or bentley.harris@akerman.com. Jonathan Turner is an associate in Akerman's Los Angeles office. He can be reached at (213) 533-5915 or jonathan.turner@akerman.com. This chapter should not be construed as giving legal advice. If you would like to receive legal advice, contact Akerman LLP. The views expressed in this chapter are the views of the authors and are not necessarily the views of Akerman LLP.

to close that week. Biff was somewhat familiar with the project, which had primarily been handled by Betty Branch Manager, who was on vacation that week. Biff did not want to disturb Betty's vacation and thus decided to handle the transfer himself.

The email included a remittance application signed with Customer's signature. In accordance with Bank's wire transfer procedures, Biff compared the signature on the remittance application to the signature on file for Customer. While Biff had not previously handled any transactions for Customer, he made sure to familiarize himself with the signature on file before comparing it with the signature on the remittance application. The signatures were a match, and Biff proceeded to process the wire transfer.

Over the next few days, Biff received additional emails from Customer requesting larger and larger amounts to be transferred to the same offshore account as a part of the investment deal. Because the signatures continued to match the signature in Customer's file, Biff continued to process the transfers. In total, $1 million was transferred to the offshore account.

It wasn't until a week later when Customer visited Bank to inquire about its account that Biff realized what had happened. Customer stated that no wire transfers had been requested that week, and Biff immediately understood that Bank and Customer were victims of a wire fraud scam.

Bank immediately launched an investigation, and the investigators determined that an international criminal organization had gained access to Customer's email servers and sent out what were determined to be forged remittance applications. Unfortunately, the $1 million had already been transferred to the offshore account and was now untraceable.

II. WIRE FRAUD UNDER THE UNIFORM COMMERCIAL CODE

A bank's customer will bear the loss of a disputed wire transfer if the transfer at issue was made pursuant to the customer's authorized payment order. Under the Uniform Commercial Code, a payment order received by a bank is the authorized payment order of the person identified as sender "if that person authorized the order or is otherwise bound by it under the law of agency."[1]

Even if it is shown that a disputed wire transfer was not an authorized payment order from a customer, the customer's bank may still avoid

1. UNIFORM COMMERCIAL CODE § 4A-202(a).

liability if the bank and the customer agreed that payment orders would be verified pursuant to a security procedure and (1) the security procedure is a commercially reasonable method of providing security against unauthorized payment orders, and (2) the bank proves that it accepted the payment order in good faith and in compliance with the security procedure.[2]

A. The Forged Remittance Applications Were Not Authorized Payment Orders

In Biff's case, it is unlikely that any of the remittance applications would be deemed authorized payment orders of the client.[3] Here, the remittance applications were determined to be forgeries sent by criminals who had gained access to Customer's email servers. Even though Bank's investigation found that the remittance applications had been sent using Customer's email servers, Customer will not be found liable and Bank will be forced to incur the loss if the sender of the payment order had no authority to act for Customer.[4] However, as will be discussed in greater detail in the following section, Bank may nevertheless avoid liability if it followed an agreed-upon security procedure to verify the transfer requests.[5]

B. Agreed-Upon Security Procedures

As discussed previously and in greater detail below, even though the forged remittance applications were not authorized payment orders, Bank may still avoid liability if it can show that (1) Bank and Customer agreed upon a security procedure to verify the transfer requests, (2) the security procedure was commercially reasonable, and (3) the security procedure was executed in good faith.[6]

---

2. *See* Uniform Commercial Code § 4A-202(b).

3. *See* Patco Const. Co. v. People's United Bank, 684 F.3d 197, 208 (1st Cir. 2012); *see also* Precision Computer Servs., Inc. v. Newtown Sav. Bank, No. AANCV186029468S, 2021 WL 5370456, at *6 (Conn. Super. Ct. Oct. 26, 2021).

4. *See Patco,* 684 F.3d at 208; *see also Precision Computer Servs.,* 2021 WL 5370456, at *6.

5. *See Patco,* 684 F.3d at 208; *see also* Robert W. Ludwig, Jr., Salvatore Scanio, and Joseph S. Szary, *Malware and Fraudulent Electronic Funds Transfers: Who Bears the Loss?,* 16 Fidelity L.J. 101, 108 (2010).

6. *See* Uniform Commercial Code § 4A-202(b).

Was There an Agreed-Upon Security Procedure?

For Bank to avoid liability, the law requires that Bank demonstrate that Bank and Customer agreed to a security procedure to be used in executing wire transfers from Customer's account. The Uniform Commercial Code defines security procedure as

> a procedure established by agreement of a customer and a receiving bank for the purpose of (i) verifying that a payment order or communication amending or cancelling a payment order is that of the customer, or (ii) detecting error in the transmission or the content of the payment order or communication.[7]

Additionally, the Uniform Commercial Code further clarifies that a security procedure "may require the use of algorithms or other codes, identifying words or numbers, encryption, callback procedures, or similar security devices. Comparison of a signature on a payment order or communication with an authorized specimen signature of the customer is not by itself a security procedure."[8]

Generally speaking, a bank's internal security policies will not be considered an agreed-upon security procedure for purposes of escaping liability under the Uniform Commercial Code.[9] Because a security procedure under the Uniform Commercial Code must be related to detecting fraudulent transfers, courts will generally not consider procedural requirements that were designed to avoid mistakes, overdrafts, or multiple transfers to be security procedures for purposes of shifting liability for fraudulent wire transfers.[10]

In this case, though Bank had a procedure in place in which its employees compared remittance application signatures with those in a client's file,

---

7. *Id.* § 4A-201.

8. *Id.*

9. *See* Chavez v. Mercantil Commercebank, N.A., 2011 WL 5285713 (S.D. Fla. Nov. 1, 2011) (refusing to consider "any procedural requirements that were not consistent with the primary purpose of a security procedure under Article 4A, which is 'to verify that the identity of the anonymous person on the other side of an electronic transmission is in fact the person who is authorized to make transfers to and from the account'").

10. *See id.* at *4; *see also* Sterling Sav. Bank v. Poulsen, 2013 WL 3945989, at *19 (N.D. Cal. July 29, 2013) (noting that bank policies aimed at compliance with the U.S. Patriot Act and Banking Secrecy Act were "to protect the banks and the government from money-laundering and other criminal activity by their customers," not to protect bank customers).

Bank would need to show the existence of an agreement between Bank and Customer under which Bank agreed to verify remittance applications in this manner. As will be discussed in greater detail, Bank will also need to show that the security procedure was commercially reasonable and that Bank properly carried out the verification in accordance with its agreement with Customer.

Was the Security Procedure Commercially Reasonable?

Even if it is assumed that Bank and Customer had an agreement under which Bank would verify payment orders (here, the remittance applications), Bank will need to demonstrate that the verification procedure was a "commercially reasonable method of providing security against unauthorized payment orders."[11] Generally speaking, the commercial reasonableness of a security procedure is a question of law.[12] In determining the commercial reasonableness of a particular security procedure, a court will consider

> the wishes of the customer expressed to the bank; the circumstances of the customer known to the bank, including the size, type, and frequency of payment orders normally issued by the customer to the bank; alternative security procedures offered to the customer; and security procedures in general use by customers and receiving banks similarly situated.[13]

Importantly, a court will not reject a security procedure as unreasonable simply because another procedure might have been better.[14] However, the bank will bear the burden of showing that the procedure was sufficient, given that "they generally determine what security procedures can be used and are in the best position to evaluate the efficacy of procedures offered to customers to combat fraud."[15]

Here, even if it is assumed that Bank agreed to compare remittance application signatures prior to executing Customer's wire transfers, it is unclear whether this procedure alone would be deemed commercially reasonable. As previously indicated, commercial reasonableness depends on

---

11. Uniform Commercial Code § 4A-202(b).

12. *See id.* § 4A-202(c).

13. *Id.*

14. *Id.* § 4A-203, cmt. 3.

15. *Id.*

such factors as the wishes of the customer expressed to the bank, the circumstances of the customer known to the bank (including the size, type, and frequency of payment orders normally issued by the customer), as well as security procedures in general use by customers and receiving banks similarly situated.[16] Given the total amount transferred, as well as the fact that many banks in the United States have implemented multifactored verification processes for initiating and completing wire transfers, it is likely that a court in Biff's case would find that signature verification alone was not commercially reasonable.[17]

Was the Security Procedure Executed in Good Faith?

Lastly, the security procedure must have been executed by the bank in good faith.[18] Here, if Bank and Customer agreed that Bank would compare remittance application signatures prior to executing Customer's wire transfers, it is likely that the signature comparison was completed in good faith. Biff made sure to familiarize himself with Customer's signature so that he could make a proper comparison before he executed the wire transfers, and ultimately determined that the two signatures were a match. It is therefore likely that a court would find that the good-faith requirement has been met.[19]

C. Liability of the Beneficiary Bank

Biff Banker also wondered whether he could advise Customer to recover the funds from the bank that received Customer's funds (i.e., the beneficiary bank or receiving bank). Unfortunately, a customer's remedies against a

---

16. *See Id.* § 4A-202(c).

17. *See* Fed. Ins. Co. v. Benchmark Bank, No. 2:17-CV-135, 2020 WL 635654, at *10 (S.D. Ohio Feb. 11, 2020) (noting that the Federal Financial Institutions Examination Council guidelines, on which courts rely as a touchstone for commercially reasonable security procedures, "endorse[] the use of both layered security and multifactor authentication for high-risk transactions"); *see also* Choice Escrow & Land Title, LLC v. BancorpSouth Bank, 754 F.3d 611, 620 (8th Cir. 2014) (noting that even multifactor authentication "may have been an inadequate safeguard").

18. Uniform Commercial Code § 4A-202(b).

19. *See Choice Escrow & Land Title*, 754 F.3d at 622–23 (Good faith "means honesty in fact and the observance of reasonable commercial standards of fair dealing. . . . [T]he bank must abide by its procedures in a way that reflects the parties' reasonable expectations as to how those procedures will operate.").

beneficiary bank are limited. First, in processing a payment order, courts have held that a beneficiary bank is usually required only to ensure that the account number on a remittance application matches with the account number receiving the funds.[20] For example, in *Lucky Star Enterprises v. Wells Fargo Bank*, the court found that the beneficiary bank was not liable even though the beneficiary bank deposited wired funds into an incorrect customer account. According to the court, when a payment order describes the beneficiary by both name and account number, a bank "may rely on the number as the proper identification of the beneficiary of the order" if it "does not know that the name and number refer to different persons."[21] The beneficiary bank "may accept the wire transfer without determining if the name and number refer to the same person, as long as the bank does not know about the name-number mismatch. A plain reading supports that actual knowledge is required, constructive knowledge is not enough."[22] In the instant case, the beneficiary bank would likely not be liable for accepting the transfer of funds, given that there is no indication that the beneficiary bank had actual knowledge that any of the beneficiaries listed on the remittance applications were incorrect. Even if it is assumed that the name and account numbers within the remittance applications did not match, the beneficiary bank will be liable only if it can be shown that the beneficiary bank had actual knowledge that the account belonged to a different person.[23]

Second, from a practical standpoint, once a wire transfer is complete, there is generally no effective way to cancel or recall a wire transfer beyond simply asking the beneficiary bank to return the funds. And, even in that case, the beneficiary bank is generally limited to simply requesting that the recipient customer agree to return the funds. Moreover, every bank has its own limitations and processes when it comes to receiving and sending

20. *See, e.g.*, Lucky Star Enterprises III, LLC v. Wells Fargo Bank, N.A., 585 F. Supp. 3d 1297 (W.D. Wash 2022).

21. *Id.* at 1302.

22. Flaherty v. Wells Fargo Bank Nat'l Ass'n, 623 F. Supp. 3d 1124, 1131 (D. Nev. 2022).

23. *Id.* ("When the payment order describes the beneficiary both by name and bank account number and the name and account number identify different persons, the beneficiary's bank may rely on the number as the proper identification of the beneficiary of the order if it does not know that the name and number refer to different persons."); *see also* Zeal Glob. Servs. Priv. Ltd. v. SunTrust Bank, 508 F. Supp. 3d 1303, 1310 (N.D. Ga. 2020) (holding that beneficiary bank is under no duty to determine whether the name and number on an account match).

wire transfers, which may impact the feasibility of returning the mistakenly transferred funds. The difficulties in retrieving funds are even greater when money has been transferred internationally, as reversal or cancellation of the transfer will also depend on the laws in place within the foreign jurisdiction.

III. UNIFORM COMMERCIAL CODE LIKELY PREEMPTS ANY COMMON LAW CLAIMS

Importantly, courts have limited a customer's recovery for claims of fraudulent wire transfer exclusively to recovery under the Uniform Commercial Code.[24] The Uniform Commercial Code "is the primary source of commercial law rules in areas that it governs . . . [W]hile principles of common law and equity may supplement provisions of the Uniform Commercial Code, they may not be used to supplant its provisions, or the purposes and policies those provisions reflect."[25] In the absence of an explicit provision to the contrary, "the Uniform Commercial Code preempts principles of common law and equity that are inconsistent with either its provisions or its purposes and policies."[26] Generally speaking, displacement of a customer's common law claims (such as fraud or misrepresentation) will occur whenever the Uniform Commercial Code "articulates a loss distribution scheme that applies to fact patterns" alleged by the customer.[27]

Here, any claim by Customer against Bank would seek to allocate the loss from the fraudulent wire transfers from Customer to Bank, a loss distribution already articulated under the Uniform Commercial Code's Issuance and Acceptance of Payment Order provisions.[28] Accordingly, the Uniform Commercial Code provides the sole means of recovery for Customer's claims against Bank.

---

24. *See Chino*, 190 Cal. App. 4th at 1170 ("the UCC expressly displaces common law, to the extent that its 'particular provisions' apply"); *see also* Uniform Commercial Code § 1-103, cmt. 2.

25. Uniform Commercial Code § 1-103, cmt. 2.

26. *Id.*

27. *See* Lee Newman, M.D., Inc. v. Wells Fargo Bank, 87 Cal. App. 4th 73, 79–80 (2001).

28. *See* Uniform Commercial Code § 4A-201 *et seq.*

3 Credit and Debit Card Claims

Will Newman†

Cindy Customer is having trouble with Money Bank, where she maintains a checking account, and with Credit Bank, which issued her credit card. Several years ago, Cindy set up an auto-pay feature with Money Bank, authorizing it to make a payment to her Credit Bank account at the end of every month.

The trouble begins when a scammer finds Cindy's credit card number online. The scammer uses the credit card number to buy luxury goods for himself, running up charges on Cindy's account. When Cindy notices that her credit card statement reflects numerous purchases she never made, she calls Money Bank and tells a customer service representative to stop its monthly wire transfer to Credit Bank, and she sends an email to Biff Banker at

† Will Newman is a commercial litigator who practices at Oberheiden P.C. in New York. He is an associate editor of *Litigation News* and the author of the litigation blog *Unpredictable*. He has represented litigants (including investors and financial institutions) in disputes in multiple states. Will can be reached at will@federal-lawyer.com. This chapter should not be construed as giving legal advice. The views expressed in this chapter are the views of Will Newman alone and are not necessarily the views of anyone else.

Credit Bank notifying him that she is disputing several purchases that appear on her latest account statement.

Money Bank, however, proceeds to transfer Cindy's money to Credit Bank, and Biff Banker believes that Cindy really did make the purchases she now denies. Biff believes this because in reviewing the charges that Cindy disputes and comparing them against charges Cindy admits she made, he notes the disputed charges were at stores that Cindy had patronized in the past. Further, Biff knows that each of those stores follow procedures to detect fraudulent purchases. Biff thus directs Credit Bank to keep the payment it received from Money Bank.

When Cindy receives her next credit card statement from Credit Bank, she does not see a credit for the disputed charges, and she deducts the amount of those charges from her next payment since she believes she is not responsible for them. Since Credit Bank does not receive its minimum payment from Cindy the following month, it charges her a fee, raises her interest rate, and notifies a credit reporting agency.

Upset about this, Cindy calls Biff and complains, and the conversation between the two becomes heated. Cindy accuses Biff of stealing her social security payments, and Biff responds that Credit Bank does not want customers like Cindy who cause trouble.

After the call, Biff cancels Cindy's credit card but still expects Cindy to pay the balance on her account, so he calls Cindy and leaves a voice message that she needs to pay her account balance or she may go to jail.

Once she hears the message, Cindy calls Lisa Lawyer for help. She wants to know what she can do to address what her banks have done. Lisa knows that numerous statutes and regulations govern how banks provide services to consumers, so she starts outlining potential claims and what she will need to show to prove those claims. Although Lisa briefly considers various state law claims that may apply to Cindy's situation, she decides to focus first on federal statutes.

I. HOW BANKS ARE DIFFERENT THAN OTHER DEFENDANTS

Lisa litigates numerous statutory claims against various people and entities, but two things distinguish banks from other defendants. First, banks have many customers who may experience the exact same treatment as any one plaintiff. Accordingly, many plaintiffs bring class action lawsuits against banks, and there is a greater likelihood that informative precedent already exists about similar claims. Second, banks frequently litigate, which may affect how they negotiate a settlement.

A. Banks Have Large Numbers of Customers That They Treat in the Same Manner

Plaintiffs frequently bring class action lawsuits against banks because the conduct about which a plaintiff complains likely affects many other customers as well.[1] This is because many statutory claims against banks arise from the sufficiency of notices they provide, which banks often standardize and repeatedly use.[2] And many statutory claims arise from conduct that is meant to protect a class of customers who are equally vulnerable to the same misconduct.[3]

Many statutes that enable litigation against banks have fee-shifting provisions and allow for class action lawsuits. Accordingly, plaintiffs often consider bringing claims against banks even when they have only lost a small amount of money.[4] And others bring claims alleging a bank violated technical rules, even if those violations did not directly cause a plaintiff to lose money.[5] Plaintiffs pursue these actions because lawyers are willing to litigate them with the understanding that applicable laws may require the banks to pay their litigation fees.[6] This prompts Lisa to consider not

1. *See, e.g.*, Kleiner v. First Nat'l Bank, 97 F.R.D. 683, 694 (N.D. Ga. 1983); Sarafin v. Sears, Roebuck & Co., 73 F.R.D. 585 (N.D. Ill. 1977).

2. *See, e.g.*, *Kleiner*, 97 F.R.D. at 694; *Sarafin*, 73 F.R.D. 585 (class actions alleging improper disclosures).

3. *See, e.g.*, Coleman v. GM Acceptance Corp., 220 F.R.D. 64 (M.D. Tenn. 2004) (alleging lender policies discriminated against Black consumers); Buycks-Roberson v. Citibank Fed. Sav. Bank, 162 F.R.D. 322, 331 (N.D. Ill. 1995) (same).

4. *See, e.g.*, Krieger v. Bank of America, N.A., 890 F.3d 429 (3d Cir. 2017) (litigation brought in an individual capacity concerning a $657 charge); Purtle v. Eldridge Auto Sales, 91 F.3d 797, 800 (6th Cir. 1996) (affirming award of attorney's fees for a $1,000 statutory violation).

5. *See, e.g.*, Obenauf v. Frontier Fin. Group, Inc., 785 F. Supp. 2d 1188, 1206 (D.N.M. 2011) (awarding nominal damages in connection with Fair Debt Collection Practices Act violation); Adiel v. Chase Fed. Sav. & Loan Ass'n, 630 F. Supp. 131, 134 (S.D. Fla. 1986) (awarding statutory damages for a Truth in Lending Act violation). *But see* TransUnion LLC v. Ramirez, 141 S. Ct. 2190 (2021) (holding that Fair Credit Reporting Act plaintiffs need to have sustained a concrete injury to have standing to sue in federal court).

6. *See, e.g.*, Watkins v. Simmons & Clark, Inc., 618 F.2d 398, 400 (6th Cir. 1980) (discussing the purpose of the class action provisions of the Truth in Lending Act); *see also* In

just whether a claim arises from the banks' conduct specifically involving Cindy, but also whether the banks' general policies complied with various statutes.

Since many plaintiffs and their lawyers may identify the same potential violations, there are often multiple lawsuits that concern the same conduct. These other lawsuits may produce judicial decisions that inform future litigants, including the bank itself, about the merits of similar legal claims and the specific factors that courts may consider when evaluating a case. This leads Lisa to research decisions brought against Cindy's banks for similar claims.

B. Banks Frequently Litigate

Banks are frequent litigants because they have many customers in a highly regulated industry,[7] and because they have notoriously deep pockets, which makes them attractive defendants to plaintiffs.[8]

Since banks cannot escape litigation, they have plenty of litigators ready to defend them. And because of the size of their business, they are often able to negotiate favorable billing arrangements with their outside counsel.

Lisa may conclude that a bank's status as a frequent litigant may make it more difficult to procure a settlement. While many litigants settle cases early to avoid the burdensome cost and disruption of a lawsuit, banks constantly endure that burden, and the legal fees related to one additional lawsuit may be negligible for a bank. Accordingly, some factors that may encourage early settlements against other defendants may carry less weight against a bank. Thus, when Lisa prepares the budget for Cindy's lawsuit, she seriously considers the costs involved in protracted litigation, given the likelihood that the lawsuit will not settle early.

---

re FDCPA Mailing Vendor Cases, 2021 WL 3160794 (E.D.N.Y. July 23, 2021) (criticizing abusive litigation by plaintiffs seeking attorney fees for technical violations).

7. Lisa considers whether to notify regulators that Money Bank and Credit Bank may have violated the law. It may be less expensive for the regulators to prosecute claims against the banks instead of Lisa doing it herself. Moreover, the banks may be more responsive to litigators than to an individual plaintiff. But Lisa also believes that a bank may pay a greater settlement to a plaintiff than a regulator may distribute to a consumer as restitution. As a result, she decides to discuss this option with Cindy before making a final decision.

8. *See, e.g.*, Bondi v. Grant Thornton Int'l, 2007 U.S. Dist. LEXIS 11767, at *3 (S.D.N.Y. Feb. 22, 2007) (noting "deep-pocket banks").

II. ELECTRONIC FUNDS TRANSFER ACT CLAIMS

Lisa begins her analysis with the first act that led to Cindy's losses: Money Bank's transfer of funds from Cindy's checking account to Credit Bank. The statute that governs that transfer is the Electronic Funds Transfer Act (EFTA).[9] Section 1693(h)(a) of the EFTA sets forth three types of failures to act that constitute a violation of the law. The first two are failures to transfer funds as instructed except in certain specified situations.[10] And the third is a failure to stop payment on a preauthorized transfer when a consumer instructs it to do so in accordance with the account's terms and conditions.[11]

Lisa considers whether Money Bank committed the third type of failure with Cindy's account: failing to stop payment upon Cindy's request. She begins by reviewing Regulation E,[12] the federal regulation that provides details concerning the application of the EFTA, and the clause that specifically sets forth the requirements for banks to cancel a remittance transfer.[13] In particular, the regulation protects the right of a bank customer to cancel certain transfers orally or in writing at least three business days before the scheduled transfer.[14] While much of the case law that interprets this statute concerns whether a defendant is a financial institution subject to the EFTA, there are also judicial decisions that provide insight into the type of conduct that courts hold may violate the law.[15]

To evaluate a potential claim, Lisa must first confirm that Cindy properly notified Money Bank that it should cancel the transfer to Credit Bank by reviewing the terms and conditions of Cindy's account to learn the

---

9. 15 U.S.C. § 1693.

10. *See id.* § 1693(h)(a)(1) and (2).

11. *See id.* § 1693(h)(a)(3).

12. *See* 12 C.F.R. § 1005. Prior to 2011, this regulation was set forth at 12 C.F.R. § 205. *See* 76 FR 81019 (2011).

13. *See* 12 C.F.R. § 1005.34.

14. *See id.* § 1005.10(c)(1).

15. *See, e.g.*, Stock v. Firstmark Servs., 2018 U.S. Dist. LEXIS 209874, at *13–14 (C.D. Cal. Dec. 12, 2018); *but see* Murphy v. Law Offices of Howard Lee Schiff P.C., 2014 U.S. Dist. LEXIS 24402 (D. Mass. Feb. 26, 2014) (denying a motion to dismiss, considering both whether the defendant was a financial institution and considering whether the plaintiff otherwise properly pled a claim for failure to properly honor a cancellation); Baldukas v. B&R Check Holders, Inc., 2012 U.S. Dist. LEXIS 186777 (D. Colo. Oct. 1, 2012) (same).

procedural rules for requesting that the bank stop a payment, and also by interviewing Cindy to learn exactly how and when she made the request and whether she has supporting documentation.

III. TRUTH IN LENDING ACT CLAIMS

The next stage of Lisa's analysis concerns Credit Bank's actions. She begins to tackle this subject by researching a major law that applies to credit card companies: the Truth in Lending Act (TILA).[16] The TILA has many components, and Lisa reviews it thoroughly to see which, if any, apply to Cindy's case.

A. The Fair Credit Billing Act

Congress amended the TILA in 1974 with the Fair Credit Billing Act (FCBA).[17] This law requires, among other things, that (1) credit card issuers permit consumers to dispute charges on their accounts by sending written notice,[18] (2) the credit card issuer acknowledge the dispute within thirty days,[19] and (3) within ninety days the credit card issuer must investigate the dispute and either remove the charge from the consumer's account or provide a written explanation for why the charge is valid.[20]

Here, Cindy disputed the scammer's charges on her account in writing, but instead of sending the dispute in a written letter, Cindy notified Credit Bank of her dispute in an email to a bank employee. Although the FCBA requires that the written dispute be made to an address set forth on Cindy's credit card bills, it also permits other types of notification if the bank notifies consumers that it will accept them.[21] Lisa must investigate whether Credit Bank notified Cindy that it would accept or had accepted her dispute by email to Biff.

16. 15 U.S.C. § 1601.

17. *See* Am. Express Co. v. Koerner, 452 U.S. 233, 234 (1981) (citing 15 U.S.C. § 1666).

18. *See id.*

19. *See id.*

20. *See id.*

21. *See* Savitz v. Citizens Bank, N.A., 2020 U.S. Dist. LEXIS 4602, at *11 (W.D. Pa. Jan. 10, 2020) (denying motion to dismiss FCBA claim because notification was oral since bank led consumer to believe it accepted the notification).

B. The Disclosure Requirements

Regulation Z sets forth rules on how credit card issuers must disclose the interest it charges to consumers. Part of Regulation Z, 12 C.F.R. § 226.5a, specifies some of the disclosures that a credit card issuer must clearly and conspicuously make.[22] It requires an issuer to disclose in its applications or solicitations whether it will impose a penalty rate for consumers.[23] Regulation Z has several exemptions, however; for example, it does not apply to credit extended to a business entity or to certain loans over $25,000.[24]

Here, Lisa investigates whether Credit Bank properly disclosed that it would impose a penalty rate on Cindy for failing to make a payment. But first, she considers whether Regulation Z applies. While Cindy is a natural person, Lisa remembers to confirm that Cindy's credit card was not a business card and that her credit limit did not exceed $25,000.

IV. FAIR CREDIT REPORTING ACT CLAIMS

The Fair Credit Reporting Act, 15 U.S.C. § 1681 (FCRA), regulates credit reporting agencies and also contains provisions that regulate the furnishers of information to credit reporting agencies, such as credit card companies.[25] In particular, it imposes an obligation on a credit card company to investigate errors on a credit report when a credit reporting agency notifies the credit card company that a consumer disputed its report.[26] The FCRA also requires that the credit card company's investigation be reasonable.[27]

Lisa makes a list of the information she needs to determine whether Credit Bank has complied with the FCRA. First, Cindy must have seen a negative entry on her credit report arising from the scammer's charges. Second, she must have reported the dispute to the credit reporting agency. Third, Lisa needs to know whether Credit Bank notified Cindy

---

22. *See* Rubio v. Capital One Bank, 613 F.3d 1195, 1200 (9th Cir. 2010) (holding that the determination of whether a particular disclosure was clear and conspicuous could not be decided as a matter of law).

23. 12 C.F.R. § 226.5a(b)(iv).

24. *Id.* § 226.3.

25. *See* Boggio v. USAA Fed. Sav. Bank, 696 F.3d 611, 616–19 (6th Cir. 2012); Whisenant v. First Nat'l Bank & Trust Co., 258 F. Supp. 2d 1312, 1314 (N.D. Okla. 2003).

26. *See Whisenant*, 258 F. Supp. 2d at 1314 (holding that FCRA does not apply to furnishers of information prior to a consumer complaint).

27. *See Boggio*, 696 F.3d at 616–19.

that it investigated the issue. And fourth, she needs to examine whether Credit Bank performed a reasonable investigation. Since Cindy has not yet informed Lisa about her dispute with the credit reporting agency, an FCRA claim may be premature, but Lisa can advise Cindy on how to initiate a dispute that will require Credit Bank to investigate.

V. FAIR DEBT COLLECTION PRACTICES ACT CLAIMS

The Fair Debt Collection Practices Act, 15 U.S.C. § 1692 (FDCPA), is the subject of much litigation.[28] The act contains several restrictions on how creditors can collect debts,[29] but it applies only to debt collectors,[30] a term that generally excludes credit card issuers and applies instead to third parties who may collect debts on another creditor's behalf.[31]

Subsection (e)(2) of the FDCPA prevents a debt collector from falsely representing "the character, amount, or legal status of any debt," and Subsection (e)(10) prevents debt collectors from using "any false representation or deceptive means to collect or attempt to collect any debt or to obtain information concerning a consumer." It also prevents debt collectors from leaving messages concerning the debt with third parties who are not the debtor,[32] and restricts the use of prerecorded messages and voicemails to collect the debt.[33]

---

28. *See, e.g.*, In re FDCPA Mailing Vendor Cases, 2021 WL 3160794 (citing "[l]egions of FDCPA cases"); Zortman v. J.C. Christensen & Assocs., 870 F. Supp. 2d 694 (D. Minn. 2012) (collecting FDCPA decisions); Reynolds v. EOS CCA, 2016 U.S. Dist. LEXIS 161706, at *10 (S.D. Ind. Nov. 22, 2016) (noting one attorney's involvement in "numerous FDCPA cases"); Padilla v. Clovis & Roche, Inc., 2007 U.S. Dist. LEXIS 88293, at *11 (N.D.N.Y. Nov. 29, 2007) (citing "numerous cases" involving the FDCPA).

29. *See* Miljkovic v. Shafritz & Dinkin, P.A., 791 F.3d 1291, 1298 (11th Cir. 2015) (citing 15 U.S.C. § 1692–1692p).

30. *See Miljkovic*, 791 F.3d at 1298 (noting the law applies to debt collectors and citing the applicable definition, 15 U.S.C. § 1692(a)(6)).

31. *See* MacDermid v. Discovery Fin. Servs., 488 F.3d 721, 734–35 (6th Cir. 2007); Stafford v. Cross Country Bank, 262 F. Supp. 2d 776, 793–94 (W.D. Ky. 2003).

32. *See* West v. Nationwide Credit, 998 F. Supp. 642, 644–45 (W.D.N.C. 1998) (citing 15 U.S.C. § 1692c(b)).

33. *See Zortman*, 870 F. Supp. 2d at 700–01 (citing decisions that interpret the FDCPA as prohibiting voicemails); Berg v. Merch. Ass'n Collection Div., 586 F. Supp. 2d 1336, 1340–44 (S.D. Fla. 2008) (denying motion to dismiss FDCPA claim arising from a prerecorded message).

Lisa believes that it is unlikely that Credit Bank is subject to the FDCPA for communications it made to collect its own debts, but she asks Cindy whether any third party contacted her about her Credit Bank charges. In particular, she examines whether anyone made any false statements to collect a payment from Cindy. She also asks Cindy about each instance in which anyone contacted her about her unpaid balance, including any voicemails or any instances in which a message was left for her with a third party. She also inquires whether Cindy ever answered the telephone and heard a prerecorded message about her Credit Bank balance instead of the voice of a live person. Lastly, Lisa considers whether she could characterize Biff Banker as a third party and allege that his threat that Cindy may face jail time for failure to pay her bills may be a false statement.[34]

VI. EQUAL CREDIT OPPORTUNITY ACT CLAIMS

The Equal Credit Opportunity Act, 15 U.S.C. § 1691 (ECOA), permits consumers to sue credit card companies when the credit card companies discriminate on certain specified bases,[35] including race, religion, sex, marital status, and age,[36] or when they discriminate based on whether a consumer benefits from a public assistance program.[37]

Lisa considers whether Credit Bank discriminated against Cindy when it refused to credit her account for the unauthorized charges she identified and when it subsequently cancelled her credit card. Cindy is in a protected class because she is a woman, but Lisa notes that two other classes may also apply to Cindy because she disclosed to Credit Bank that she receives social security benefits. This exposes Credit Bank to the claim that it discriminated against Cindy based on her age and because of her receipt of public assistance. Lisa decides to investigate whether Credit Bank's knowledge of

34. Courts have differed in deciding whether an employee of a debt collection company is a separate debt collector. *See* Bray v. Cadle Co., 2010 U.S. Dist. LEXIS 109470, at *18 (S.D. Tex. Oct. 12, 2010) (citing conflicting rulings on the subject but noting that most hold that an employee is a debt collector). But courts have rejected FDCPA claims against credit card company employees. *See, e.g.*, MacDermid v. Discover Fin. Servs., 488 F.3d 721, 735 (6th Cir. 2007); Murray v. J.P. Morgan Chase, N.A., 2010 U.S. Dist. LEXIS 84808, at *11–12 (C.D. Ill. Aug. 18, 2010).

35. *See* Midlantic Nat'l Bank v. Hansen, 48 F.3d 693, 699 (3d Cir. 1995).

36. 15 U.S.C. § 1691(a)(1).

37. *Id.* § 1691(a)(2).

Cindy's age and social security payments prompted its decision to reject the merits of Cindy's dispute and to cancel Cindy's credit card, and whether Credit Bank treats older customers or social security recipients differently from younger customers or those not receiving social security payments.

VII. LISA TAKES THE CASE TO COURT

After Lisa considers numerous claims, she must decide which to assert. If she tries to plead all of them, she may dilute the strength of powerful claims with weaker claims and risk losing credibility or the court's attention. If she misses the opportunity to file a class action, she may miss out on substantial negotiation leverage and the opportunity to fund a vigorous prosecution of the case, but in representing a class, she may not be able to make strategic decisions in the litigation that focus solely on Cindy's interests, and she may face significantly complicated procedural issues.

Lisa decides to assert an EFTA claim against Money Bank for its failure to cancel Cindy's wire payment, despite Cindy exercising her statutory right to do so. Since Lisa is unaware of other similar incidents in which Money Bank failed to cancel a customer's wire payment or a general bank policy that led to the cancellation, Lisa decides not to pursue the claim as a class action.

Lisa also decides to assert an FCBA claim. While the express terms of Cindy's credit card agreement did not permit her to submit disputes by email, Lisa believes that she can argue that Credit Bank tacitly accepted emailed disputes through its course of conduct with Cindy. In support of this claim, Lisa cites other instances in which Credit Bank communicated with Cindy by email that may have reasonably led her to believe the bank consented to electronic notice.[38] While she expects Credit Bank to dispute the relevance of those other communications, she believes Cindy's reasonable reliance to be a factual issue that may survive summary judgment and thus give Credit Bank incentive to settle to avoid the high costs and risks of trial.

Lisa decides to assert the FCBA claim as a class action because it arises from the bank's general practices. Lisa alleges that Credit Bank's general practice was to communicate with customers by email and then reject disputes that customers submit by email. She claims that this practice harmed an entire class of customers.

38. *See Savitz*, 2020 U.S. Dist. LEXIS 4602, at *11 (denying motion to dismiss FCBA claim where bank led consumer to believe it accepted the notification).

Lisa also decides to assert a claim under Regulation Z because Credit Bank failed to disclose the penalty rate it imposed on Cindy on her monthly statements. Lisa hesitated in asserting this claim because Cindy did not have all the literature that Credit Bank had provided to her about the account, and thus it was possible that one of Credit Bank's numerous mailings prior to Cindy's first purchase on the account properly disclosed the penalty rate, which would be sufficient to defeat the Regulation Z claim.[39] Lisa nevertheless pursues the claim because Cindy is confident that she did not see such a disclosure, though Lisa harbors doubts that Cindy would have read and considered all of the fine print that comes with a credit card agreement. Still, Lisa believes that she may obtain copies of Credit Bank's correspondence during discovery to confirm whether Credit Bank made the proper disclosures.

Like her FCBA claim, Lisa asserts the Regulation Z claim as part of a class action because any defective disclosure would likely not have affected Cindy individually but would have affected an entire class of customers who failed to receive the proper penalty rate notice.

Lastly, Lisa asserts ECOA claims against Credit Bank, alleging that it refused to credit Cindy's claims of identity theft and because it ultimately canceled her account because she is a woman. To prepare this claim, Lisa researched Credit Bank's differing treatment of male and female cardholders. While she could not find publicly available information about the demographics of the bank's cardholders generally or information on how Credit Bank considered their complaints, she did read an article in a prominent newspaper about sexist remarks made by the bank's leadership, and she spoke with a male cardholder who had no difficulty in getting Credit Bank to reverse similar fraudulent charges. Based on this differential treatment, and with the color provided by the news article, Lisa asserted a gender discrimination claim.

Lisa also alleges that Credit Bank discriminated against Cindy based on her age and receipt of social security payments. To support this claim, Lisa cites her conversation with the male cardholder who was younger than Cindy and did not receive public assistance. She also cites Biff Banker's comments, which suggested a discriminatory intent.

Lisa chooses not to assert the ECOA claims as a class action. While Lisa believes that Credit Bank's discriminatory attitudes likely led it to treat women, the elderly, and social security recipients worse than other customers, she believes that the specific discriminatory conduct here—Credit

39. *See* 12 C.F.R. § 226.5a(b)(1).

Bank's refusal to credit Cindy's account for fraudulent charges and its cancellation of her account—may pose specific factual questions that are not common to the discriminatory treatment other customers may have faced.[40] Accordingly, she asserts these claims on Cindy's individual behalf.

Lisa does not pursue an FCRA claim because there is no negative entry on Cindy's credit report arising from the disputed charges. As a result, Lisa believes the claim is premature, but she makes a note in her calendar to check with Cindy in a few months to see if Credit Bank's dispute has affected her credit report, and if it has, she can consider amending the complaint.

Lisa also decides not to assert an FDCPA claim because it likely does not impose liability on Credit Bank arising from its efforts to collect its own debts.

VIII. THE BANK'S MOTION TO DISMISS

Lisa is accustomed to receiving phone calls from opposing counsel to discuss settlement after she serves a complaint, so she is not surprised to receive a call from the banks' attorney. The lawyer does not want to discuss settlement, however; she wants to propose a schedule for the parties to brief the banks' forthcoming motion to dismiss.

A few weeks later, Money Bank submits its motion to dismiss the EFTA claim, asserting a safe harbor affirmative defense pursuant to 15 U.S.C. § 1693m(d)(1), which shields it from liability for "any act done or omitted in good faith in conformity with any rule, regulation, or interpretation thereof" by various government agencies. Money Bank argues that pursuant to 12 C.F.R. § 1005.10(c)(2), it was authorized to disregard Cindy's request to stop the payment because she failed to provide written confirmation of her dispute within fourteen days.

At the same time, Credit Bank also moves to dismiss the complaint. Its motion begins with the FCBA claim and argues that the statute does not protect Cindy because she submitted her dispute in an email instead of in writing. Credit Bank cites express language in its account agreement and in its monthly statements that requires cardholders to submit any disputes in writing mailed to a specific address. The motion cites case law

40. *See, e.g.*, Phillips v. Sheriff of Cook Cnty., 828 F.3d 541, 550–51 (7th Cir. 2016) (affirming refusal to certify a class on the grounds that alleged mistreatment did not raise common questions of fact).

that supports the argument that the express terms of the cardholder agreement supersede any contrary understanding Cindy may have obtained through her course of dealing with the bank.[41]

Credit Bank also moves to dismiss the Regulation Z claim. The motion contends that Cindy's claim is barred by a one-year statute of limitations that began running once Credit Bank allegedly failed to make its disclosure.[42] Since Cindy had her credit card for more than a year before filing her claim, Credit Bank argues that she missed her chance to claim that it failed to make a necessary disclosure. Its motion also cites a sworn declaration by Biff Banker that the bank timely disclosed its penalty rate, and it attaches a copy of a proper disclosure that Biff swears is a true and correct copy of a document the bank mailed to Cindy when it solicited her business.

Lastly, Credit Bank does not move to dismiss the ECOA claims. Courts often dismiss ECOA claims that rely on a disparate impact theory, comparing the aggregate treatment of customers against those in a protected class.[43] Credit Bank may have had strong grounds to move to dismiss Cindy's ECOA claims had they relied solely on claims that the bank's policies generally resulted in better outcomes for customers who were not in protected classes. But because Cindy can cite Biff Banker's statements as evidence of discriminatory intent and can also cite the bank's differing treatment of individual customers as evidence of disparate treatment, Credit Bank faces a major obstacle to a motion to dismiss.[44]

Instead, Credit Bank plans to take discovery and then move for summary judgment on the ECOA claims. When considering such a motion, federal courts often apply the same burden-shifting analysis that they apply in Title VII claims.[45] A plaintiff first has the burden to demonstrate that the

---

41. *See* Tian Long Fashion Co. v. Fashion Ave. Sweater Knits, LLC, 2016 U.S. Dist. LEXIS 96734, *14 (S.D.N.Y. July 25, 2016) (citing Uniform Commercial Code § 2-208).

42. *See* Schiavone v. Bank of Am., 2019 U.S. Dist. LEXIS 135971, at *7–8 (D. Del. Aug. 13, 2019) (citing 15 U.S.C. § 1640(e)).

43. *See* Duarte v. Quality Loan Serv. Corp., 2018 U.S. Dist. LEXIS 77642, at *22 (C.D. Cal. May 8, 2018); *but see* Palmer v. Homecomings Fin., LLC, 677 F. Supp. 2d 233, 242 (D.D.C. 2010) (granting motion to dismiss disparate impact claim permitting plaintiff to replead with allegations that the defendant discriminated against other similarly situated individuals).

44. *See* Swierkiewicz v. Sorema N.A., 534 U.S. 506, 508 (2002).

45. *See* Rosa v. Park West Bank & Trust Co., 214 F.3d 213, 215 (1st Cir. 2000); *but see* Sims v. New Penn Fin. LLC, 2018 U.S. Dist. LEXIS 51657, at *28–29 (N.D. Ind. Mar. 28, 2018) (explaining that, in the Seventh Circuit, plaintiffs need to provide "direct evidence of discrimination, disparate impact analysis, or disparate treatment analysis").

defendant has implemented a discriminatory policy.[46] Once established, the burden shifts to the defendant to provide "legitimate, non-discriminatory reasons" for its policy.[47] The plaintiff then assumes the burden to demonstrate that "such reasons are pretextual."[48]

Here, Credit Bank will concede that it has a policy of refusing to credit claims of identity theft when its systems observe that allegedly fraudulent purchases were made in the same places as purchases that a customer admits making. It will also concede that it cancels accounts when customers use combative language with a bank employee. Credit Bank will demonstrate that these policies have legitimate purposes: the former is to relieve the bank from false claims and to discourage customers from making such claims; the latter is to protect the bank's staff from a hostile work environment. At that point, Cindy will have the burden to establish that Credit Bank did not maintain its policies for these reasons, and to do so, she may present internal bank emails that discuss the policies, the testimony of bank employees that created and implemented the policies, or evidence that the bank did not apply the policies in the same manner for customers who were not in protected classes.[49]

IX. HOW DOES THIS LITIGATION END?

The merits of the claims are one factor among several that dictate the outcome of the dispute between Cindy Customer, Money Bank, and Credit Bank. On the one hand, Lisa Lawyer has a lot of work to do to research numerous complex statutory claims, gather evidence from numerous witnesses, and review a mountain of documents. That work costs money that Cindy Customer may not have and that Lisa Lawyer may never see if the defendants prevail. But on the other hand, Money Bank and Credit Bank are exposed to the risk of a large financial judgment and significant negative publicity for their treatment of a customer, which could attract sympathy from the public. While banks may have teams of lawyers ready to defend them, the defense in this case may require the participation of numerous employees who must therefore temporarily cease working on otherwise profitable activities. As a result, Cindy and Credit Bank each

46. *See* Chiang v. Schafer, 2008 U.S. Dist. LEXIS 64654, at *75 (D.V.I. Aug. 20, 2008).

47. *See id.*

48. *Id.*

49. *Id.* at *78.

have strong motivation to settle, especially since Credit Bank is not moving to dismiss the ECOA claims and therefore cannot escape the cost of discovery. If Money Bank does not succeed on its motion to dismiss, it too has a strong incentive to settle. But whether the parties actually reach an agreement depends on whether they and their lawyers are practical and clear-eyed about the costs of litigation and the strengths and weaknesses of their cases.

Lender Claims

4

Josephine M. Bahn and Braden Riley[†]

Andy the Aging Athlete is a former college basketball star who, after admitting to himself that his dreams of going pro were unlikely to be realized, decided to attend law school. After graduation from law school, Andy worked for a local law firm and practiced commercial litigation for several decades before retiring from the practice of law. Never one to sit still for long, Andy decided to open a local gymnasium, Andy's Athletics, as an investment. Andy is the owner-manager of Andy's Athletics and handles all the finances himself. He set up Andy's Athletics, LLC, in which he is the sole member. At the ripe age of 85, Andy is staying busy but is starting to wonder if he can keep up with all the important day-to-day operations of the gym. His daughter, Caroline, tries to help where she can, but Andy

---

† Braden Riley is a litigator who practices in the areas of commercial litigation and torts at Morrow & Sheppard LLP in Houston, Texas. Prior to joining Morrow & Sheppard, Braden practiced commercial litigation at Cozen O'Connor and was also an assistant district attorney at the Harris County District Attorney's Office. As a prosecutor in one of the largest district attorney's offices in the country, Braden prosecuted a wide variety of felonies and misdemeanors, including those related to financial crimes and embezzlement. He can be reached at briley@morrowsheppard.com.

is a cantankerous old man and refuses her offers of help. Caroline is concerned that Andy in his advancing age will be taken advantage of and that the gym is too much for him to handle.

One day, Caroline sends her good friend, Lisa Lawyer, an email with an ominous tone. The subject line reads, "Call me." Lisa telephones Caroline to ask what is wrong. Distraught, Andy's daughter tells Lisa that she thinks something went terribly wrong at Andy's Athletics. She tells Lisa that she thinks her father will have to file for bankruptcy soon, and she is worried about what will happen to him. Lisa schedules a meeting with Caroline and Andy to discuss the situation.

Andy and Caroline visit Lisa's office the following day, and Andy starts to tell Lisa the story of what has happened with his business. Cash flow is typically tight at Andy's Athletics. Members are charged a monthly fee, but Andy pays for a lease on the building and taxes on the property. Additionally, the gym requires periodic maintenance. Andy also maintains a small staff, comprised of several front desk managers, an administrative assistant, and several trainers. Though Andy makes a profit on the gym, there is not much left over at the end of each month.

Andy recently wanted to make renovations to the gym and also wanted to upgrade the equipment, particularly the cardio machines. Andy expected that the renovations and the new equipment would attract a new crowd of young professionals who would be likely to pay a higher monthly membership fee. Andy made plans to move forward with the renovations but determined that his current cash flow would not be enough to cover the expenses. He needed a loan.

Josephine M. (Jo) Bahn is a commercial litigator who practices in Cozen O'Connor's Washington, D.C., office. Prior to joining Cozen, she was a senior attorney in the enforcement section of the Federal Deposit Insurance Corporation (FDIC). There, Jo focused on banking laws and regulations, including the Federal Deposit Insurance Act, Dodd-Frank Wall Street Reform and Consumer Protection Act, Equal Credit Opportunity Act, Federal Housing Act, Real Estate Settlement Procedures Act, and section 5 of the Federal Trade Commission Act. She managed, investigated, and developed legal strategy for 10c enforcement litigation matters and investigations involving deceptive and unfair practices to consumers and fraud or other risk-related harm to FDIC-insured institutions. She worked with the FDIC's seven regional offices and examiners in the FDIC's Division of Consumer Protection and Risk Management Supervision. She can be reached at (202) 280-6484 or jbahn@cozen.com.

This chapter should not be construed as giving legal advice. If you would like to receive legal advice, contact Braden or Jo. The views expressed in this chapter are Braden's and Jo's and are not necessarily the views of Cozen O'Connor.

Andy grew up in the same small town as Biff Banker. The two of them were childhood friends, and Andy relied on Biff for his advice in both personal and professional matters. In fact, Biff had helped Andy set up Andy's Athletics, LLC, had looked at the financial statements of Andy's Athletics on several occasions, and frequently gave Andy unsolicited advice on how to grow his business. Andy knew that Biff would be able to help him acquire financing for the renovations to Andy's Athletics. Andy reached out to Biff and scheduled a time to meet with him at Biff's bank. Caroline asked Andy if she could join Andy to make sure he understood everything before signing any financial commitments, but Andy, stubborn as ever, refused.

I. CLAIMS ARISING OUT OF THE LOAN APPLICATION PROCESS

Andy arrived on the day of the meeting and began discussing his plans with Biff. Biff listened intently and seemed to take careful notes. Andy told Biff that he estimated that he would need a loan for $150,000 to complete the renovations and might need additional capital in the future. "This is going to be expensive, isn't it?" Andy asked. Biff, eager to make the sale, told Andy not to worry about the costs and that the bank can offer him "special rates" that charge "very low interest," and even stated that these rates could be "as low as 3 percent interest." When Andy asked Biff what the interest rate would be, exactly, Biff rebuffed Andy and again told him to "not worry about it" and that he would "take care of Andy."

Biff gave Andy the loan application, and Andy immediately had questions. The loan application indicated Andy was applying for a loan and a line of business credit. Additionally, the paperwork indicated the application was for a loan "up to $300,000." Andy expressed concern that he may not be able to afford the interest on such a high loan, but Biff assured him that they are just building in additional capital should Andy need it. Biff further reassured Andy that "Andy's Athletics is in the driver's seat here" and that he should just "trust" Biff, who would be there with him every step of the way. Biff continued, telling Andy that he knew Andy's Athletics, that he had "run the numbers," and that the expansion was the only way forward for the business. As part of the loan process, Biff also referred Andy to Craig Contractor to help with the renovations. Biff told Andy that Craig has worked with several of Biff's clients and has always done a great job.

A week later, Andy received a letter from Biff informing him that he has been approved for a $300,000 loan and is eligible for an additional personal line of credit up to $150,000. When Andy read the fine print, he discovered that the loan was being charged a 20 percent interest rate. The loan was also collateralized by Andy's Athletics and the profits made on member revenue. Despite having reservations, Andy signed the loan paperwork and made his first payment.

At this point, Lisa stops Andy so she can write down some initial thoughts about Andy's potential claims.

A. Issues with Formation of the Contract

First, the lender should always know who they are going into business with. Lisa knows, from years of being around Caroline, that Andy's age has really crept up on him. She suspects that, due to his age, he is particularly susceptible to being convinced of things that are not necessarily good for his business. Lisa makes a note to ask Andy who else was present during his meeting with Biff, whether Biff committed things to writing or just made oral promises, and whether Andy really seemed to comprehend everything Biff was saying when they were discussing how Andy's Athletics would be impacted by the loan.

Lisa briefly considers whether any pretransaction discussions between Andy and Biff could negate the contract entirely for lack of a meeting of the minds over an agreement. Lisa quickly dismisses this possibility, as noncommittal preliminary exchanges normally do not constitute binding agreements.[1] Further, as Lisa will examine when she looks at Andy's claims for breach of contract, oral promises in lender liability claims are particularly problematic. Lisa also contemplates whether Biff issued any preliminary letters of intent, but then dismisses this possibility as a source of Andy's claims, as she suspects that the bank, being a diligent lender, would have included a merger clause, which typically states that the final loan agreement provided to the debtor reflects the entire agreement between the parties and that all prior agreements are null and void. Indeed, Lisa finds such a clause upon further inspection.

---

1. *See* Frutico S.A. de C.V. v. Bankers Trust Co., 833 F. Supp. 288, 297–98 (S.D.N.Y. 1993) (no contractual agreement when parties did not intend to be bound absent contractual agreement); Kyle v. Apollomax, LLC, No. CV 12-152-RGA, 2013 WL 5954782, at *3 (D. Del. Nov. 1, 2013) ("[P]reliminary discussions and negotiations cannot form the basis for a valid contract, and without a contract there can be no breach of contract.").

B. Negligence

Lisa ponders whether a general claim for negligence might also make sense. She quickly realizes, however, that negligence may be the least helpful path for her to follow to advocate on Andy's behalf.

A typical negligence case will require Lisa to show (1) the bank owed Andy a cognizable duty of care as a matter of law, (2) the bank breached that duty, and (3) Andy suffered damage as a proximate result of that breach.[2] While that seems straightforward, Lisa thinks that several problems might give her pause to bring this claim. First, it will be an uphill battle to prove the bank owed an ordinary duty of care to Andy.[3] For that reason, this claim may get dismissed at the pleadings stage, making the rest of Andy's claims seem less substantiated. Second, and relatedly, in many jurisdictions the economic loss rule will prevent Andy from bringing this claim at all; that is, "[i]n general, there is no recovery in tort for negligently inflicted 'purely economic losses,' meaning financial harm unaccompanied by physical or property damage."[4] Courts limit these negligence theories because such claims would "disrupt the parties' private ordering, render contracts less reliable as a means of organizing commercial relationships, and stifle the development of contract law."[5]

Lisa also knows that in the jurisdictions that would allow such a claim, there is generally no duty for the borrower to competently handle a loan application.[6] Lisa thinks Andy may be out of luck with respect to a pure negligence cause of action, but she may still be able to claim certain kinds of torts, even those that somewhat sound in negligence, specifically negligent misrepresentation. Lisa will have to show that these causes of action

---

2. Millennium Partners, L.P. v. U.S. Bank Nat'l Ass'n, No. 12 Civ. 7581(HB), 2013 WL 1655990, at *4 (S.D.N.Y. Apr. 17, 2013).

3. *See, e.g.*, Wilcox v. Sec. State Bank, 2023 WY 2, ¶ 36, 523 P.3d 277, 286 (Wyo. 2023), reh'g denied (Feb. 14, 2023) (refusing to recognize a noncontractual "reasonably competent banker" duty on lender).

4. *See, e.g.*, Sheen v. Wells Fargo Bank, N.A., 12 Cal. 5th 905, 922, 505 P.3d 625, 632 (2022), reh'g denied (June 1, 2022); Mayotte v. U.S. Bank Nat'l Ass'n as Tr. for Structured Asset Inv. Loan Tr. Mortg. Pass-Through Certificates, Series 2006-4, 985 F.3d 1248, 1251 (10th Cir. 2021).

5. *Sheen*, 12 Cal. 5th at 922, 505 P.3d at 627–28.

6. *See* House v. U.S. Bank Nat'l Ass'n, 2021 MT 45, ¶ 18, 403 Mont. 287, 300, 481 P.3d 820, 828 (Mont. 2021) ("[a]lleged errors or omissions by a lender in the servicing or administration of a mortgage loan is thus generally compensable only in contract on a claim for breach of express contract terms or the covenant of good faith and fair dealing").

did not "arise from—or are . . . independent of the parties' underlying contracts."[7] Therefore, negligent misrepresentation, fraud, and breach of fiduciary duty, just to name a few, may still be viable tort theories against Biff and the bank.

C. Negligent Misrepresentation

Lisa also identifies that Biff made material misrepresentations to Andy in the placing of the loan and wonders whether Biff might be liable for negligent misrepresentation.

To prove the tort of negligent misrepresentation, Andy would need to show (1) a representation made by Biff and the bank in the course of their business or in a transaction in which the bank has a pecuniary interest, (2) the representation conveyed false information for the guidance of others in their business, (3) Biff and the bank did not exercise reasonable care or competence in obtaining or communicating the information, and (4) Andy suffered pecuniary loss by justifiably relying on the representation.[8]

Lisa believes there is no doubt that Andy relied on Biff and his representation in taking out the loan. However, Lisa is aware that Andy will likely again run into issues proving this claim because of the nature of the oral misrepresentations that were made.

Even if Andy relied on Biff's representations regarding the low interest rate, many courts hold that the contradicting terms of the contract prevail, which would prevent Andy from claiming he materially relied on the contradicting oral promise.[9] Additionally, as Lisa previously determined, there are a multitude of hurdles in presenting a cause of action alleging reliance on oral promises in the context of lender claims.

First, Lisa is aware that many states have enacted credit agreement statutes that prevent debtors such as Andy from bringing claims arising out of oral promises related to credit agreements.[10] Even if Lisa successfully

---

7. *Sheen*, 12 Cal. 5th at 922, 505 P.3d at 633.

8. *See* J.P. Morgan Chase Bank, N.A. v. Orca Assets G.P., L.L.C., 546 S.W.3d 648, 653–54 (Tex. 2018).

9. *See, e.g.*, Silver v. Countrywide Home Loans, Inc., 760 F. Supp. 2d 1330, 1341 (S.D. Fla. 2011), aff'd, 483 F. App'x 568 (11th Cir. 2012) (finding that any reliance upon alleged oral misrepresentations expressly contradicted by the terms of a loan is "objectively unreasonable as a matter of law").

10. *See, e.g.*, 815 Ill. Comp. Stat. 160/2. (Illinois Credit Agreement Act); La. Rev. Stat. Ann. § 6:1122 (2005) (Louisiana Credit Agreement Statute).

navigates the case past one of these credit agreement statutes, Andy's testimony regarding the oral promises might still be barred by his jurisdiction's applicable statute of frauds and, failing that, by the parol evidence rule. Finally, the bank would likely argue that Biff's statements were mere puffing or opinion. Lisa concludes that alleging negligent misrepresentation will not bear much fruit at this stage.

D. Fraud and Fraudulent Inducement

Lisa also considers whether Biff's actions might amount to fraud. In many jurisdictions, a claim of fraud will require her to show that Biff either intentionally or recklessly[11] made misrepresentations by clear and convincing proof.[12] Generally, it will also require Andy to show that Biff made specific statements that he relied upon, to show when and where those statements were made, and to explain why those statements were fraudulent.[13] In any event, Lisa realizes she will encounter some of the same problems as she did trying to prove the negligence causes of action, and she thinks a court would likely not find Biff's reference to a rate "as low as 3 percent" to be sufficiently specific to give rise to a cause of action for fraud.

E. Breach of Fiduciary Duty

Finally, Lisa wonders how a court might classify the relationship between Andy and Biff, and whether Biff owed Andy certain duties above and beyond that of an ordinary banker. Lisa knows that most consider the lender-borrower relationship to be that of creditor-debtor, and not a fiduciary relationship.[14] Lisa also knows that, in determining whether a fiduciary relationship was established, courts will not only look to the degree to which Andy relied on Biff's advice, but also to the "common disparity in pertinent knowledge and expertise" between the lender and the borrower.[15]

---

11. *See* Of A Feather, LLC v. Allegro Credit Servs., LLC, No. 19CV9351 (DLC), 2020 WL 3972752, at *6 (S.D.N.Y. July 14, 2020).

12. *See* Freeman v. Pittsburgh Glass Works, LLC, 709 F.3d 240, 256–57 (3d Cir. 2013).

13. *See* Loreley Fin. (Jersey) No. 3 Ltd. v. Wells Fargo Sec., LLC, 797 F.3d 160, 171 (2d Cir. 2015).

14. *See* In re Bailey Tool & Mfg. Co., No. 16-30503-SGJ-7, 2021 WL 6101847, at *41 (Bankr. N.D. Tex. Dec. 23, 2021).

15. *See House*, 2021 MT at ¶ 18, 403 Mont. at 300, 481 P.3d at 829.

Lisa wonders how Andy's prior expertise as a commercial litigator might affect a court's likelihood of finding that a fiduciary relationship was established. Given these challenges, she anticipates that she will likely need to get an expert to explain financial advisory guidelines and the reasonableness of Andy's reliance on Biff's advice. Lisa decides she might need to revisit this claim after she learns more about the relationship between Biff and Andy.

Lisa considers it ironic that, had Biff not gone through with the loan at all, Andy wouldn't be in the position he is in, and may not have even been able to hold the bank and Biff liable for failing to extend the loan to him.[16]

F. Redlining Is Still Prevalent

Redlining is a discriminatory practice that first emerged in the early 20th century and remains in effect,[17] and it has had a profound impact on shaping the spatial, social, and economic landscape of the United States. Redlining has kept individuals out of more affluent or desirable neighborhoods based on their race. With the creation of the Home Mortgage Disclosure Act, redlining was formally outlawed by banking regulators.[18] Though most jurisdictions have foregone the complete designation of areas related to a specific race, the practice of redlining still continues, but in a subtle and less complex way in the banking industry,[19] making it harder for regulators to identify. Following is an example of redlining with Amanda, who is attempting to secure a loan from her local community bank, only to be offered a loan from the bank at a higher interest rate than her friend, Fran, because of where the home address is.

Redlining Example

Amanda, a young millennial in her early thirties with a stable job as a nurse, wants to become a homeowner. She saved up several years' worth of wages to make a down payment and has been fiscally responsible and

16. *See, e.g.*, Albino Constr. Co. v. Wells Fargo Bank, Nat'l Ass'n, No. CV 21-35, 2021 WL 2529811, at *4 (E.D. Pa. June 17, 2021) (lender generally owes no duty of care to borrower in processing of loan application).

17. *See, e.g.*, *Redlining*, Consumer Credit and the Law (June 2023).

18. *Id.*

19. *See* Khristopher J. Brooks, *Redlining's Legacy: Maps Are Gone, but the Problem Hasn't Disappeared*," CBS News (June 12, 2020), https://www.cbsnews.com/news/redlining-what-is-history-mike-bloomberg-comments.

possesses no current outstanding debts. Amanda wants to purchase her home in a vibrant, up-and-coming neighborhood with a great school system and local amenities.

When she is ready to finance her chosen home, Amanda applies for a mortgage from a local bank. Her application notes her great credit history, her income as a nurse, and provides all the necessary documentation needed. She submits the application to her local banker, Biff, for his review.

Biff is an experienced banker with over thirty years of experience in the banking industry. He has personally worked on more than 1,000 applications for mortgages and prides himself on his client interaction and service. Biff reviews Amanda's application, assesses the supporting documents she provided, and then begins looking at the home's location. The property is in a predominantly minority neighborhood, and Biff is concerned that the home will not appreciate in value as other homes in other parts of the local community. Biff feels he is left with no choice but to apply a strict approach to Amanda's application.

Biff agrees that the bank should approve Amanda's mortgage application, but under terms that are different from those she expected. Because of the property's location, Biff offers the mortgage to Amanda at a high interest rate that requires a large down payment. The interest rate and the down payment are higher than what she expected or saved for, and more than what someone in her income bracket and with her credit score would normally require. As Biff relays to Amanda the proposed loan terms, Amanda gets the sense that Biff is attempting to discourage her from pursuing the loan. He just keeps talking about concerns for the neighborhood's future development.

Amanda is concerned about the bank's assessment of the neighborhood, and she's worried she will not be able to afford the home she's had her eye on for years. She applies for another mortgage loan with another local bank, providing the same information she provided to Biff. In the meantime, Amanda asks her friend Fran to reach out to Biff to test his interest in providing Fran with a loan. Fran applies for a loan with Biff and provides him with information that is essentially the same as the information Amanda included with her loan application, except that Fran's chosen property is in the more affluent part of town. While Amanda waits for the second bank to provide the terms of her loan, Fran has been preapproved for a loan with Biff's bank at an interest rate that is a half percentage point better than the one Biff offered to Amanda.

Amanda realizes that Biff's biases against her chosen neighborhood is a classic example of redlining and contacts the consumer protection group at the bank's primary regulator.

II. CLAIMS ARISING DURING THE LIFE OF THE LOAN

Andy started making payments on the loan. Several months later, a junior banker calls Biff and says he has some bad news about the loan to Andy's Athletics. When Biff inquires as to the situation, the junior banker tells him that something went wrong during the due diligence period and that they miscalculated Andy's monthly revenue. The younger banker explains that Andy's monthly revenue is only about half of what they expected. Worse, when the risk is adjusted for Andy's updated revenue projections, the bank simply cannot afford to extend a personal line of credit to Andy. Despite his concerns, the junior banker knows that Biff is insistent on the bank profiting on the loan, and that Biff change his image as a manager who makes bad loans to the bank's detriment.

Biff calls Andy and explains that Andy's Athletics was actually "overleveraged" and that, as a result, the bank would need additional capital to continue financing the loan or Andy could be in default. Andy is perplexed, but Biff reassures Andy and tells him this happens all the time. Andy doesn't recall any terms in his loan that defined what it meant for Andy to be "overleveraged," and as Lisa later discovers, that term was not defined anywhere in the paperwork. Biff just needed Andy to put up another $15,000 in cash and the bank could then continue to finance the original loan on the same terms. Biff assures Andy that the additional capital is just temporary and that the bank would hold the $15,000 for Andy as additional security on the loan. Andy, distressed, starts to think about how he can secure this additional funding. He reaches out to Larry the Local Lender, who specializes in bridge loans. Larry assesses Andy's outstanding debt and offers to loan the additional funds to Andy at a 30 percent interest rate and requires the loan to be repaid within a year. Without any other options, Andy accepts. He receives the loan proceeds and pays them over to Biff, who says nothing to Andy about the personal line of credit being unavailable but does reiterate that he has "run the numbers" and that this deal continues to make sense for Andy's Athletics.

Meanwhile, the contractors reach out to Andy to let him know that they reviewed the construction plans and would be able to add a yoga studio, a sauna, and a rehabilitative whirlpool at Andy's Athletics for an additional $75,000. Fortunately, the contractors are willing to take credit from cash-strapped Andy. Andy, unaware that the personal credit line had been rejected, accepts the contractors' proposal.

A. Modification of the Loan Terms

Lisa's first thought is whether the additional $15,000 collateral is enforceable. Of course, even if she can get the additional collateral obligation reversed, this would not necessarily clear Andy's obligation with Larry the Local Lender. But Lisa thinks she might have other strategies for getting Andy out of that obligation, or at least she might be able to have Biff and the bank pay for it. Lisa again faces the problem of whether an oral promise made by a lender is enforceable. In this case, however, Lisa thinks the parol evidence—i.e., Andy's testimony regarding the modification of the loan—could be admissible because some jurisdictions allow parol evidence to be admitted for purposes of proving an oral modification of a written contract.[20] If the bank were smart, Lisa thinks, they would have insisted that the original loan agreement contain a clause forbidding oral modifications. Further, the bank could have insisted that the loan modification documentation require Andy to reaffirm his original obligations under the loan and waive any defenses or offsets to his obligations under the loan. None of those things were done, and Lisa thinks there could be traction here. But what about Andy's obligation to repay Larry the Local Lender?

B. Promissory Estoppel

Lisa feels optimistic about her chances of making the bank cover the bridge loan to Larry the Local Lender under a theory of promissory estoppel. Typically, promissory estoppel would require Andy to show (1) a promise; (2) that the promisor, as a reasonable person, could foresee would induce conduct of the kind that has occurred; (3) actual reliance on the promise; and (4) that results in a substantial change in position.[21] Here, Andy clearly

20. Barinaga v. J.P. Morgan Chase & Co., 749 F. Supp. 2d 1164, 1173 (D. Or. 2010).

21. *See* Dane v. U.S. Bank, N.A., No. 3:12-CV-00333-ST, 2013 WL 11319046, at *2 (D. Or. May 31, 2013).

changed his position by obligating himself to Larry based on the promise made by Biff and the bank that the additional collateral payment would be held in trust. If the bank goes back on its word as to the additional $15,000 collateral, Lisa should be able to get Andy out of the obligation. Lisa thinks the same analysis could apply to Andy's decision to obligate himself to the tune of an additional $75,000 to the contractors.

C. Breach of Contract

Lisa begins to contemplate claims Andy might assert arising out of issues with the additional collateral and the unfulfilled personal credit line. It seems to Lisa that the request for additional collateral and the unfulfilled line of credit could be a clear breach of contract by the bank. Although breach of contract is perhaps the most intuitive cause of action for lender liability, Lisa knows that, in practice, the complexity of loan agreements and the many provisions they contain in favor of the lender make these claims difficult if not impossible to pursue.[22] She knows that Biff probably did not do his due diligence if he was claiming Andy's Athletics was overleveraged only months after the initial loan paperwork was signed. She also knows that parol evidence might not work in Andy's favor to prove that the contract did not actually mean what it said. Further, the loan agreement provides that the bank can declare Andy in default at any time.

Lisa also starts to have doubts about the unfulfilled personal line of credit. While it is true that the bank issued a letter approving Andy for the line of credit, it is not clear whether the contract guaranteed that the credit would be automatically available or whether it was subject to further approval by the bank. After all, Andy had not actually used the line of credit yet; he had only relied on the likelihood that he could access those funds when he chose to accept the contractors' proposal for the additional construction. But Andy might have a strong case for negligent misrepresentation.

---

22. *See, e.g.*, In re Bailey Tool & Mfg. Co., No. 16-30503-SGJ-7, 2021 WL 6101847, at *37 (Bankr. N.D. Tex. Dec. 23, 2021) ("While this court believes that [the lender's] conduct was in many ways tortious (and shocking), the breach of contract analysis here is actually quite vexing . . . the [loan] Agreements are amazingly one-sided [and] there seem to be very few breaches of contract. In other words, many of the alleged bad acts articulated by the Trustee were seemingly permitted by the terms of the Agreements.").

III. ISSUES WITH WORKOUTS

Andy thinks he is in the clear, and for a while, things seem to have calmed down. Unfortunately, Andy's prosperity does not last. Some of the gym members are frustrated with the construction work in the gym and the resulting inconveniences, and a newer, cheaper gym opened on the other side of town. Andy started to lose members. Cash flow dipped again, and Andy again fell behind on his loan payments to the bank.

One day, Andy received a call from Biff. "We're going to have to foreclose on the gym," Biff told him. Biff also told Andy that the bank would have to seize all the member revenues directly. Biff also said that if Andy wanted the bank to forbear on foreclosing on the gym until he got back on his feet, Andy would need to install one of the bank's employees as CFO of Andy's Athletics. Finally, to further protect their outstanding debt, the bank would control how Andy's Athletics disbursed funds to some of the equipment suppliers from whom he had bought equipment on credit. Biff told Andy he would send a revised loan addendum that reflected these terms. Andy, anxious about the state of his business, was quick to tell Biff that he would sign anything to keep the business, but Biff never sent him an addendum. Nonetheless, Andy complied with the terms, and the bank appointed Biff as CFO of Andy's Athletics.

A. Breach of the Duty of Good Faith and Fair Dealing

As Lisa listens to Andy, she realizes there may be some red flags raised by Biff and the bank's insistence on being overly involved in the day-to-day affairs of Andy's Athletics. Though it is not uncommon for a lender to take extra precautions to protect its investment when it is imperiled, she also knows that, when it comes to lender liability claims, one of the most frequently litigated issues is the lender being overly involved in the borrower's business decisions. In particular, actions such as taking over the borrower's business, controlling the business's workforce, and controlling the priority and distribution of the business's profits and debt payments raise red flags that might cause a court to find that the lender's actions support one or more causes of action alleged by the borrower.[23]

23. *See, e.g.*, In re Bailey Tool & Mfg. Co., No. 16-30503-SGJ-7, 2021 WL 6101847, at *40–41 (Bankr. N.D. Tex. Dec. 23, 2021).

Moreover, Lisa knows that a lender's undue influence over a borrower's business operations is an important concept in lender liability, and one that courts might apply to support several different causes of action other than just a breach of the duty of good faith and fair dealing.

First, Lisa recalls that most if not all states require contracts to be performed in good faith,[24] and that this might be a basis on which to assert liability against the bank for undue influence over Andy's Athletics. The covenant of good faith and fair dealing is implied in contracts by state law, and it "prevents one party from 'unfairly frustrating the other party's right to receive the benefits' of the contract."[25] The covenant generally comes into play in the parties' discretion in their exercise of contractual rights and looks to the "agreed common purposes and consistency with the justified expectations of the other party."[26]

Lisa is also aware that she will need to be intimately aware of the contours of her jurisdiction's law, because the duty of good faith and fair dealing varies greatly among jurisdictions. For example, Lisa could bring this claim as an independent cause of action in some states, but not in others.[27] In those states where she could bring the claim as an independent cause of action, Lisa might be required to show that Andy and Biff were in a fiduciary relationship with each other.[28] Additionally, some jurisdictions will require Andy to show a breach of an express provision of the contract before he can assert a breach of the duty of good faith and fair dealing, while other jurisdictions will not require such a showing.[29]

---

24. *See, e.g.*, LA. CIV. CODE ART. 1983; Grisaffi v. Dillard Dep't Stores, Inc., 43 F.3d 982, 983 (5th Cir. 1995) ("Good faith performance is an implied requirement of every contract under Louisiana law."); Klamath Off-Project Water Users, Inc. v. Pacificorp, 237 Or. App. 434, 445, 240 P.3d 94 (2010) (Under Oregon law, "every contract has an obligation of good faith in its performance and enforcement under the common law.").

25. Villegas v. Wells Fargo Bank, N.A., No. C 12-02004 LB, 2012 WL 2931343, at *9 (N.D. Cal. July 17, 2012).

26. Amoco Oil Co. v. Ervin, 908 P.2d 493, 498 (Colo. 1995).

27. *Compare* Nicholson v. United Pacific Ins. Co., 219 Mont. 32, 710 P.2d 1342, 1348 (1985), *with* Williams v. Fed. Home Loan Mort'g Corp., No. PWG-13-2453, 2013 WL 6713278, at *4 (D. Md. Dec. 18, 2013).

28. *See* Pension Trust Fund v. Fed. Ins. Co., 307 F.3d 944, 955 (9th Cir.2002) (applying California law); Morrow v. Bank of Am., N.A., 2014 MT 117, ¶ 31, 375 Mont. 38, 45, 324 P.3d 1167, 1176.

29. *Compare* Silver v. Countrywide Home Loans, Inc., 760 F. Supp. 2d 1330, 1344 (S.D. Fla. 2011) ("A duty of good faith 'is not an abstract and independent term of a contract' but must relate to performance of an express contractual obligation."), *with* Elizabeth Retail

It seems to Lisa that the bank's actions in appointing Biff as CFO of Andy's Athletics, in addition to controlling the majority of the revenues and expenses of Andy's Athletics, crossed the line of what could be considered good faith and fair dealing under the loan agreement. Although a lender is entitled to have some say in the borrower's hiring and firing of corporate officers, the borrower is typically also "entitled to have its affairs managed by competent directors and officers who would maintain a high degree of undivided loyalty to the company,"[30] and here, it is questionable whether Biff, an employee of the bank with the bank's interests first in mind, would fit that bill. Further, the closer the lender gets to "assum[ing] actual, participatory, total control of" the borrower, the more likely a court is to find impermissible overreaching by the lender.[31] Lisa also realizes that the bank has made a major mistake by not memorializing the change of terms in the written loan workout agreement. Such an agreement could include a waiver of claims against the lender and make clear that the changes in operating procedure were a condition of the bank's forbearance on defaulting the loan. Though a court might cast a skeptical eye towards the bank's overinvolvement, the lack of a written agreement worsens the bank's position here because it makes the additional conditions seem arbitrary and perhaps outside the boundaries of the original contract terms to which Andy and the bank agreed.

Lisa is mindful of the bank's duty of good faith and fair dealing as she assesses the events related to Andy's Athletics. Some courts hold that this duty attaches as early as the contractual negotiations stage.[32] Lisa realizes that Biff and the bank may have breached their duty of good faith and fair dealing when they failed to inform Andy that they would not be extending to him the personal line of credit.[33]

Properties LLC v. KeyBank Nat'l Ass'n, 83 F. Supp. 3d 972, 990 (D. Or. 2015) (a "party may violate its duty of good faith and fair dealing without also breaching the express provisions of a contract") (citing Elliott v. Tektronix, Inc., 102 Or. App. 388, 396, 796 P.2d 361 (1990)).

30. State Nat'l Bank of El Paso v. Farah Mfg., 678 S.W.2d 661, 690 (Tex. App.1984), writ dism'd by agr. (called into question on other grounds by Wal-Mart Stores, Inc. v. Sturges, 52 S.W.3d 711, 724 (Tex. 2001)).

31. *See* Schwan's Sales Enterprises, Inc. v. Com. Bank & Tr. Co., 397 F. Supp. 2d 189, 195 (D. Mass. 2005).

32. *See, e.g.*, High v. McLean Fin. Corp., 659 F. Supp. 1561, 1569 (D.D.C. 1987) (holding that duty of good faith and fair dealing could arise between loan broker and loan applicant).

33. *See* K.M.C. Co., Inc. v. Irving Trust Co., 757 F.2d 752, 1 Fed. R. Serv. 3d 1095, 92 A.L.R. Fed. 661 (6th Cir. 1985).

B. Duress

Andy recounts to Lisa how incredibly distraught he was when he received the phone call from Biff. Pushed to his wit's end, Andy would have signed anything to keep the gym open. Lisa wonders whether she could convince a judge that Biff took advantage of Andy, and thus have rescinded what Andy agreed to due to duress.

A showing of duress typically requires (1) a threat to do something a party has no legal right to do, (2) an illegal exaction or some fraud or deception, and (3) an imminent restraint that destroys the victim's free agency and leaves him without a present means of protection.[34] Lisa realizes not all jurisdictions will recognize duress as an independent cause of action. At most, it might be considered an affirmative defense to enforcement of the bank's rights related to the loan. The other problem Lisa acknowledges is that, as much as Andy was likely stressed out, it is not entirely clear that Biff and the bank took actions that they were not entitled to under the loan agreement. Even if the loan agreement did not provide specifically for the bank's overinvolvement in the day-to-day operation of Andy's Athletics, the loan itself was collateralized by the gym and allowed the bank to foreclose on the gym in the event of a default. Lisa is not sure that a claim for duress is viable because it requires her to show that the bank threatened an action it had no legal right to enforce.[35]

IV. CLAIMS ARISING OUT OF DEFAULT ON THE LOAN

Once more, things spiral out of control for Andy's Athletics. The construction continues to run into delays, and the contractors begin to demand that Andy start making payments on the additional projects. Andy, believing the bank granted him the personal line of credit, goes to the bank to draw on that credit line. He is, unfortunately, informed that he has no line of credit. To make matters worse, Biff stops paying Andy's trainers. The trainers quit and Andy loses more clients who had stayed on as members

---

34. *See* Lockwood Int'l, Inc. v. Wells Fargo, Nat'l Ass'n, No. 20-40324, 2021 WL 3624748, at *3 (5th Cir. Aug. 16, 2021) (citing Wright v. Sydow, 173 S.W.3d 534, 544 (Tex. App.—Houston [14th Dist.] 2004, pet. denied).

35. *See, e.g.*, Leal v. Bank of Am., N. A., No. CIV.A. M-11-346, 2012 WL 1392089, at *5 (S.D. Tex. Apr. 20, 2012).

specifically for training sessions. To save what they can on their loan, the bank directs Biff to stop paying Larry the Local Lender and Andy's equipment suppliers.

When Andy's Athletics misses two payments on the bridge loan, Larry the Local Lender puts Andy's in default. Andy continues to lose gym members as he now cannot keep up with operations and maintenance. Even with the bank's accommodations, Andy again falls behind on the loan payments to the bank.

Biff is nervous and plans to put Andy's in default, figuring that he can seek to foreclose on the gym, sell it, and sell all the equipment to make up for the loan. Biff is concerned that the default he caused by not paying Larry could be an issue in foreclosing on the gym. To ensure there will be no problems, Biff enlists his friend, an appraiser, to conduct an appraisal of Andy's Athletics and asks him to "make the numbers work for him" by devaluing the business.

Biff and the bank then claim Andy is in violation of the lending agreement because of the default declared on other debt obligations owed to Larry the Lender and because of a decline in the value of collateral securing the bank's loan. The bank thus puts Andy's Athletics in default and claims that the entirety of the balance on Andy's loan is now accelerated and due.

Andy is in dire financial straits and out of options. The loan had years left to be repaid. He feels as though Biff misled him, and he wants to seek rescission of the loan in its entirety. Lisa contemplates Andy's options.

A. Breach of Contract

Lisa begins to evaluate the possibility of alleging breach of contract for the bank's attempted default on the loan. She knows that the bank has the right to default on the loan under the contract and that the terms of allowable default are generic—the bank can move to default any time if there was an "event of default" under the loan, defined as Andy's "failing to observe or perform any of the covenants, conditions and agreements contained herein or in any of the other Financing Documents."[36] The conditions of Andy's loan agreement require him not to experience (1) an "insolvency event," which includes any event in which Andy's Athletics defaults on a debt obligation; or (2) a "material adverse change" in the financial condition of

36. In re Bailey Tool & Mfg. Co., No. 16-30503-SGJ-7, 2021 WL 6101847, at *37 (Bankr. N.D. Tex. Dec. 23, 2021).

Andy's Athletics.[37] Because these conditions are worded so broadly, Lisa determines that the bank likely did not breach its contract with Andy by moving for default based upon the financial condition of Andy's Athletics and after receiving notice of default on his loan from Larry the Lender.

"How could that be?" Andy asks Lisa. "This just isn't fair. Isn't there something else we can claim?"

B. Breach of Duty of Good Faith and Fair Dealing

Lisa considers the circumstances that led to the bank finally putting Andy's Athletics in default, and questions whether a court would find that the bank breached its duty of good faith and fair dealing. It certainly seems that the bank's directing Biff to cease paying Larry the Local Lender crosses the line of control and places the bank's interests above preserving Andy's Athletics. Lisa thinks the same analysis should apply to the bank's decision to stop paying the trainers. In fact, she is reasonably certain that some courts would find this to be grossly overreaching conduct that ultimately caused Andy's Athletics to suffer damages.[38] Lisa also recalls that the specific reason Andy even needed the loan from Larry was due to the bank declaring that Andy was "overleveraged," a term that was undefined in the loan agreement and which seemed like nothing more than an excuse to require Andy to front additional collateral on the bank's loan.

Further, when Lisa learns that Biff asked the appraiser to devalue the gym, it becomes clear that the bank and Biff committed a "dishonest or unreasonable deviation from prevailing commercial standards of reasonableness in the trade, thereby denying [Andy] the benefit of the bargain."[39]

C. Breach of Fiduciary Duty

Lisa jots down some thoughts about whether Biff and the bank would now be considered to have been in a fiduciary relationship with Andy in light of the entirety of the developments between the bank and Andy's Athletics.

---

37. *Id.*

38. *Id.* at *41.

39. House v. U.S. Bank Nat'l Ass'n, 2021 MT 45, ¶ 18, 403 Mont. 287, 304, 481 P.3d 820, 831 (Mont. 2021); *But see* Silver v. Countrywide Home Loans, Inc., 760 F. Supp. 2d 1330, 1344 (S.D. Fla. 2011), aff'd, 483 F. App'x 568 (11th Cir. 2012) ("under Florida law, there can be no cause of action for breach of implied covenant of good faith and fair dealing absent an allegation that an express term of the contract has been breached").

Lisa thinks it likely that Andy "repose[d] trust in a bank and rel[ied] on the bank for financial advice,"[40] or at least that special circumstances here made the bank Andy's fiduciary.[41] Assuming that to be true, the bank should have "refrain[ed] from misleading or concealing information" from Andy, and the bank was "required to make decisions in the best interests of the borrower, even if contrary to the best interest of the lender."[42]

Lisa considers the relationship between Andy and Biff. Biff certainly hid information from Andy. Andy had also come to heavily rely on Biff's financial advice through the years, and a court would likely find that Andy's reliance on Biff's advice was reasonable. Certainly, it seems as though Biff did nothing to disabuse Andy of the notion that Biff was his financial adviser. Lisa believes that Andy's claims for breach of fiduciary duty will be bolstered by the excessive control and influence exerted by the bank on Andy's Athletics.[43] Lisa will have to show, however, that Andy's relationship with Biff transcends the "mere fact that [he] subjectively trusts [Biff]."[44] Assuming she can do so, Lisa believes she can certainly prove the bank put its interests ahead of Andy's and his business: the bank fabricated the "overleveraged" classification to extract additional collateral; it touted the alleged "personal line of credit" as inducement for Andy to enter into the loan; it ultimately seized control of Andy's finances and operational control of his business to the bank's benefit and to the detriment of Andy's Athletics; and the bank's actions caused Andy's Athletics to default on both the bank loan and the bridge loan from Larry.

D. Tortious Interference

In some states, Andy could have a claim against Biff and the bank for tortious interference with his business relationships. This is particularly so

40. Black Creek Station Homeowner Ass'n, Inc. v. MUFG Union Bank, N.A., No. 2:22-CV-132-MHH, 2023 WL 3111727, at *4 (N.D. Ala. Apr. 26, 2023) (citing K & C Dev. Corp. v. AmSouth Bank, 597 So. 2d 671, 675 (Ala. 1992)).

41. *See id.*; *See also* High v. McLean Fin. Corp., 659 F. Supp. 1561, 1568 (D.D.C. 1987); Christianson v. First Nat'l Bank Alaska, No. S-13985, 2012 WL 6062124, at *21–22 (Alaska Dec. 5, 2012).

42. In re Bailey Tool & Mfg. Co., No. 16-30503-SGJ-7, 2021 WL 6101847, at *41 (Bankr. N.D. Tex. Dec. 23, 2021).

43. *See* Bowman v. CitiMortgage Inc., No. 3:14-CV-4036-B, 2015 WL 4867746, at *7 (N.D. Tex. Aug. 12, 2015) (citing In re Absolute Res. Corp., 76 F. Supp. 2d 723, 734 (N.D. Tex. 1999)).

44. Smith v. Deneve, 285 S.W.3d 904, 911 (Tex. App.—Dallas 2009, no pet.).

when the lender intentionally interferes with things such as management selection and the borrower's business contracts.[45] A typical cause of action for tortious interference might require Andy to show (1) a contract subject to interference exists, (2) the act of interference was willful and intentional, (3) the intentional act proximately caused the plaintiff's damage, and (4) actual damage or loss occurred.[46] The fact that Biff was installed as CFO of Andy's Athletics and his subsequent directives to stop paying the trainers and Larry the Local Lender will not serve the bank's case. The bank could be subject to additional liability if it also upset the contracts between Andy's Athletics and its equipment suppliers due to its control of Andy's finances.

E. Fraud, Fraudulent Inducement, and Consumer Protection Act Violations

Finally, Lisa turns to other potential tort-based claims. To establish fraud, Lisa would have to prove that (1) the lender made a representation to the borrower; (2) the representation was material; (3) the representation was false; (4) when the lender made the representation, it either knew the representation was false or positively asserted the representation recklessly and without knowledge of whether it was true; (5) the lender made the representation with the intent that the borrower act on it; (6) the borrower did rely on the representation; and (7) the representation caused the borrower injury.[47] Fraudulent inducement is a closely related cause of action that requires a showing of the same elements, in addition to an allegation that the fraud perpetrated caused the plaintiff to fraudulently enter into a contract.[48] Lisa carefully evaluates these elements. While Biff said many false statements, she is unsure whether a jury would find these representations to be willfully or intentionally misleading, rather than simply negligent. However, Lisa feels more confidence with respect to the appraisal. In using the fraudulently obtained lower-than-market-value appraisal as a basis to default Andy's Athletics on the loan, it is likely that Biff committed an actionable fraud.[49]

45. *See* In re Bailey Tool & Mfg. Co., No. 16-30503-SGJ-7, 2021 WL 6101847, at *41 (Bankr. N.D. Tex. Dec. 23, 2021).

46. *See id* at *47.

47. *See id.* at *44.

48. *See* Kevin M. Ehringer Enters., Inc. v. McData Servs. Corp., 646 F.3d 321, 325 (5th Cir. 2011).

49. *See In re Bailey Tool & Mfg. Co.*, 2021 WL 6101847, at *54.

Finally, Lisa entertains whether she might bring a consumer protection claim under the jurisdiction's applicable statutes. Most jurisdictions have such protections, but the extent to which they apply to loan transactions varies.[50] Lisa thinks this claim is less likely to be successful.

V. LITIGATION AND DAMAGES

So what? That's the question that strikes Lisa after all this back and forth. So what if all of this happened? What does Andy get out of it? How is it likely to play out?

Lisa first figures she needs to set realistic expectations for Andy. Discovery in a case such as this can be burdensome. It could take more than a year from the date of filing a complaint against Biff and the bank for the dispute to wind its way through the courts. Even if they are successful, Andy's business may be long gone by the time he sees a nickel.

On the other hand, the bank will almost certainly need to hire counsel to defend against the litany of claims that Andy will seek to bring against the bank and Biff. The bank should begin by assessing liability at an early stage by conducting interviews with those people associated with Andy's loan, and in particular with Biff. The bank should be careful about sending internal communications regarding Andy's loan because any such communications could be discoverable. This is particularly important if there is a chance that Andy can prove any cause of action that requires malicious intent, such as fraud. These subsequent statements could give a jury insight into the mind of the bank and its employees to determine how they thought of Andy, of Biff, and of Andy's Athletics. The bank should also examine Biff's prior course of conduct and what the bank knew or should have known about his business practices prior to his dealings with Andy's Athletics. If Biff's practices fell outside the bank's ordinary practices and procedures, the bank should strategically consider whether to argue Biff was outside the course and scope of his employment and authority to

50. *See e.g.*, Guajardo v. J.P. Morgan Chase Bank, N.A., 605 F. App'x 240, 249 (5th Cir. 2015) (dismissal of claims under the Texas Deceptive Trade Practices Act regarding a mortgage loan transaction upheld on appeal as pure loan transactions are generally not considered to be a good or service and thus claimant not considered to be a consumer under Texas law); Dellos Farms, Inc. v. Sec. State Bank, 2022 WY 107, ¶ 15, 516 P.3d 846, 849–50 (Wyo. 2022) (in case involving promissory notes securing agricultural loans, Supreme Court of Wyoming found that loans did not fall within Wyoming Consumer Protection Act because the notes pertained only to commercial operations and not consumer transactions).

transact in the manner in which he did with Andy. The bank should be prepared to defend against Andy's claim that, regardless of the bank's position, Biff had actual or apparent authority to act in the way that he did.

When the bank receives a copy of Andy's lawsuit, it should immediately forward it to its counsel for review. Biff is likely to be named as a defendant along with the bank, and chances are that Biff is a citizen of the same state as Andy. If Biff and the bank happen to be citizens of a different state than Andy (i.e, diverse citizens), there will be limited time to remove the case to federal court.

Although pleading practice may draw out the litigation, the fewer claims that are viably pled against the bank, the less Andy can pry into the bank's operations during discovery. Nonetheless, the bank should be prepared to do damage control in the discovery phase. Andy will likely be entitled to a wide range of documents, policies, and correspondences relating to his loan and potentially also relating to others like his. The bank should be prepared to depose Andy, certainly, but it should also be aware that Andy will seek to depose bank employees as well as a corporate representative of the bank.

The bank should take inventory of how much Andy's business is worth and what he is claiming is the lost value of his business as a going concern. Even for a modest business, the lost "legacy" value may amount to millions of dollars. Additionally, if Andy can plead a cause of action for an intentional tort, such as fraud, he may be entitled to punitive damages. If the bank takes inventory of the facts likely to come out during discovery and finds that they are likely to hurt its case, the bank may consider attempting early resolution of Andy's claims. Perhaps the bank can consider what Andy really wants (rescission of the loan) and try to put Andy back in the same condition he was in prior to the loan, without paying additional damages for Biff's actions. The bank otherwise should be prepared for extensive and hard-fought litigation, in which case it will need a good lawyer.

This is all just the tip of the iceberg, and Lisa knows that there may be additional facts she has not yet uncovered that give rise to liability against Biff and the bank under other causes of action.[51] She thanks Andy for coming in, walks him out of the office, and calls it a day. She has a lot of work ahead of her.

---

51. For example, depending on what Lisa discovers, Biff may have violated provisions of the Truth in Lending Act or other state-specific regulations.

5

Navigating Commercial Real Estate Loan Defaults: From Classification to Collection and Foreclosure

Robert S. McWhorter†

I. INTRODUCTION: COLLECTION OF DEFAULTED REAL ESTATE LOANS

This chapter examines the complex dynamics of defaulted commercial real estate loans. Understanding the distinct nature of defaults—monetary and nonmonetary—is a vital first step in this journey. The terms may seem self-explanatory, but there is a considerable level of nuance in understanding the ability to redeem or reinstate a defaulted loan. This chapter delves into the realm of collecting loans secured by real property under California law, which is a representative example of the foreclosure process. In California, a lender must make an election of remedies, which

† Robert S. McWhorter is a shareholder of Buchalter, A Professional Corporation. Having practiced law for almost thirty years, he serves as the chair of Buchalter's Sacramento litigation practice group, specializing in representing financial institutions in collecting commercial loans and defending lender liability actions. He also specializes in handling bankruptcies under Chapters 7, 9, and 11 of the Bankruptcy Code. He obtained his Bachelor of Arts from the University of Chicago, a Juris Doctorate from Wayne State University Law School, and his Master of Business Administration from the Ross School of Business, University of Michigan.

involves the choice between two divergent paths of foreclosure proceedings: judicial and nonjudicial. While both routes share the common goal of resolving defaulted loans, their associated processes, pros and cons, and legal implications vary significantly. For judicial foreclosure, we explore the one-action rule, anti-deficiency statutes, and receiverships, providing a practical guide for anyone navigating these legal waters. This chapter aims to provide a well-rounded comprehension of real estate loan defaults, enabling you to take informed actions in the event of a default.

II. NATURE OF DEFAULT: MONETARY VS. NONMONETARY DEFAULTS

A lender may exercise remedies upon an event of default under the loan documents.[1] Defaults are typically monetary or nonmonetary. The debtor's[2] failure to pay principal and interest is the most typical monetary default.[3] Other monetary defaults include failing to pay taxes, assessments, or insurance premiums when due.[4] A monetary default imposes an immediate financial loss to, or increases the obligations of, the lender.

California law allows a debtor to cure monetary defaults and avoid property loss. Under California Civil Code section 2924c, a debtor may cure monetary defaults and reinstate the loan by paying the delinquent sums plus the costs incurred in enforcing the note at any time until five "business days" before the initial date on which the property is scheduled to be sold to satisfy the loan.[5] This statute does not expressly provide a

1. *See* CAL. CIV. PROC. CODE § 726(a) (foreclosure is the sole action for recovery of a debt secured by real property).

2. For simplicity's sake, we will refer to the trustor/mortgagor or their successors as the "debtor."

3. *See* Coltrin v. James B. Nutter & Co., No. 2:19-cv-00483-JAM-DMC, 2019 U.S. Dist. LEXIS 85631, at *10 (E.D. Cal. May 20, 2019) (noting that typical default occurs when the borrower fails to make monthly payments to the lender).

4. *Id.* (borrower's failure to pay government taxes and insurance constituted a default); Sec. First Nat'l Bank v. Lamb, 212 Cal. 64, 68 (1931) ("if the mortgagor fails to pay due taxes and assessments, under provisions similar to those set forth above, the mortgagee may pay the same, and add the amount so paid to the mortgage debt, and if the mortgagor refuses to refund the same, he is in default, and the mortgagee may foreclose").

5. *See* CAL. CIV. CODE §§ 2924c(a)(1); *see also* Morris v. J.P. Morgan Chase Bank, N.A., 78 Cal. App. 5th 279, 293 (2022) ("During the foreclosure process, the debtor/trustor is given several opportunities to cure the default and avoid the loss of the property. First, the trustor is entitled to a period of reinstatement to make the back payments and reinstate

right of reinstatement after a nonmonetary default.[6] The statute states in pertinent part:

> (a)(1) Whenever all or a portion of the principal sum of any obligation secured by deed of trust or mortgage on real property . . . therein hereafter executed has, prior to the maturity date fixed in that obligation, become due or been declared due by reason of default in payment of interest or of any installment of principal, or by reason of failure of trustor or mortgagor to pay, in accordance with the terms of that obligation or of the deed of trust or mortgage, taxes, assessments, premiums for insurance, or advances made by beneficiary or mortgagee in accordance with the terms of that obligation or of the deed of trust or mortgage, the trustor or mortgagor . . . may pay to the beneficiary . . . the entire amount due, at the time payment is tendered, with respect to (A) all amounts of principal, interest, taxes, assessments, insurance premiums, or advances actually known by the beneficiary to be, and that are, in default and shown in the notice of default, under the terms of the deed of trust or mortgage and the obligation secured thereby, (B) all amounts in default on recurring obligations not shown in the notice of default, and (C) all reasonable costs and expenses, subject to subdivision (c), that are actually incurred in enforcing the terms of the obligation, deed of trust, or mortgage, and trustee's or attorney's fees . . . and thereby cure the default theretofore existing . . .[7]

Under this statute, if the sale is postponed for more than five business days, the right of reinstatement is revived.[8] In addition to the right of reinstatement, the debtor possesses equity of redemption, which permits the debtor to pay all sums due before the sale of the property at foreclosure and thus avoid the sale.[9]

Nonmonetary defaults are defaults that the payment of money cannot cure. Such defaults include the failure to maintain or repair improvements, the destruction or removal of improvements, the failure to furnish

---

the terms of the loan. . . . This period of reinstatement continues until five business days prior to the date of the sale, including any postponement.").

6. *See* Cal. Civ. Code § 2924c(a)(1).

7. *See id.* § 2924(c).

8. *See id.* § 2924c(e).

9. *See id.* §§ 2903, 2905; *Morris*, 78 Cal. App. 5th at 293.

financial statements, the failure to comply with financial covenants, the cancellation of a lease, or the failure to comply with applicable laws.

Not every nonmonetary default under the terms of the loan documents justifies foreclosure. Unlike a monetary default, a nonmonetary default may not cause the lender to incur a financial loss or obligation. A court can relieve a debtor from a technical nonmonetary default unless the beneficiary has suffered or there is a threat to an impairment of its security.[10] In *La Sala v. American Savings & Loan Association*, the court concluded that the burden is on the lender to show that a monetary default created a "danger of impairment of security" to justify the acceleration of the debt and foreclosure on the property.[11] *La Sala* involved a due-on-encumbrance clause that accelerated the debtor's loan if a junior encumbrance was revoked against the property.[12] The California Supreme Court, in *Tucker v. Lassen Savings & Loan Association*, later affirmed the *La Sala* principle.[13] In *Brown v. Avemco Investment Corp.*, the Ninth Circuit echoed the rationale of the *La Sala* court while examining Texas law and found that acceleration is an equitable remedy that focuses on whether a default impairs the collateral securing the loan, stating:

> Acceleration clauses are designed to protect the creditor from actions by the debtor which jeopardize or impair the creditor's security. They are not to be used offensively, e.g., for the commercial advantage of the creditor. Acceleration is a harsh remedy with draconian consequences for the debtor. Acceleration is a matter of equity and the courts . . . have historically been careful to evaluate the fairness of acceleration in the particular facts of a case.[14]

Other courts have followed this rationale to prohibit acceleration and foreclosure based on nonmonetary default. In *Bart v. Streuli*, the court

---

10. *See, e.g.*, Schoolcraft v. Ross, 81 Cal. App. 3d 75, 80 (1978) (impairment required); Brown v. Avemco Inv. Corp., 603 F.2d 1367, 1376 (9th Cir. 1979) (acceleration is a matter of fairness; acceleration of debt aimed to protect against impairment of creditor's security). Acceleration of a loan based on a nonmonetary default may violate the implied covenant of good faith and fair dealing.

11. *See* La Sala v. American Sav. & Loan Ass'n, 5 Cal. 3d 864, 882 (1971).

12. *Id.* at 869.

13. *See* Tucker v. Lassen Sav. & Loan Ass'n, 12 Cal. 3d 629, 640 (1974) (examined acceleration based on due-on-sale clause; found acceleration based on "due-on" clause was an unreasonable restraint on alienation).

14. *Brown*, 603 F.2d at 1376.

prohibited foreclosure when the default caused no harm to the lender. In that case, the loan documents prohibited demolishing or removing any portion of the building on the encumbered property and affirmatively required the borrowers to cultivate, fertilize, and prune the growing trees.[15] Without the lender's approval, the borrowers removed the front porch and also failed to cultivate, fertilize, or prune the trees. The court found that the lender was barred from foreclosing "because [lender] was not injured in any way, and was in fact benefited by [borrowers'] acts."[16] The court ruled that it "had the power to relieve against the effect of any technical violation of covenants" in the loan documents.[17]

In *Baypoint Mortgage Corp. v. Crest Premium Real Estate Investments Trust*, the court ruled that equity would not allow "the drastic sanction of foreclosure to be used to enforce compliance with payment on the 'due date.'"[18] In that case, the borrower agreed under the promissory note to make payments on the first day of each month and to pay a late fee if payment was not received on the tenth day.[19] The borrower habitually made payments on the thirteenth day of the month.[20] The lender notified the borrower that it would commence foreclosure proceedings if it did not receive payment by the first of each month.[21] When a payment was not received by the first of the month, the lender recorded a notice of default on the fifth day after the payment was due.[22] The court enjoined the sale. The court found that the provision imposing a late fee after ten days determines "to what degree time is of the essence" in making payments by the due date.[23] As such, the court held that a payment made within the period before late charges accrue cannot normally be deemed a default justifying foreclosure.[24]

If a lender decides to accelerate the loan and foreclose based on nonmonetary default, the lender will need to closely examine whether such

15. *See* Bart v. Streuli, 5 Cal. 2d 67, 67–68 (1935)

16. *Id.* at 68.

17. *Id.* (citing Ebbert v. Mercantile Tr. Co., 213 Cal. 496, 499 (1931) (equity may prevent a foreclosure)).

18. Baypoint Mortg. Corp. v. Crest Premium Real Estate Inv. Trust, 168 Cal. App. 3d 818, 827 (1985).

19. *See id.* at 822.

20. *See id.*

21. *See id.*

22. *See id.* at 823.

23. *See id.* at 826.

24. *See id.* at 825.

default impaired the value of its collateral.[25] That may not be easy to determine and will depend on the factual circumstances. The mere reduction of the property's value may or may not be sufficient depending on the circumstances, including the amount of the unpaid debt, the equity in the property, the market trend (i.e., are property values decreasing), and the magnitude of the reduction. If the property has substantial equity or if the equity in the property has grown since the loan originated, a debtor could argue that the mere reduction in property value is irrelevant, given that there is a sufficient equity cushion to ensure that the lender is paid in full. A lender could argue that an impairment occurs when nonmonetary default decreases the bargained-for equity cushion or loan-to-value ratio. A lender may also argue that a nonmonetary default decreasing the value of property exists, even if there is an equity cushion when the equity cushion is being eroded by accruing interest or depreciation.

PRACTICE TIP

Foreclosures are equitable proceedings. Before foreclosing, a lender should provide written notice to the borrower of its intent to foreclose, identifying every monetary and nonmonetary default. When nonjudicially foreclosing, a lender should specifically identify each monetary and nonmonetary default in the notice of default, which should match the written notice to the borrower. If the lender only identifies monetary defaults (without identifying nonmonetary defaults in the notice of default), the borrower may be able to reinstate the loan by curing the monetary default.

III. COLLECTION OF COMMERCIAL LOANS SECURED BY REAL PROPERTY

A. Election of Remedies: Judicial and Nonjudicial Foreclosure

Under California law, two types of foreclosure proceedings may enforce a defaulted loan secured by real property: (1) a judicial foreclosure action; and

25. The impairment of collateral issues is analogous to issues that arise in the Bankruptcy Code involving the use of cash collateral or relief from the automatic stay due to a lack of equity. *See* 11 U.S.C. §§ 362(d)(1), 363.

(2) a nonjudicial foreclosure sale (also referred to as a trustee sale). A nonjudicial foreclosure proceeding is generally faster and less expensive than a judicial foreclosure. In many states, there is no postsale right of redemption by the debtor after a nonjudicial foreclosure sale. In contrast, a debtor typically possesses a right of redemption after a judicial foreclosure sale.

A deed of trust that does not expressly contain a "power of sale" clause can only be foreclosed by court proceedings.[26] A power of sale clause is a contractual provision that authorizes a trustee to conduct a public sale of the property upon default outside of court.[27] Courts liberally construe a clause in a deed of trust to grant the power of sale.[28] A creditor's right to conduct a public sale without judicial proceedings is irrevocable, even if the trustor dies.[29] If the deed of trust contains a power of sale clause, the secured creditor may simultaneously exercise the dual judicial and nonjudicial foreclosure remedies.[30] As such, a secured creditor whose deed of trust contains the power of sale may pursue a judicial and nonjudicial foreclosure sale singularly or simultaneously (commonly referred to as dual tracking).[31] The secured creditor may commence a nonjudicial foreclosure proceeding and then discontinue it in favor of pursuing judicial foreclosure without prejudice.[32] Alternatively, a secured creditor may file a judicial action and dismiss the action in favor of selling the real property at a public auction via a nonjudicial foreclosure proceeding so long as no judgment

26. *See* Cal. Civ. Code §§ 2931, 2932; Cal. Civ. Code § 725a.

27. *See* Garfinkle v. Superior Court, 21 Cal. 3d 268, 277 (1978); Davidson v. Corp. of America, 16 Cal. App. 6, 13 (1936); *see also* Estate of Jones v. Live Well Fin., Inc., 902 F.3d 1337, 1340 (11th Cir. 2018) (power of sale clause permits "private parties to sell at auction, without any court oversight, property pledged as security by a debtor who has come into default").

28. *See* Fogarty v. Sawyer, 17 Cal. 589, 591 (1861).

29. *See* Weber v. McCleverty, 149 Cal. 316, 323 (1906); Athearn v. Ryan, 154 Cal. 554, 556 (1908).

30. *See* Cal. Civ. Code § 725a.

31. *See* Flack v. Boland, 11 Cal. 2d 103, 107–08 (1938); Commercial Ctr. Realty Co. v. Superior Court of San Francisco, 7 Cal. 2d 121, 129 (1936) ("The remedy which the mortgagee has elected to pursue to the exclusion of the other remedy therefore is the exercise of the power of sale contained in the mortgage. Moreover, if it be conceded merely for the sake of argument that the mortgagee elected to proceed by foreclosure, such election did not preclude the subsequent exercise of the power of sale").

32. *See* Shin v. Superior Court, 26 Cal. App. 4th 542, 547 (1994) ("the mere *commencement* of an action by the creditor that does not include a foreclosure of all the real property security is not in violation of the rule since the creditor may dismiss the action before judgment or amend the complaint to include a foreclosure of all of the security").

or adverse action beyond collateral is taken.[33] A secured creditor is not deemed to have elected its remedy until the trustee sale is conducted or a judgment is obtained.[34]

A secured creditor may benefit from dual-tracking judicial and nonjudicial foreclosure proceedings. A secured creditor may file a judicial foreclosure action to obtain a receiver to collect rent or manage the real property pending foreclosure.[35] By filing dual proceedings, a secured creditor preserves its right to obtain a deficiency until it better understands the debtor's financial condition or the property's value. The value of the real property collateral will largely determine which remedy a secured creditor will pursue. If the property's value exceeds the debt owed under the loan, the secured creditor should probably pursue a nonjudicial foreclosure. Conversely, if the property's value is less than the debt and the debtor or guarantor is collectible, a judicial foreclosure should probably be pursued to obtain a deficiency judgment, which cannot be obtained through a nonjudicial foreclosure.

B. Nonjudicial Foreclosure

Recording of the Notice of Default

When the trustor defaults on any obligation secured by a deed of trust containing a power of sale, the beneficiary has the right to declare a default and proceed with a foreclosure sale under the power of sale. A nonjudicial foreclosure sale is a two-stage process. The first stage begins with recording a notice of default and election to sell.[36] A notice of default is not effective until it is recorded.[37]

---

33. In *Shin*, 26 Cal. App. 4th at 550, the court held that a "judgment be entered before the sanction of the 'one form of action' rule applies to bar further recovery on collateral for a debt." The court further held that prior to judgment, "an attachment of a debtor's unsecured property as a means to enforce an obligation secured by the debtor's real property is so contrary to public policy that its creation justifies the forfeiture of the secured creditor's security interest." *See also* McDonald v. Smoke Creek Live Stock Co., 209 Cal. 231, 240 (1930) (foreclosure judgment deemed res judicata as to the issues decided and was binding upon one claiming title to the property).

34. *See* Carpenter Title Ins. & Trust Co., 71 Cal. 2d 593 (1945); Vlahovich v. Cruz, 213 Cal. App. 3d 317, 321 (1989).

35. *See* Turner v. Superior Court, 72 Cal. App. 3d 804, 818 (1977) (authorizes the appointment of a rents and profits receiver to sell the estate prior to foreclosure sale).

36. *See* Cal. Civ. Code § 2924(a)(1).

37. *See* U.S. Hertz v. Niobrara Farms, 41 Cal. App. 3d 68, 85 (1974).

The notice of default serves to notify the trustor, junior lienholders, and other interested persons that a default occurred and the nature of the default to allow them to reinstate the loan.[38] In *R.E. Loans, LLC v. Investors Warranty of America, Inc.*, the court ruled that notice of default containing the "mandatory language" disclosing the amount owed is "directed to the property owner, not the holder of a junior trust deed."[39] However, given that a junior lienholder is permitted to reinstate a defaulted loan, the notice of default facilitates the purpose of allowing the junior lienholder to protect its interest in the property.[40]

Courts have described foreclosure as a "drastic sanction" and a "draconian remedy."[41] As such, the form and content of the notice of default are statutorily mandated and must be complied with strictly.[42] The notice of default must contain (a) the name of the trustor, (b) a description of the secured property or the instrument number or book/page number of the originally recorded deed of trust, (c) declaration that a breach of the obligation occurred and the nature of each breach, and (d) a statement of the beneficiary's election to sell the property to satisfy the obligation or other obligation secured by the deed of trust.[43] The notice of default must set forth "the nature of each breach actually known to the beneficiary."[44] The secured creditor's omission of all "known defaults" in the notice of default does not constitute a waiver and may be relied upon in subsequent notices of default.[45] If the default identified in the notice of default is curable, the notice of default must specify the amount due, the reinstatement period, and certain statutory warnings.[46] A statutorily deficient notice of

38. *See* Cal. Civ. Code § 2924c.

39. R.E. Loans, LLC v. Investors Warranty of America, Inc., 212 Cal. App. 4th 1432, 1439 (2013).

40. *See* Miller & Starr, California Real Estate § 13:224, pp. 13–922 n.20 (4th ed. 2021).

41. *See* Ozkay v. Equity Wave Lending, Inc., No. 20-cv-08263-JST, 2020 U.S. Dist. LEXIS 242879, at *3 (N.D. Cal. Dec. 28, 2020) ("Foreclosure is a 'drastic sanction' and a 'draconian remedy'"); Baypoint Mortg. Corp. v. Crest Premium Real Estate etc. Tr., 168 Cal. App. 3d 818, 827 (1985) ("drastic sanction of foreclosure").

42. *See Ozkay*, No. 20-cv-08263-JST, 2020 U.S. Dist. LEXIS 242879, at *3 (statutory requirements "must be strictly followed"); Bisno v. Sax, 175 Cal. App. 2d 714, 720 (1959) (Civil Code section 2924 "must be strictly followed"); Kleckner v. Bank of Am. Nat'l Tr. & Sav. Ass'n, 97 Cal. App. 2d 30, 34 (1950).

43. Cal. Civ. Code §§ 2924(a)(1)(A)–(C).

44. *Id.* § 2924(a)(1)(D).

45. *Id.* § 2924(e).

46. *See id.* §§ 2924(a)(1)(D), 2024c(b)(1).

default is invalid and may be set aside if the trustor can establish that prejudice resulted from the error.[47] In short, to set aside a nonjudicial sale, the trustor must establish that the foreclosure sale was procured by fraud, was "improperly, unfairly or unlawfully conducted, or tainted by fraud," or "where there has been such a mistake that to allow it to stand would be inequitable to purchaser and parties."[48]

Service of the Notice of Default

Within ten business days after the notice of default is recorded, the notice of default must be mailed by registered or certified mail, postage prepaid, to the trustor and to all other persons who requested notice and whose request for special notice was recorded before the recordation of the notice of default.[49] An additional copy of the notice of default must be mailed to the trustor by first-class mail, postage prepaid.[50] If "the last business or residence physical address actually known" differs from that address, the notice must be sent to that address.[51] Further, the notice of default must be mailed to the trustor even if an attorney represents the trustor.[52] A trustee complies with notice requirements by mailing the notice to the trustor at their last known address. In *Estate of Yates*, the trustee mailed a notice of default to the trustor, who had died before such mailing.[53] The court ruled that a trustee who does not know that a trustor has died complies with statutory notice by mailing a notice of default to the trustor at their last known address. However, if the trustee knows that a trustor has died and the public administrator is administering the deceased's estate, the trustee must notify the public administrator of default.[54]

---

47. *See* Kleckner v. Bank of Am. Nat'l Tr. & Sav. Ass'n, 97 Cal. App. 2d 30, 34 (1950) (trustor bears the burden of establishing that prejudice caused by error in the notice of default).

48. Lona v. Citibank, N.A., 202 Cal. App. 4th 89, 103 (2011) ("It is the general rule that courts have power to vacate a foreclosure sale where there has been fraud in the procurement of the foreclosure decree or where the sale has been improperly, unfairly or unlawfully conducted, or is tainted by fraud, or where there has been such a mistake that to allow it to stand would be inequitable to purchaser and parties.").

49. *See* Cal. Civ. Code § 2924b(b)(1).

50. *See id.* § 2924b(b)(1), (3).

51. *See id.*

52. *See* Ellison v. Fullett Rosenlund Anderson P.C., 347 F. Supp. 3d 370, 380 (N.D. Ill. 2018) ("California law requires the trustee to mail the notices of default and sale directly to the borrower, and makes no exception for borrowers who are represented by counsel.").

53. *See* Estate of Yates, 25 Cal. App. 4th 511, 521 (1994).

54. *See id.*

The person who mails the notice must execute and retain an affidavit identifying the notice mailed, showing the name and residence or business address of that person, that they are over eighteen years of age, the date of deposit in the mail, the name and address of the trustor or mortgagee to whom sent, and that the envelope was sealed and deposited in the mail with postage fully prepaid.[55] In the absence of fraud, the affidavit required by this subdivision establishes a conclusive presumption of mailing.[56]

If the deed of trust does not contain the trustor's address and if the trustor's address is not known, the notice of default must be published once a week for four successive weeks starting ten business days after the recordation of the notice of default in a newspaper of general circulation in the county where the property is located.[57]

The failure to mail (or publish) the notice to the trustor as statutorily required may constitute grounds to set aside the subsequent trustee sale.[58] The trustor must establish that the lack of notice prejudiced the trustor. Mere inadequacy of price, even a gross disparity, is insufficient for setting aside a sale legally made absent proof of fraud, unfairness, or oppression.[59] A court will not likely set aside a completed sale to a bona fide purchaser for value (where the trustee's deed has been delivered to the purchaser) even if there is a substantial disparity between the sale price and the property's value.[60] The California Supreme Court explained the trustor's ability to challenge the purchase of property by a bona fide purchaser for value, stating:

> The purchaser at a foreclosure sale takes title by a trustee's deed. If the trustee's deed recites that all statutory notice requirements and procedures required by law for the conduct of the foreclosure

---

55. *See* Cal. Civ. Code § 2924b(e).

56. *See id.*

57. *See id.* § 2924b(d).

58. *See* Estate of Yates, 25 Cal. App. 4th at 523 (failure to give proper notice constitutes ground to set aside sale); Ram v. OneWest Bank, FSB 234 Cal. App. 4th 1, 10–11 (2015) ("wrongfulness" element of cause of action to set aside trustee's sale can be satisfied by noncompliance with notice requirements).

59. *See* Sargent v. Shumaker, 193 Cal. 122, 130 (1924) (mere inadequacy of price insufficient to set aside even if trustor is not provided notice of sale).

60. *See* Estate of Yates, 25 Cal. App. 4th 511, 523 (1994) ("Where . . . the trustee's deed recites that all requirements of law have been complied with, . . . failure to comply with the notice requirements is a ground to cancel the sale only as against a party who is not a bona fide purchaser.").

> have been satisfied, a rebuttable presumption arises that the sale has been conducted regularly and properly; this presumption is conclusive as to a bona fide purchaser . . . But "the conclusive presumption does not apply until a trustee's deed is delivered."[61]

Thus, if a defect in the procedure is discovered after the bid is accepted but before delivery of the trustee's deed, the trustee may abort a sale to a bona fide purchaser, return the purchase price, and restart the foreclosure process.[62]

In *Biancalana*, the trustee mistakenly communicated to the auctioneer an incorrect opening bid that was less than 10 percent of the actual amount of the credit bid submitted by the foreclosing beneficiary.[63] The trustee discovered the error before it delivered the trustee's deed to the bona fide purchaser at the sale.[64] As such, the court ruled that the conclusive presumption does not apply, and the gross inadequacy of price coupled with the unfairness and irregularity serves as a sufficient basis to set aside the sale.[65] The bid was an irregularity sufficient to set aside the sale.[66] In setting aside the sale, the court noted that the trustee's error is not imputed to the beneficiary because "the trustee under a deed of trust is an agent of the beneficiary only in a limited sense," in which the trustee plays a passive, statutory role.[67]

C. Judicial Foreclosure

Overview of Mechanics Lien for Filing Judicial Foreclosure Action

A beneficiary, trustee, or their successor under a deed of trust may file an action in Superior Court to recover the debt owed or enforce the obligation secured by the deed of trust.[68] Such an action is a proceeding in equity.[69]

---

61. Biancalana v. T.D. Serv. Co., 56 Cal. 4th 807, 814–15 (2013) (citations omitted).

62. *See id.*

63. *See id.* at 812.

64. *See id.* at 814.

65. *See id.*

66. *See id.* at 818.

67. *See id.*

68. *See* Cal. Civ. Proc. Code §§ 86, 725a, 726(a); Cal. Civ. Code § 2931.

69. *See* Nelson v. Orosco, 117 Cal. App. 3d 73, 76 (1981).

The action must be filed in the county where all or part of the property is located.[70] The complaint should set forth a statement of facts identifying the underlying obligation, the deed of trust, its date of recordation, and the property being foreclosed upon in the foreclosure action. The complaint should also accurately set forth the legal description of the property.

The current record titleholder of the encumbered property must be named a defendant, even if the titleholder was not the trustor and did not assume the debt.[71] Prior owners who neither assumed any obligations to the bank nor were current titleholders should not be named as defendants.[72] The failure to name the current owner "of record" deprives the court of the ability to take action against that owner. In *Burton v. Lies*, the trustor sold the encumbered property to a married purchaser who later died.[73] The plaintiff filed a judicial foreclosure action against the trustor and the purchaser's estate but failed to name the purchaser's surviving wife as defendant, even though she owned an undivided one-half interest.[74] The court declined to extend any relief impacting the wife's interest in the property, including the right to possession.[75]

All persons liable for a deficiency judgment should be named defendants in the action, such as guarantors and co-obligors. Similarly, all junior lienholders should be named as a defendant to extinguish their rights to foreclose their rights.[76] If the junior lienholder is included, its interests in the encumbered property will be generally terminated upon a sale conducted under judicial action.[77] If a junior lienholder is omitted, the junior lienholder's rights are not terminated, including, but not limited to, the right to redeem the property under California Civil Code sections 2903 through 2905 and section 2924c.[78] However, the purchaser, an assignee of

---

70. *See* Cal. Civ. Proc. Code § 392(a)(2); *see also* Appel v. Hubbard, 155 Cal. App. 2d 639, 641 (1957).

71. *See* Cal. Civ. Proc. Code § 726(c).

72. *See* Johnson v. Home Owners' Loan Corp., 46 Cal. App. 2d 546, 548–49 (1941).

73. *See* Burton v. Lies, 21 Cal. 87, 90 (1862).

74. *See id.*

75. *See id.* at 92.

76. *See* Cal. Civ. Proc. Code § 726(c); Cal. Civ. Code §§ 2903–2905.

77. *See* Cal. Civ. Proc. Code § 701.630.

78. *See* Fox v. Cal. Title Ins. Co., 120 Cal. App. 264, 266 (1932) (if junior lienholder is not joined, his rights are not affected by judgment and sale under the foreclosure suit); *see* Cal. Civ. Proc. Code § 726(c).

the senior lien, may file a separate foreclosure action or a quiet title action to terminate the junior lienholder's rights.[79]

Certain parties do not need to be named defendants in a judicial foreclosure action. A plaintiff does not need to name senior lienholders as defendants; if named, the senior lienholder may file a cross-complaint to foreclose on its senior lien.[80] A person holding an unrecorded lien need not be named as a defendant, as such a person is conclusively bound by the foreclosure judgment, even if the plaintiff knows the unrecorded interest.[81]

Upon filing a complaint for judicial foreclosure, the plaintiff should record a lis pendens in each county where all or part of the property is located.[82] The filing of a lis pendens provides constructive notice of the foreclosure action.[83] "In the absence of notice, actual or constructive, one who takes title from the defendant pending the action is not bound by the judgment if not a party thereto."[84]

Foreclosure Judgment and Sale

Once the complaint for judicial foreclosure is filed, it is handled like any other civil ligation. A plaintiff may seek a default judgment if a defendant fails to answer the complaint or may move for summary judgment or summary adjudication.[85] If necessary, the action may proceed to trial. If a court finds in favor of a plaintiff through default, summary judgment, or trial, the court will enter a judgment of foreclosure.[86] This judgment should (1) declare the amount of the secured debt owed to the plaintiff; (2) direct issuance of a writ of sale, requiring the levying officer to sell the encumbered property; (3) direct application of the sale proceeds to pay court costs, levy and sale expenses, and the amount due to the plaintiff, including reasonable attorneys' fees and costs if permitted under the loan documents; (4) direct any excess sale proceeds to be paid to defendants whom the court determines are entitled to receive such excess proceeds; and (5) identify

79. *See* Diamond Benefits Life Ins. Co. v. Troll, 66 Cal. App. 4th 1, 10 (1998) (purchaser filed quiet title action against omitted junior lienholder).

80. *See* Van Loben Sels v. Bunnell, 131 Cal. 489, 494 (1901).

81. *See* CAL. CIV. PROC. CODE § 726(c); Hager v. Astorg, 145 Cal. 548, 549–51 (1904).

82. *See* CAL. CIV. PROC. CODE § 405.20.

83. *See* Foster v. Warren, 39 Cal. App. 2d 470, 475 (1940) (lis pendens provides constructive notice).

84. *Id.*; *see also* Page v. W. W. Chase Co., 145 Cal. 578, 582 (1904).

85. *See* CAL. CIV. PROC. CODE §§ 437c, 585–87.

86. *See id.* § 726(a)–(b).

the defendants who may be liable for any deficiency judgment if the sale proceeds are insufficient to pay the outstanding obligation.[87] Upon entry, the plaintiff should serve notice of entry of the foreclosure judgment under Code of Civil Procedure section 664.54(a). The court clerk should then issue a writ of sale under the judgment.[88] The plaintiff should prepare a notice of levy and notice of sale consistent with the judgment and deliver them to the levying officer.[89] The levying officer must then record the writ of sale and the notice of levy and serve them upon the judgment debtor and any occupants of the property.[90] At least twenty days before the sale date, the levying officer must post, publish, mail, and serve notice of the sale as required under Code of Civil Procedure section 701.540.

The sale must be held in the county where the property is located between 9:00 a.m. and 5:00 p.m.[91] A sale may only be postponed if the judgment debtor and creditor agree to such postponement.[92] The judgment creditor may credit bid any amount up to the amount owed; a creditor that bids more than the amount owed must pay cash, certified check, or cashier's check to cover the excess.[93] All other bidders must pay with cash, certified check, or cashier's check.

If the deficiency judgment is allowed under the judgment, the levying officer issues a certificate of sale to the purchaser.[94] If the proceeds are insufficient to satisfy the indebtedness owed to the judgment creditor, the borrower will generally have one year after the sale to redeem the property for a redemption price equal to the purchase price, subject to certain statutory adjustments.[95] If the proceeds are sufficient to satisfy the indebtedness owed, the applicable redemption is three months.[96] Once the redemption period expires, the levying officer executes and delivers a deed of sale to

87. *See id.* §§ 726(a)–(b), 727, 730.

88. *See id.* §§ 699.520, 716.010–.020, 712.010–.060.

89. *See id.* §§ 699.540–.545, 700.015, 701.540, 701.547.

90. *See id.* §§ 700.015, 701.540, 716.020(a).

91. *See id.* § 701.570(a).

92. *See id.* § 701.580.

93. *See id.* § 2924h; Central Sav. Bank v. Lake, 201 Cal. 438, 447 (1927). Prior to the foreclosure sale, the judgment creditor should appraise the property to determine its value.

94. *See id.* § 729.040.

95. *See id.* § 729.030(b).

96. *See id.* § 729.030(a).

the purchaser.[97] If the property is redeemed, the levying officer executes and delivers a recordable redemption certificate to the redeeming party.[98]

Upon completion of the sale, the levying officer distributes the sale proceeds according to the terms of the judgment.[99] They then file a return of the writ of sale setting forth the sale price and the distribution of the sale proceeds.[100] If the sale did not satisfy the indebtedness, the judgment creditor must apply for a fair-value determination and entry of a deficiency judgment.[101] Such an application must be filed within three months after the date of the sale.[102] This three-month period constitutes a statute of limitations for seeking a deficiency judgment.[103] As such, this deadline may not be extended by application of equitable consideration or under California Code of Civil Procedure section 473 for mistake, inadvertence, surprise, or excusable neglect.[104]

A court must conduct a hearing to determine the fair value of the property.[105] At this hearing, the parties must submit evidence as to the fair value of the real property sold.[106] An "owner of the property," including a person entitled to possession, may opine on the property's value, provided that an adequate foundation can be laid for the owner's testimony.[107] For instance, in *Jones v. Wachovia Bank*, the court excluded an owner's property valuation at a fair-value hearing, finding that the owner lacked foundation and information upon which to base such valuation.[108] Permitting an owner to testify as to value is premised on the notion that an owner acquires sufficient information and knowledge of the property to estimate its value.[109] Rather than merely relying on the owner's testimony, both the judgment creditor and defendants may call certified appraisers to testify as

97. *See id.* § 729.080(a).

98. *See id.* § 729.080(b).

99. *See id.* §§ 716.020(c), 726(a).

100. *See id.* §§ 699.560, 712.050.

101. *See id.* § 726(b)

102. *See id.*

103. *See* Life Sav. Bank v. Wilhelm, 84 Cal. App. 4th 174, 178 (2000) (three-month period is a statute of limitations).

104. *See id.* at 177.

105. *See* Cal. Civ. Proc. Code § 726(b).

106. *See id.*

107. *See* Cal. Evid. Code §§ 813(a)(2), 813(c)(1), 814.

108. *See* Jones v. Wachovia, 230 Cal. App. 4th 935, 950–51 (2014).

109. *See* City of Pleasant Hill v. First Baptist Church, 1 Cal. App. 3d 384 (1969).

to the value of the property. Alternatively, the court may appoint a probate referee to appraise the property, submit the appraisal into evidence, and testify at the fair hearing subject to cross-examination.[110]

The fair-value hearing was a product of the Great Depression and seeks to protect the defaulting trustor.[111] "The 'fair value' of foreclosed property is . . . its intrinsic value. Under normal conditions, this intrinsic value will often coincide with its fair market value, the value a willing purchaser will pay a willing seller in an open market."[112] The fair value must also consider all the circumstances affecting the underlying worth of the property at the time of the sale without considering the impact of foreclosure proceedings on this value.[113] If the fair value of the property is less than the sale price, the deficiency judgment amount is limited to the actual deficiency (i.e., outstanding indebtedness less the sale price).[114] If the fair value of the property is more than the sale price, then a deficiency judgment is entered between the indebtedness and the fair value.[115]

One-Action Rule: Overview

All lenders must be aware of the "one-action" rule, which limits a lender's ability to enforce and collect debts secured by real property.[116] Many states have modeled their one-action rule after California's one-action rule (also called "One Form of Action Rule"), found in section 726(a) of the California Code of Civil Procedure. This section provides:

> (a) There can be but one form of action for the recovery of any debt or the enforcement of any right secured by mortgage upon real property or an estate for years therein, which action shall be in accordance with the provisions of this chapter. In the action the court may, by its judgment, direct the sale of the encumbered real property or estate for years therein (or so much of the real property or estate for years as may be necessary), and the application of the proceeds of the sale to the payment of the costs of court, the

---

110. *See id.*

111. *See* Rainer Mortg. v. Silverwood, 163 Cal. App. 3d 359, 365 (1985).

112. *Id.* at 366.

113. *See id.* at 367.

114. *See* Cal. Civ. Proc. Code § 726(b).

115. *See id.*

116. *See, e.g.*, Cal. Civ. Proc. Code § 726; Mich. Comp. Laws § 600.3204(1)(b).

> expenses of levy and sale, and the amount due plaintiff, including, where the mortgage provides for the payment of attorney's fees, the sum for attorney's fees as the court shall find reasonable, not exceeding the amount named in the mortgage.

Under the one-action rule, a creditor must first exhaust its security before seeking a money judgment on a debtor secured by a deed of trust or mortgage.[117] In a nutshell, "[a] secured creditor can bring only one lawsuit to enforce its security interest and collect its debt."[118] The one-action rule was enacted to safeguard borrowers who default on a loan secured by real property.[119] It protects borrowers from multiple lawsuits from creditors and requires creditors to first exhaust their security before seeking a money judgment against the debtor for a deficiency.[120]

The one-action rule under section 726 can serve as a shield or a sword.[121] As a shield, a debtor may interpose the one-action rule as an affirmative defense to suit brought by the secured creditor.[122] The effect of the affirmative defense is to bar the action and force the creditor to exhaust the security before seeking a personal judgment against the debtor for a deficiency.[123] As a sword, this rule can be wielded as a sanction against the secured creditor.[124] The debtor may use the one-action rule to argue that the secured creditor elected its remedies by not foreclosing and waiving the security.[125] As one court noted, "[i]f the secured creditor does not resort to all its security before obtaining money judgment on the underlying debt, the secured creditor may be deemed to have made an 'election of remedies'

---

117. *See* Hartman v. Smith, 219 Cal. App. 2d 415, 417 (1963).

118. Coker v. J.P. Morgan Chase Bank, N.A., 62 Cal. 4th 667, 690–91 (2016).

119. *See id.* at 673.

120. *See* Felton v. West, 102 Cal. 266, 269 (1894) (one-action rule remedied the "evil" of "multiplicity of suits, and the harassing of the debtor by two actions"); Sav. Bank of San Diego Cty. v. Cent. Mkt. Co., 122 Cal. 28, 36 (1898) (one-action rule prevents a multiplicity of suits and compels the creditor to first exhaust his security); Sec. Pac. Nat'l Bank v. Wozab, 51 Cal. 3d 991, 997 (1990) (*Wozab*) (creditor "forced to exhaust the security before he may obtain a money judgment against the debtor for any deficiency").

121. *See Wozab*, 51 Cal. 3d at 997; *see also* In re Kearns, 314 B.R. 819, 822 (B.A.P. 9th Cir. 2004).

122. *See Wozab*, 51 Cal. 3d at 997.

123. *See id.*; *see also* Walker v. Community Bank, 10 Cal. 3d 729, 734 (1974).

124. *See Wozab*, 51 Cal. 3d at 997; *In re Kearns*, 314 B.R. at 822.

125. *See id.*

and to have waived the balance of its security."[126] The creditor may not foreclose but can recover a money judgment against the debtor.[127] If the debtor does not raise the one-action rule as a defense, the debtor waives the right to have the security exhausted before becoming personally liable for the debt.[128]

One "Action." Section 726 is both a "security-first" and "one-action" rule: "It compels the secured creditor, in a single action, to exhaust his security judicially before he may obtain a monetary 'deficiency' judgment against the debtor."[129] In determining whether a secured creditor violated section 726, a court must examine whether the creditor commenced an "action."[130] First, Section 726 limits the creditor to one "action" to recover its debt.[131] Section 22 of the California Code of Civil Procedure defines the word "action" as "an ordinary proceeding in a court of justice by which one party prosecutes another for the declaration, enforcement, or protection of a right, the redress or prevention of a wrong, or the punishment of a public offense."[132] In short, a "proceeding in a court of justice" generally constitutes an "action."[133] As a result, a trustee sale under a power of sale is not an "action" under the one-action rule because there is no court involvement.[134] As the California Supreme Court recognized in *Dreyfuss v. Union Bank of California*, "a creditor may proceed seriatim in foreclosing [non judicially] against multiple items of collateral without commencing a judicial action to determine the fair market value of each item sold and crediting that amount to the debt, before proceeding with foreclosure sales of any additional collateral."[135] The presenting of a claim to a labor commission outside of a court of law does not constitute an "action."[136] The

---

126. *In re Kearns*, 314 B.R. at 822.

127. *See Wozab*, 51 Cal. 3d at 997.

128. *See* Scalese v. Wong, 84 Cal. App. 4th 863, 869–70 (2000).

129. Black Sky Capital, LLC v. Cobb, 12 Cal. App. 5th 887, 896 (2017).

130. *See Wozab*, 51 Cal. 3d at 998.

131. *See id.* at 999.

132. CAL. CIV. PROC. CODE § 22.

133. *Id.*

134. *See* Black Sky Capital, LLC v. Cobb, 12 Cal. App. 5th 887, 896 (2017) ("Because there is no court involvement in a nonjudicial foreclosure, section 726 does not apply.").

135. Dreyfuss v. Union Bank of California, 24 Cal. 4th 400, 406 (2000).

136. Triad Data Serv., Inc. v. Jackson, 153 Cal. App. 3d Supp. 1, 12–13 (1984), overruled on other grounds by Smith v. Rae-Venter Law Grp., 29 Cal. 4th 345, 368 (2002).

setoff of funds is not "a 'proceeding in a court of justice' and therefore is not an 'action,'" but may violate the one-action rule as discussed below.[137]

The California Legislature and the courts have created multiple exceptions to what constitutes an action to recover a debt under the one-action rule. For instance, a secured creditor may seek an appointment of a receiver to take possession of the property, collect rents and profits, and take related actions under an assignment of rents clause without violating the one-action rule.[138] California Code of Civil Procedure section 564(d) states: "Any action by a secured lender to appoint a receiver under this section shall not constitute an action within the meaning of subdivision (a) of Section 726."[139] This section furthers the policies underlying the one-action rule because the appointment of a receiver merely preserves and protects the security under the supervision of the court. The rents are additional security for the debt payment, which the receiver would collect and apply the rents toward the debt if the foreclosure sale produces an insufficient amount for the entire loan.

A related exception exists under California Civil Code section 2938, which provides that upon default of an assignor under an obligation secured by an assignment of leases, rents, issues, and profits, the assignee may "collect and receive all rents, issues, and profits that have accrued but remain unpaid and uncollected by the assignor or its agent or for the assignor's benefit on that date, and all rents, issues, and profits that accrue on or after the date" by taking any of the following actions: (1) seek appointment of a receiver to collect rents; (2) obtain possession of the rents, issues, or profits; (3) deliver a written demand for turnover rents to tenants; or (4) deliver a written demand for turnover rents to the assignor.[140] Section 2938 states that taking any of the preceding activities does not violate the one-action rule.[141] Section 2938 authorizes the assignor to file an enforcement action to collect rents and profits without violating the one-action rule.[142]

Another exception to the one-action rule exists for certain fraud actions. Case law establishes that a claim for damages based on fraudulent

137. *See Wozab*, 51 Cal. 3d at 998.

138. *See* Ca. Civ. Proc. Code 564(d).

139. *Id.*

140. *See* Cal. Civ. Code § 2938(c)(1)–(4).

141. *See id.* § 2938(c).

142. *See id.* § 2938(f)(1).

inducement to make the loan is not barred by the one-action rule.[143] The legislature also established a specific statutory exception for

> a federal association, an affiliate of an association or federal association, a service corporation, or any successor in interest thereto, that originates, acquires, or purchases, in whole or in part, any loan secured directly or collaterally, in whole or in part, by a mortgage or deed of trust on real property, or any interest therein, may bring an action for recovery of damages, including exemplary damages not to exceed 50 percent of the actual damages, against a borrower where the action is based on [actual] fraud under Section 1572 of the Civil Code and the fraudulent conduct by the borrower induced the original lender to make that loan.[144]

This exception does not apply to "loans secured by single family, owner-occupied residential real property, when the property is actually occupied by the borrower as represented to the lender in order to obtain the loan and the loan is for an amount of one hundred fifty thousand dollars ($150,000) or less," as adjusted annually by the Consumer Price Index.[145]

Security-First Principle. Next, to determine whether the one-action rule is violated, the court must examine whether the secured creditor exhausted its security before seeking to recover its secured obligation.[146] This concept is referred to as the "security-first principle."[147] If a creditor possesses multiple security interests for a single debt, the creditor must exhaust all of those interests. If a secured obligation is secured by both personal property and real property, the secured creditor may conduct separate private sales or a private sale followed by a foreclosure action.[148] In *Walker v. Community Bank*, the bank made a loan secured by personal property and a second loan secured by real property.[149] When the debtor

---

143. *See* Alliance Mortg. Co. v. Rothwell, 10 Cal. 4th 1226, 1236–37 (1995) (one-action rule "[does] not preclude an action against a borrower for fraud in the inducement of a loan").

144. Cal. Civ. Proc. Code § 726(f); Cal. Fin. Code §§ 1301(a), 7460(a), 15102(a).

145. *See* Cal. Civ. Proc. Code § 726(g); Cal. Fin. Code §§ 1301(b), 7460(b), 15102(b).

146. *See Black Sky Capital, LLC*, 12 Cal. App. 5th at 896.

147. *Wozab*, 51 Cal. 3d at 1008.

148. *See* Ramsey v. Furlott, 14 Cal. App. 2d 145, 147 (1936) (private sale of personal property did not bar subsequent foreclosure action).

149. *See* Walker v. Community Bank, 10 Cal. 3d 729, 732 (1974).

defaulted, the bank commenced a judicial foreclosure action regarding the personal property and requested a deficiency judgment without mentioning the second loan or its real property security.[150] Before the entry of the deficiency judgment, the debtor sold the real property to a third party (Walker), and the bank recorded a notice of default on the real property under the second loan. Walker commenced an action to quiet title on the real property and to enjoin a trustee's sale claiming a violation of the one-action rule. The *Walker* court held:

> where 'there is a single debt secured by both real and personal property and the creditor elects to foreclose only on the personal property judicially, he thereby loses his security interest in the real property as against all parties even though the debtor does not raise the one form of action rule (§ 726) as an affirmative defense in the judicial foreclosure proceedings.[151]

In *Wozab*, the court recognized that "under section 726(a), a bank is not allowed to take a unilateral setoff of funds in a borrower/depositor's demand account against a debt secured by the depositor's interest in real property."[152] While the setoff does not constitute an "action" because it does not involve a "proceeding in a court of justice," it violates the "security-first" principle embodied under the one-action rule.[153] The bank must proceed against its security before resorting to the borrower's personal assets—i.e., bank deposits.[154] When a bank improperly sets off a deposit account violating the one-action rule, the bank waives any right to resort to the security, even if the borrower/depositor fails to object before the bank's setoff.[155] The borrower retains the right to require the bank to return the improper setoff and proceed against the security interest before the bank attempts to recover the underlying debt.[156] If the bank refuses the debtor's demand and retains the setoff funds, the security-first principle precludes the bank from foreclosing on the security interest or proceeding on the underlying debt without waiving the security. If the bank complies with

150. *See id.*

151. *Id.* at 741.

152. *Wozab*, 51 Cal. 3d at 1000.

153. *See id.* at 999–1000.

154. *See id.* at 1005.

155. *See id.*

156. *See id.* at 1006.

the borrower's demand and returns the funds, the borrower cannot claim that the bank waived the security interest.[157]

Waiver of the One-Action Rule. The benefits of the one-action rule may not be waived in advance by a borrower. Any purported waiver at the time of the loan transaction is void.[158] However, this rule does not preclude a trustor from subsequently waiving the one-action rule under certain circumstances.[159]

Anti-Deficiency Statutes

In addition to the one-action rule, the California legislature enacted anti-deficiency statutes (California Code of Civil Procedure sections 580a to 580d) to protect borrowers who default on real property loans.[160] Enacted during the Depression, California's anti-deficiency statutes "limit or prohibit lenders from obtaining personal judgments against borrowers where the lender's sale of real property security produces proceeds insufficient to cover the amount of the debt."[161] In other words, these statutes limit the right to recover deficiency judgments for the amount the debt exceeds the security value.[162] The legislature enacted these statutes to "prevent an overvaluation of the security," "prevent the aggravation of an economic recession which would result if creditors lost their property and were also burdened with personal liability," and "prevent the creditor from making an unreasonably low bid at the foreclosure sale, acquire the asset below its value, and also recover a personal judgment against the debtor."[163]

A borrower may not waive the anti-deficiency statutes in advance "because the anti-deficiency legislation was established for a public reason and cannot be contravened by a private agreement."[164] However, as

---

157. *See id.*

158. *See* Ca. Civ. Code § 2953.

159. *See* Salter v. Ulrich, 22 Cal. 2d 263, 266–67 (1943) (a borrower may waive his or her rights under section 726 after the loan is made, when all rights have been established and there remains only the enforcement of those rights).

160. *See* Coker v. J.P. Morgan Chase Bank, N.A., 62 Cal. 4th 667, 673 (2016).

161. Talbott v. Hustwit, 164 Cal. App. 4th 148, 151 (2008).

162. *See* In re Hoag Urgent Care Tustin, Inc., No. SACV 19-2343-MWF, 2021 U.S. Dist. LEXIS 61233, at *15 (C.D. Cal. Mar. 30, 2021).

163. *Id.*

164. United States v. Kumar, 2016 WL 7369863, at *5 (N.D. Cal. Dec. 20, 2016); *see also* Freeland v. Greco, 45 Cal. 2d 462, 467 (1955); Union Bank v. Wendland, 54 Cal. App. 3d 393, 408 (1976); California Bank v. Stimson, 89 Cal. App. 2d 552, 554 (1949).

discussed below, a guarantor may waive the anti-deficiency statutes and the one-action rule.[165]

For commercial loans, there are two key anti-deficiency statutes. The first statute is Code of Civil Procedure section 580a, which limits any deficiency judgment that a beneficiary of a deed of trust may obtain after a nonjudicial foreclosure sale to the difference between the fair market value of the property and the amount of the outstanding debt.[166] Section 580a states:

> Whenever a money judgment is sought for the balance due upon an obligation for the payment of which a deed of trust or mortgage with power of sale upon real property or any interest therein was given as security, following the exercise of the power of sale in such deed of trust or mortgage, the plaintiff shall set forth in his or her complaint the entire amount of the indebtedness which was secured by the deed of trust or mortgage at the time of sale, the amount for which the real property or interest therein was sold and the fair market value thereof at the date of sale and the date of that sale. . . .

As one court of appeal recognized, section 580a appears "superfluous" or "diminished," since a creditor is not entitled to a deficiency judgment after a nonjudicial sale.[167]

The second statute, Code of Civil Procedure section 580d, precludes a lender from obtaining a deficiency judgment against the borrower after a nonjudicial foreclosure sale. This statute states, in pertinent part:

> (a) Except as provided in subdivision (b), no deficiency shall be owed or collected, and no deficiency judgment shall be rendered for a deficiency on a note secured by a deed of trust or mortgage on real property or an estate for years therein executed in any case in which the real property or estate for years therein has been sold by the mortgagee or trustee under power of sale contained in the mortgage or deed of trust.

---

165. *See* CAL. CIV. CODE § 2856.

166. *See* CAL. CIV. PROC. CODE § 580a; In re Marriage of Oropallo, 68 Cal. App. 4th 997, 1003 (1998). California Code of Civil Procedure section 726(b) contains a similar fair-value limitation.

167. *See In re Marriage of Oropallo*, 68 Cal. App. 4th at 1003.

The intended effect of adding "no deficiency shall be owed or collected" is "that the borrower would not be liable for a deficiency."[168]

The Defenses and Protections Afforded to Guarantors

The one-action rule is inapplicable to a suit by a secured creditor against a guarantor, endorser, or other surety.[169] Similarly, "the anti-deficiency statutes' protections generally do not extend to guarantors."[170] As one court noted, "[A] lender may recover a deficiency judgment from a guarantor who waives his or her anti-deficiency protections, even though the anti-deficiency statutes would bar the lender from recovering that same deficiency from the primary borrower."[171] As one treatise explains, "guarantors are generally not protected by the anti-deficiency statutes because those statutes concern only actions on the principal obligation, as distinguished from actions against guarantors."[172] For example, courts have uniformly ruled that Code of Civil Procedure section 580a "has no application to guarantors" because this section is limited to actions for recovery of deficiency judgments on the principal obligation.[173] California courts generally do not directly extend the anti-deficiency protections under Code of Civil Procedure section 580d to guarantors.[174] Accordingly, courts have permitted lenders to sue a guarantor after nonjudicially foreclosing on a deed of trust or mortgage encumbering real property.[175]

---

168. Cal. Ass. Comm. on Judiciary, Analysis of Sen. Bill No. 426 (2013-2014 Reg. Sess.), as amended June 11, 2013, p. 3.

169. *See* Union Bank v. Gradsky, 265 Cal. App. 2d 40, 43–44, fn. 3 (1968) (Gradsky); Loeb v. Christie, 6 Cal. 2d 416, 418–19 (1936); Bank of Am., N.A. v. Shetty, 2016 WL 4482865, at *2 (Cal. Ct. App. Aug. 25, 2016).

170. LSREF2 Clover Prop. 4, LLC v. Festival Retail Fund I, LP, 3 Cal. App. 5th 1067, 1075 (2016).

171. *Id.*

172. 555 California Pleading and Practice § 555.32[5][a], pp. 555–99.

173. *See Talbott*, 164 Cal. App. 4th at 151; Mariners Sav. & Loan Ass'n v. Neil, 22 Cal. App. 3d 232, 234 (1971).

174. *See* Bauman v. Castle, 15 Cal. App. 3d 990, 994 (1971) ("the protective provisions of the Code of Civil Procedure (sections 580b and 580d) shield only the principal debtor and not the guarantors, such as defendants, who were separately and independently liable to plaintiff"); Chequers Inv. Assocs., JI v. Heil, 2001 WL 1521935, at *2 (Cal. Ct. App. Nov. 29, 2001).

175. *See* In re Pon, 164 B.R. 322, 323 (Bankr. N.D. Cal. 1994) (lender obtained judgment against guarantor after nonjudicially foreclosing).

One line of cases deviates from the general principle that section 580d does not apply to guarantors. In *Gradsky*, the court indirectly applied section 580d to prevent recovery against a guarantor based on the principles of estoppel and election of remedies. Specifically, the court ruled that where the lender conducts a nonjudicial foreclosure, it is estopped from pursuing the guarantor unless the guaranty contains an express waiver of the anti-deficiency statute. The *Gradsky* court stated:

> The creditor's recovery is not directly barred by section 580d. . . . It is barred by applying the principles of estoppel. The estoppel is raised as a matter of law to prevent the creditor from recovering from the guarantor after the creditor has exercised an election of remedies which destroys the guarantor's subrogation rights against the principal debtor. The destruction of the guarantor's subrogation rights follows from the combination of the creditor's election to subject the security to nonjudicial sale and the operation of section 580d, which prevents both the creditor and the guarantor from obtaining any deficiency judgment against the debtor after nonjudicial sale of the security. . . . The language of the guarantee agreement does not specifically waive the guarantor's defense based upon an election of remedies which destroys both the guarantor's subrogation rights and his right to proceed against the principal obligor for reimbursement. In the absence of an explicit waiver, we shall not strain the instrument to find that waiver by implication. [176]

Following *Gradsky*,[177] the legislature enacted Civil Code section 2856(b), enabling the guarantor to waive many of its rights "without regard to the inclusion of any particular language or phrases in the contract." One unpublished decision suggests that this statute "may well have been intended to supersede the holdings in *Gradsky*."[178]

176. *Gradsky*, 265 Cal. App. 2d at 41, 48.

177. *See also* Cathay Bank v. Lee, 14 Cal. App. 4th 1533 (1993) (required certain strict waiver language).

178. Copenbarger v. McNaughton, 2014 WL 2815695, at *5 (Cal. Ct. App. June 23, 2014).

Letters of Credit—The One-Action Rule and Anti-Deficiency Statutes

Letters of credit are governed by Article 5 of the Uniform Commercial Code (U.C.C.) and the Uniform Customs and Practices for Documentary Credits (U.C.P.), a body of rules adopted by the bankers of the International Chamber of Commerce.[179] The U.C.C. defines a letter of credit as "a definite undertaking . . . by an issuer to a beneficiary at the request or for the account of an applicant . . . to honor a documentary presentation by payment or delivery of an item of value."[180] The parties to a letter of credit effectively substitute the creditworthiness of an issuing bank for that of the applicant or a third party.[181]

The typical letter of credit involves three parties: applicant, issuer, and beneficiary.[182] However, a four-party letter of credit is valid.[183] In such circumstances, there are three separate transactions: (1) the contract between the issuing bank and its customer (applicant) to issue a letter of credit; (2) the letter of credit in which the issuing bank agrees to pay the beneficiary when the conditions contained in the letter of credit are complied with; and (3) the underlying contract between the beneficiary and a third party designated by the applicant in a letter of credit.[184] The issuer's obligation under the letter of credit is independent of any underlying contract between the applicant and the beneficiary.[185]

Generally, there are two types of letters of credit: commercial and standby. For over 700 years, a commercial letter of credit has been used in commercial sales to reduce the risk of nonpayment for goods, in which the issuing bank promises to pay a seller upon satisfaction of certain

---

179. *See* CAL. COMM. CODE § 5103(a) ("This division applies to letters of credit and to certain rights and obligations arising out of transactions involving letters of credit"); 3 WHITE, SUMMERS, AND HILLMAN, UNIFORM COMMERCIAL CODE § 26:1, pp. 161–62 (6th ed. West Pub. 2014); comment to CAL. COMM. CODE § 5101.

180. *See* CAL. COMM. CODE § 5102(a)(10).

181. *See* Chuidian v. Philippine Nat'l Bank, 976 F.2d 561, 567 (9th Cir. 1992) (Fernandez, J. dissenting); *see* Leney v. Plum Grove Bank, 670 F.2d 878, 881 (10th Cir. 1982) ("By issuing the letter of credit the [issuing] bank substitutes its credit for that of its customer.").

182. *See* CAL. COMM. CODE § 5102(a)(2), (3), and (9); Ensco Envtl. Servs. v. United States, 650 F. Supp. 583, 588 (W.D. Mo. 1986).

183. *See Ensco*, 650 F. Supp. at 588; Alhadeff v. Meridian on Bainbridge Island, LLC, 144 Wash. App. 928, 936 (2008).

184. *See Alfadeff*, 144 Wash. App. at 936.

185. *See* CAL. COMM. CODE § 5103(d); Cal. Bank & Tr. v. Piedmont Operating P'ship, L.P., 218 Cal. App. 4th 1322, 1334 (2013) (recognizing independent obligation of issuer).

terms (i.e., shipment or delivery of goods).[186] In contrast, "standby letters of credit are used in the non-sale setting and serve to reduce the risk of nonperformance under a performance contract"; a bank promises to pay a credit upon documentary certification of a default in the underlying contract.[187]

A letter of credit involves a deed of trust encumbering real property in two situations: (1) an applicant that seeks issuance of a letter of credit may pledge real property as collateral to the lender issuing the letter of credit, or (2) the beneficiary of a letter of credit may be the beneficiary under a deed of trust securing a loan or other contractual obligation. Under California Code of Civil Procedure section 580.5(b), the beneficiary of a letter of credit may demand payment under a letter of credit without violating the one-action rule or the anti-deficiency laws contained in California Code of Civil Procedure sections 580a, 580b, 580d, or 726, except in the limited circumstances discussed below.[188] As such, before or after a judicial or nonjudicial foreclosure, the beneficiary of a deed of trust may demand and receive payment or enforce its rights under the letter of credit without violating the one-action rule or anti-deficiency statutes.[189] Similarly, the issuer of a letter of credit may honor a demand or payment and demand reimbursement or enforce any contractual, statutory, or other rights to reimbursement without violating the one-action rule or anti-deficiency statutes.[190]

Permitting a beneficiary or issuer to exercise its letter of credit rights does not contravene the policies under the one-action rule and the anti-deficiency statutes. Upon issuance of a letter of credit, the issuing bank owes a ministerial duty to the beneficiary, not the applicant, to comply with the letter of credit.[191] Thus, once the issuer pays on the letter or the

---

186. *See* CRM Collateral II, Inc. v. TriCounty Metro. Transp., 669 F.3d 963, 969 (9th Cir. 2012); 3 White, Summers, Hillman, Uniform Commercial Code § 26:1, p. 161 (6th ed. West Pub. 2014).

187. *See CRM Collateral II, Inc.*, 669 F.3d at 969, citing John F. Dolan, The Law of Letters of Credit ¶ 1.04 (4th ed. 2007); *Ensco*, 650 F. Supp. at 590; 3 White, Summers, Hillman, Uniform Commercial Code § 26:1, p. 161 (6th ed. West Pub. 2014).

188. *See* W. Sec. Bank v. Superior Court, 15 Cal. 4th 232, 247 (1997); Paramount Exp. Co. v. Asia Tr. Bank, 193 Cal. App. 3d 1474, 1476 n.1 (1987).

189. *See* Cal. Civ. Proc. Code § 580.5(b).

190. *See id.*

191. *See* Cal. Bank & Tr. V. Piedmont Operating P'ship, L.P., 218 Cal. App. 4th 1322, 1334 (2013); Studwell, Inc. v. Korean Exch. Bank, 55 Cal. App. 4th 1185, 1190 (1997); *see also* 3 White, Summers, & Hillman, Uniform Commercial Code. § 26:32, p. 232 (6th ed.

beneficiary receives its payment, the issuer and beneficiary may pursue the applicant/trustor who pledged the deed of trust on the real property. As such, there is no risk that the trustor will face multiple lawsuits from creditors or violate any notion that the security should be exhausted first.[192]

Added in 1994, California Code of Civil Procedure section 580.7 sets forth an exemption to the rule that letter of credit transactions do not violate the one-action rule or the anti-deficiency statutes.[193] Section 580.7 declares unenforceable letters of credit issued to avoid defaults on purchase money mortgages for owner-occupied real property containing one to four residential units.[194]

IV. LENDERS' REMEDIES BEYOND FORECLOSURE

A. Deed in Lieu of Foreclosure

A provision in a deed of trust that requires a trustor to convey title upon default is void and unenforceable.[195] After a deed of trust is recorded, a trustor who is unable to make payments grants a deed to the beneficiary of a deed of trust instead of judicial or nonjudicial foreclosure (commonly referred to as a "deed in lieu" or a "deed in lieu of foreclosure"). A deed in lieu is more expedient, less expensive, and less burdensome because the beneficiary receives title to the property immediately without incurring trustee fees, attorneys' fees, and other costs associated with foreclosure, and because the trustor avoids the embarrassment and hassle connected

---

2014); Osten Meat Co. v. First of Am. Bank-Southeast Mich., NA, 205 Mich. App. 686, 691 (1994) (issuing banks "owe a primary duty to the beneficiary, not the applicant").

192. *See* Felton v. West, 102 Cal. 266, 269 (1894) (one-action rule remedied the "evil" of "multiplicity of suits, and the harassing of the debtor by two actions"); Sav. Bank of San Diego Cty. v. Cent. Mkt. Co., 122 Cal. 28, 36 (1898) (one-action rule prevents a multiplicity of suits and compels the creditor to first exhaust his security); *Wozab*, 51 Cal. 3d 997 (creditor "forced to exhaust the security before he may obtain a money judgment against the debtor for any deficiency").

193. *See* CAL. CIV. PROC. CODE § 580.7(b); Stats. 1994, ch. 611, § 3 (SB 1612).

194. *See id.* § 580.7(b)(1)–(4); *see W. Sec. Bank*, 15 Cal. 4th at 242.

195. *See* CAL. CIV. CODE § 2889 ("All contracts for the forfeiture of property subject to a lien, in satisfaction of the obligation secured thereby, and all contracts in restraint of the right of redemption from a lien, are void.").

with the foreclosure.[196] However, as the court in *Decon Grp., Inc. v. Prudential Mortg. Capital Co., LLC*, recognized, a "deed in lieu of foreclosure may carry potential risks, however, if there are junior encumbrances against the property."[197] Contrary to a foreclosure, a trustor conveys title through a deed in lieu to the beneficiary subject to all existing liens.[198] Thus, "if the title is encumbered by two deeds of trust, a third party grantee takes subject to both."[199]

The lender must consider the merger doctrine in deciding whether to accept a loan in lieu. In short, the lender must examine whether taking the deed in lieu extinguishes the grantee's deed of trust because a merger of legal and equitable interest occurs. The merger doctrine provides that whenever the same person holds a greater and lesser estate in the same parcel of real property, without an intermediate interest or estate, the lesser estate generally merges into the greater and is extinguished.[200] When a real property loan is evidenced by a promissory note secured by a deed of trust, a merger of the lien created by the deed of trust and ownership of the property in one person generally extinguishes the lien.[201] To effect a merger, "the whole title, legal as well as equitable title, must unite in one and the same person."[202]

However, a merger "does not always follow the union of a greater and lesser estate in the same ownership."[203] The California Supreme Court noted that

---

196. *See* Decon Grp., Inc. v. Prudential Mortg. Capital Co., LLC, 227 Cal. App. 4th 665, 670 (2014) (The deed in lieu of foreclosure "may be advantageous to both parties" by, for example, allowing the beneficiary to "avoid[] the delays and costs of foreclosure" and saving the trustor "to some extent from the embarrassment and impaired credit rating a public foreclosure sale produces.").

197. *See id.*

198. *See id.* at 671; *see also* Streiff v Darlington, 9 Cal. 2d 42 (1937).

199. *Decon Grp., Inc.*, 227 Cal. App. at 671.

200. *See* Sheldon v. La Brea Materials Co., 216 Cal. 686, 689–90 (1932); Kolodge v. Boyd, 88 Cal. App. 4th 349, 361 (2001); In re Martinez, 2021 Cal. App. Unpub. LEXIS 7306, at *16 (Nov. 19, 2021); 5 Miller & Starr, Cal. Real Estate § 13:53 (4th ed. June 2021); Black's Law Dictionary (11th ed. West. Pub. 2019) (merger doctrine defined as "[t]he principle that contractual promises about the title to real property are merged into the terms of the deed when the buyer accepts the deed").

201. *See* Alliance Mortgage Co. v. Rothwell, 10 Cal. 4th 1226, 1235 (1995).

202. Estate of Washburn, 11 Cal. App. 735, 746 (1909).

203. Ito v. Schiller, 213 Cal. 632, 635 (1931); *In re Martinez*, 2021 Cal. App. Unpub. LEXIS 7306, at *16.

> equity will interpose to prevent a merger where from the circumstances it is apparent that it was not the intention of the grantee that a merger should take place; and where it appears to be for the interest of the grantee that there should be no merger of the lesser estate, such will be presumed to have been his intention.[204]

Thus, if several estates are united, courts examine the parties' intent, which is a factual question.[205]

> While it is presumed that there is no merger where the merger would work an inequity, the presumption against merger can be overcome by evidence that the parties intended a merger upon the union of two or more estates, and as to this question, the person claiming merger has the burden of proof.[206]

In general, applying these principles, when a junior lienholder is the grantee of a deed in lieu, courts presume that the junior lien is eliminated by merger and that the grantee is subject to the senior deed of trust.[207] However, courts do not apply this presumption when a senior lienholder is the grantee of a deed in lieu. When the beneficiary of a senior deed of trust is the grantee of a deed in lieu, courts hold that the senior lien and title do not merge, so the senior lienholder retains the power to foreclose and thereby eliminate the junior liens.[208] This holding is based upon the presumed intent of the parties. Under a traditional merger, if a senior lienholder is the grantee of a deed in lieu, "its lien would normally merge into its title and be destroyed, but this would have the effect of making its title subject to the (former) junior deed of trust, which is clearly not the result that the parties intend."[209]

---

204. *Sheldon*, 216 Cal. at 691.

205. *See Ito*, 213 Cal. at 635–36 (equity will block merger "if the interest of the person in whom the several estates have united, as shown from all the circumstances, would be best subserved by keeping them separate, the intent so to do will ordinarily be implied"); Strike v. Trans-West Discount Corp., 92 Cal. App. 3d 735, 743 (1979) (intent is factual question); Batten v. Kern, 16 Cal. App. 2d 414, 416 (1936) (same).

206. *Kolodge*, 88 Cal. App. 4th at 362; *In re Martinez*, 2021 Cal. App. Unpub. LEXIS 7306, at *18.

207. *See Decon Grp., Inc.*, 227 Cal. App. at 671.

208. *See id.*; *see also* Anglo-Californian Bank, Ltd. v. Field, 146 Cal. 644, 654 (1905) (a merger of senior lien and title "would operate to [its] disadvantage").

209. *Id.*; *see also Sheldon*, 216 Cal. at 690.

Given the foregoing principles, a lender accepting a deed in lieu of foreclosure should conduct a title search to determine the existence of any junior or senior lienholders. The lender should also obtain title insurance against the existence of lienholders and against other liens that may not immediately appear on the title. Finally, if the lender wants to reserve the right to foreclose on its deed of trust to extinguish any junior lienholders, the lender should include nonmerger language in the deed in lieu. As a "belt and suspenders," the lender should prepare a separate agreement that sets forth the parties' intent to prevent a merger.

Finally, it is important to note that a trustor may not force a beneficiary to accept a deed in lieu.[210] If a trustor records a deed in lieu without the beneficiary's consent, the beneficiary may record a "notice of nonacceptance," thereby annulling the recorded deed in lieu and restoring the condition of the recorded title.[211] The grantee must receive and accept the deed in lieu to be effective.[212]

B. Short Sales

Another potential avenue for a lender is to permit a "short sale" of the real property to avoid the cost and delay associated with the foreclosure. In *Coker v. J.P. Morgan Chase Bank, N.A.*, the court defined a "short sale" as follows:

> In a short sale, the lender agrees to release its lien on the borrower's property so that the borrower can sell the property to a third party. In exchange, the borrower agrees to give the lender all of the proceeds from the sale. Both parties know that the sale proceeds will fall short of the total amount that the borrower owes.[213]

In *Coker*, the court noted that during the Great Recession, banks conducted approximately 90,000 and 110,000 short sales in 2009 and 2010,

210. *See* Rollins v. Neilson (In re Cedar Funding, Inc.), 398 B.R. 346, 354 (Bankr. N.D. Cal. 2008) ("Under California law, holders of a security interest need not accept a recorded deed in their favor.").

211. *See* Cal. Civ. Code § 1058.5(a).

212. *See Rollins*, 398 B.R. at 354 (must be a "reasonable inference from plaintiffs' receipt and acceptance of the recorded demand"); *see also* Reina v. Erassarret, 90 Cal. App. 2d 418, 424 (1949).

213. Coker v. J.P. Morgan Chase Bank, N.A., 62 Cal. 4th 667, 673 (2016).

respectively, saving "banks millions in foreclosure costs."[214] In *Coker*, the court held that although a borrower could waive the one-action rule in connection with a short sale, the borrower could not waive protection under section 580b for purchase money transactions because "a law established for a public reason cannot be contravened by a private agreement."[215] In deciding whether to accept a short sale, the lender must decide whether releasing its right to a deficiency is worth the short sale proceeds, given the property's value, the indebtedness amount, and the cost/hassle avoided with foreclosure.

C. Collection of Rent

A deed of trust or mortgage typically contains an assignment of rent provision, which permits the lender, upon default, to collect rent or other income generated from real property as additional security upon default.[216] A lender that includes an absolute assignment of rents clause in a recorded deed of trust or mortgage obtains a "present and perfected transfer of the property effective on [the debtor's] default."[217]

California Civil Code section 2938 sets forth a procedure for a lender to obtain rent before foreclosure.[218] Any rent obtained under section 2938 must be applied to the secured debt.[219] Section 2938 allows the lender to obtain the appointment of a receiver to send written demand (using a statutory form) to the assignor and tenants and to file an enforcement action to collect rent.[220] It recognizes that taking these statutorily mandated actions

214. *Id.*, citing California Assem. Com. on Judiciary, Analysis of Sen. Bill No. 931 (2009–2010 Reg. Sess.) p. 61 and California Sen. Com. on Banking & Financial Institutions, Analysis of Sen. Bill No. 412 (2011–2012 Reg. Sess.) as amended Mar. 21, 2011, p. 2.

215. *Coker*, 62 Cal. 4th at 692.

216. *See* Gietzen v. Covenant RE Mgmt., Inc., 40 Cal. App. 5th 331, 341 (2019) (assignment of rents clause is a "provision in trust deeds assigning rents as additional security in the event of default").

217. *See* MDFC Loan Corp. v. Greenbrier Plaza Partners, 21 Cal. App. 4th 1045, 1054 (1994).

218. *See* Cal. Civ. Code § 2938(c).

219. *See id.*; *Gietzen*, 40 Cal. App. 5th at 341.

220. *See id.* § 2938(b)–(k); *see* Federal Nat'l Mortg. Ass'n v. Bugna, 57 Cal. App. 4th 529, 538, (1997) ("California law holds that even when an assignment is absolute, an affirmative enforcement step in addition to perfection is a prerequisite to the lender's possession of the rents, and that the lender is entitled to all the rents, issues, and profits from the time of demand upon the defaulting borrower to deliver possession and pay over the rents.").

does not violate the one-action rule, consistent with the security-first and exhaustion of collateral policies underlying the one-action rule. [221]

If a lender (assignor) exercises its rights to collect rent under an assignment of rents clause, the assignor (borrower) may make a written demand that the assignee "pay the reasonable costs of protecting and preserving the property, including payment of taxes and insurance and compliance with building and housing codes, if any."[222] Upon receipt of the demand, the lender must pay the reasonable costs of protecting and preserving the property "*to the extent*" of rent "*actually received*" by the lender.[223]

D. Appointment of a Receiver

Instead of foreclosing, a lender can seek the appointment of a receiver to collect rent, protect the property, maintain the property, and sell the property to a third-party buyer.[224] By statute, the appointment of a receiver under Code of Civil Procedure section 564 does not constitute an action within the meaning of section 726.[225] Subdivision (d) of section 564 states, "Any action by a secured lender to appoint a receiver pursuant to this section shall not constitute an action within the meaning of subdivision (a) of Section 726."[226]

There are many benefits and detriments to seeking the appointment of a receiver. On the one hand, receivers can be very costly. On the other hand, a receiver may be used to preserve, protect, and enhance the property, especially when it is abandoned or at risk. If a property generates income or rent, a receiver can install procedures to manage cash flow, collect rent, or establish accounting procedures. The receiver can also lessen a lender's liability in contested foreclosure proceedings and facilitate the potential sale of the property in an impartial manner under the court's

---

221. *See* CAL. CIV. CODE § 2928(c)(4), (f)(1).

222. *Id.* § 2938(g)(1).

223. *See id.* § 2938(g)(2).

224. *See id.* § 2938(b); CAL. CIV. PROC. CODE § 564(b)(11), (d) (acknowledges no violation of Code of Civil Procedure section 726; appointment of a receiver in "an action by a secured lender for specific performance of an assignment of rents provision in a deed of trust, mortgage, or separate assigned document").

225. *See* CIV. PROC. CODE § 564(d) ("Any action by a secured lender to appoint a receiver pursuant to this section shall not constitute an action within the meaning of subdivision (a) of Section 726").

226. CAL. CIV. PROC. CODE § 564(d).

supervision. An experienced receiver may well be worth the cost to the lender to mitigate risk and litigation costs.

The appointment of a receiver is not automatic. Because the appointment of a receiver transfers property or even a business "out of the hands of its owners" and into the hands of a receiver, courts treat the appointment of a receiver as a very "drastic," "harsh," and "costly remedy" that is to be "exercised sparingly and with caution."[227] Due to the "extraordinary" nature of this remedy and the special costs it imposes, courts are strongly discouraged, although not prohibited, from appointing a receiver unless the more intrusive oversight of a receiver is a "necessity" because other, less intrusive remedies are either "inadequate or unavailable."[228] As a practical matter, courts may examine the revenue generated by the property to determine whether there are sufficient funds to support the appointment of a receiver, especially if the case is complex and the receiver must retain separate counsel.

V. CONCLUSION

Navigating the complexities of commercial real property defaults is an intricate and nuanced task. Each defaulted commercial loan is unique and requires a custom-tailored strategy, considering such factors as the nature of the defaults (nonmonetary or monetary defaults), the equity in the property, the ability to collect a deficiency, and the property's condition. Given each case's unique challenges, an attorney specializing in this area should be consulted to ensure the most effective and efficient resolution.

227. Medipro Med. Staffing LLC v. Certified Nursing Registry, Inc., 60 Cal. App. 5th 622, 628 (2021).

228. *Id.*

Employment Claims

6

Aaron Krauss†

Lisa Lawyer is sitting in her office when she gets a call from her friend, Tom Teller, who works at the local bank. Tom says he was just fired by Betty Branch Manager. Tom goes on to whine about Betty being a horrible manager who was always second-guessing him, telling him he wasn't following policies and procedures, hassling him about his time card, and writing him up for every little thing. Betty told him he was being fired for being late, but Tom insists that can't be the real reason because Bob Baker—Betty's

---

† Aaron Krauss is a commercial litigator who practices in Cozen O'Connor's Philadelphia office. He has spent more than 30 years representing companies (or officers or directors of companies) in disputes with other companies who they used to like, but now don't. In his spare time, when he hasn't been chasing his children around, serving on nonprofit boards, or practicing law, Aaron has served in multiple leadership positions within the ABA, most recently as the chair of the Litigation Section's Health Law Litigation Committee and as a member of the Litigation Section's Book Publishing Board. This chapter should not be construed as giving legal advice. If you would like to receive legal advice, contact Aaron directly. Aaron can be reached at (215) 665-4181 or akrauss@cozen.com. The views expressed in this chapter are Aaron's alone and are not necessarily the views of Cozen O'Connor.

favorite—is late all the time and he hasn't been fired. Tom therefore wants Lisa to sue the bank. On a contingent fee, of course.

After observing that, unlike the last defendant she sued, the bank won't be judgment-proof, Lisa asks Tom to come in the next morning so she can gather the information she will need to draft a complaint. After she hangs up, she remembers the sage advice of her mentor: before you take a contingent fee case, figure out if it is likely to make money, and remember that you aren't making money if you have to put too much time into the case. So Lisa starts outlining potential claims and what she will need to show to prove those claims. She immediately thinks of discrimination and wage and hour claims. Although Lisa briefly considers a breach of employment contract claim, she lives in a nonunion town and can't remember ever having seen an employment contract that didn't say—usually in bold letters—that the employee is employed at will.[1] She also starts writing down how banks are different than other defendants, and how those differences might affect Tom's case, for better or worse.

I. HOW BANKS ARE DIFFERENT THAN OTHER DEFENDANTS

In Lisa's experience, there are three main differences between banks and most other defendants. First, banks have cameras everywhere. Second, banks seem to have more written policies than any other business. Third, banks are heavily regulated, which could explain their fondness for written policies. As she sketches out questions to ask Tom, Lisa also starts writing down questions to ask the bank.

A. Banks Have Cameras Everywhere

Banks have cameras everywhere. Indeed, some post signs on their doors telling people to "smile, because you are on camera."[2] Although the cameras are part of a bank's FDIC-required security program,[3] as a practical matter they cover most areas of the bank and are likely to have recorded anything that happened in a bank branch. As a result, Lisa knows that there is likely to be video footage of when Tom showed up for work. That

1. As a result, Lisa decides not to waste her paper (or her time) trying to come up with a breach of employment contract claim.

2. *See, e.g.*, TD Bank.

3. *See* 12 C.F.R. § 326.3.

video will quickly make or break a claim that Tom wasn't really late and that Betty Branch Manager made that up as a pretext to fire him. And while the cameras don't record sound, there might be video that would prove (or disprove) Tom's claim that Betty Branch Manager constantly berated him.[4] Lisa therefore makes a note to get a document preservation letter out to the bank as soon as she can, because she knows that banks don't keep their camera footage forever.[5]

B. Banks Have Written Policies on Just About Everything

Lisa knows that banks have written policies on just about everything. Those policies, she knows, are a double-edged sword. On the one hand, they will let the bank say that Tom was fired for violating bank policy (i.e., being late). Presumably, they will also let the bank say that whatever Betty Branch Manager did was pursuant to bank policy, even if Tom found that policy, or the application of that policy, to be distasteful. But on the other hand, Lisa might be able to show either that whatever Tom did was permitted by bank policy (or at least was not contrary to bank policy) or that the bank wasn't following its own policies. She makes a note to request the bank policies governing whatever Tom says Betty did wrong, or did in an unfair (or unequal) fashion.

C. Banks Are Heavily Regulated

Most banks are regulated by a combination of the Office of the Comptroller of the Currency,[6] the Federal Reserve,[7] and the Federal Deposit Insurance

---

4. In making her notes, Lisa acknowledges that that the lack of sound makes many pictures equivocal. Presumably, Betty Branch Manager will say she was counseling Tom on his lack of performance, rather than berating him, if the cameras show the two of them deep in conversation. Lisa does, however, remember something else her mentor told her: you want as much evidence as you can get, and if it is bad for your case, you would rather know up front before you put more time into it.

5. The length of time banks keep video varies, so it is best to send a document preservation letter as soon as possible. To be useful, the document preservation letter should specify the dates (and ideally times) for which video should be preserved. A demand that a bank preserve all its video forever is not helpful to anyone.

6. When a bank has "N.A." (or National Association) after its name, or says it is a "national bank," it is regulated by the Office of the Comptroller of the Currency. The National Credit Union Administration, as its name suggests, regulates credit unions.

7. The Federal Reserve supervises banks that are members of the federal reserve system. Most banks are members.

Corporation (FDIC).[8] Lisa wonders whether she should try and get the regulators involved. The regulators could certainly put pressure on the bank, but she knows from experience that the regulators usually won't get involved in employment claims. And even if they did, Lisa knows that she wouldn't have any control over the regulators, and the bank would not be inclined to (and might not be able to) settle with Tom (and pay Lisa's fee) if the bank is facing regulatory scrutiny. She therefore doubts it makes sense to try and approach the regulators, but Lisa decides to postpone a final decision until she talks with Tom.

II. DISCRIMINATION CLAIMS

When Lisa starts outlining potential discrimination claims, she realizes that she is really drafting a matrix. This is because there are at least two ways to bring each type of discrimination claim: as a direct claim and as a retaliation claim. Then, depending on the protected class in which the plaintiff can claim membership, a plaintiff can bring discrimination claims under Title VII,[9] Section 1981,[10] the Age Discrimination and Employment Act (ADEA) (as amended by the Older Workers Benefit Protection Act),[11] the Americans with Disabilities Act (ADA),[12] or perhaps even the Family and Medical Leave Act (FMLA).[13] Plaintiffs can also bring state law claims.[14]

A. Direct vs. Retaliation Claims

Although Lisa is naturally drawn towards bringing a direct claim on Tom's behalf—because being fired is unquestionably an "adverse employment

8. In addition to regulating state-chartered banks, the FDIC insures most banks, and therefore imposes regulations on them.

9. *See* 42 U.S.C. §§ 2000e, *et seq.*

10. *See* 42 U.S.C. § 1981.

11. *See* 29 U.S.C. §§ 621, *et seq.*

12. *See* 42 U.S.C. §§ 12101, *et seq.*

13. *See* 29 U.S.C. §§ 2601, *et seq.*

14. *See, e.g.*, Pennsylvania Human Relations Act, 43 Pa. C.S.A. §§ 951, *et seq.*

action"[15]—she has often heard that retaliation claims are actually easier to prove and more likely to win than direct discrimination claims.[16] She therefore resolves to ask Tom whether he made any complaints, either about his own situation or about his coworkers' situations, before he was fired. After all, most employees complain about something (and some employees complain about everything). Lisa figures that she might get lucky and find that Tom had made a complaint that could give rise to a retaliation claim of some sort. And if she's really lucky, that complaint will be in an email that Tom copied to his personal account. One more question for her list of things to ask Tom.

In making her list, Lisa also remembers that "discrimination statutes allow employers to discharge employees for any reason whatsoever (even a mistaken but honest belief) as long as the reason is not illegal discrimination. Thus, when an employee is discharged because of an employer's honest mistake, federal antidiscrimination laws offer no protection."[17] She therefore resolves to ask Tom about anything Betty Branch Manager said or did that would suggest she knew what she was doing, and that she was doing it because of Tom's membership in a protected class.

---

15. If Tom had quit, rather than having been fired, Lisa would have to determine if he could claim that he had been constructively discharged. A constructive discharge occurs when "the employer permitted conditions so unpleasant or difficult that a reasonable person would have felt compelled to resign." Colwell v. Rite Aid Corp., 602 F.3d 495, 502–03 (3d Cir. 2010) (citations omitted). A court employs an objective test in determining whether an employee was constructively discharged, *see Colwell*, 602 F.3d at 502, and "does not permit an employee's subjective perceptions to govern a claim of constructive discharge." Gray v. York Newspapers, Inc., 957 F.2d 1070, 1083 (3d Cir. 1992) (citations omitted). To determine whether an employee was forced to resign, a court considers whether the employee was threatened with discharge, encouraged to resign, demoted, subjected to reduced pay, benefits or responsibilities, transferred to a less desirable position, or given unsatisfactory job evaluations. *See Colwell*, 602 F.3d at 503. A constructive discharge requires a "greater severity or pervasiveness of harassment than the minimum required to prove a hostile working environment." Spencer v. Wal-Mart Stores, Inc., 469 F.3d 311, 316 n.4 (3d Cir. 2006).

16. *See, e.g.*, Eric Bachman, *Here's Why Retaliation Claims Are Easier to Prove in Court Than Discrimination Claims: The FedEx Case*, FORBES (Sept. 4, 2019), https://www.forbes.com/sites/ericbachman/2019/09/04/heres-why-retaliation-claims-are-easier-to-prove-in-court-than-discrimination-claims/?sh=19bc45657967.

17. Capps v. Mondelez Global LLC, 847 F.3d 144, 154 (3d Cir. 2017) (citation omitted).

Direct Claims

A direct discrimination claim is exactly what one would expect—a claim that a plaintiff "was treated less favorably than similarly situated employees who are not in the plaintiff's protected class."[18] The treatment giving rise to a discrimination claim can either be a specific act or a claim that the totality of the circumstances created a hostile work environment. A plaintiff bringing a hostile work environment claim must establish that "1) the employee suffered intentional discrimination because of his/her [membership in a protected class], 2) the discrimination was severe or pervasive, 3) the discrimination detrimentally affected the plaintiff, 4) the discrimination would detrimentally affect a reasonable person in like circumstances, and 5) the existence of respondeat superior liability."[19] Absent a basis for respondeat superior liability, the plaintiff must prove that the defendant had actual or constructive knowledge of the existence of the hostile work environment and failed to take prompt and adequate remedial action.[20]

To prevail on a hostile work environment claim, the discrimination must be "severe or pervasive" enough to alter the conditions of the plaintiff's employment and create an abusive working environment.[21] When determining whether a work environment is sufficiently hostile to be actionable, a court considers "the totality of the circumstances," including "the frequency of the discriminatory conduct, its severity, whether it is physically threatening or a mere offensive utterance, and whether it reasonably interferes with an employee's work performance."[22] Moreover, for a single instance to state a claim, it must be "an extreme isolated act of discrimination."[23] "An isolated incident, unless extremely serious, is not sufficient to sustain a hostile educational environment claim."[24] Indeed,

18. Doe v. C.A.R.S. Protection Plus, Inc., 527 F.3d 358, 366 (3d Cir. 2008) (citations omitted).

19. Mandel v. M & Q Packaging Corp., 706 F.3d 157, 167 (3d Cir. 2013).

20. *See, e.g.*, Vance v. Ball State Univ., 570 U.S. 421, 427 (2013); Vazquez v. Carr & Duff, Inc., 2017 WL 4310253, at *4 (E.D. Pa. Sept. 28, 2017).

21. *See, e.g.*, Castleberry v. STI Grp., 863 F.3d 259, 264 (3d Cir. 2017); Fichter v. AMG Resources Corp., 528 F. App'x 225, 230–31 (3d Cir. 2013).

22. Harris v. Forklift Sys., Inc., 510 U.S. 17, 23 (1993).

23. *Castleberry*, 863 F.3d at 265.

24. Katchur v. Thomas Jefferson Univ., 354 F. Supp. 3d 655, 664 (E.D. Pa. 2019).

an isolated incident must have been so severe that it altered the conditions of employment.[25]

In addition to denying that the allegedly hostile acts occurred (or that, if they occurred, they were sufficiently severe or pervasive), a defendant can claim that the plaintiff "unreasonably failed to take advantage of any preventive or corrective opportunities provided by the employer to avoid harm or otherwise."[26] In addition to constituting an affirmative defense, a claim that the plaintiff failed to take advantage of a complaint or corrective procedure can cast doubt on the veracity of the plaintiff's claims. Lisa agrees that a jury is likely to ask, "if it was that bad, why didn't plaintiff complain?" and to conclude that "if plaintiff didn't complain, it must not have been that bad." She therefore makes a note to ask Tom what complaint or corrective procedures were available[27] and whether—and when—he availed himself of them.

Retaliation Claims

A "prima facie case of illegal retaliation requires a showing of (1) protected employee activity; (2) adverse action by the employer either after or contemporaneous with the employee's protected activity; and (3) a causal connection between the employee's protected activity and the employer's adverse action."[28]

The "protected employee activity" must be a complaint that an objectively reasonable plaintiff would believe is about conduct that would violate the applicable statute.[29] As a result, a complaint that is not about conduct that would violate the applicable statute, or that is not objectively

25. *See* Sessoms v. Trustees of Univ. of Penn., 739 F. App'x 84, 90 (3d Cir. 2018); Roberts v. Health Partners Plans, Inc., 2017 WL 3310691, at *4–5 (E.D. Pa. Aug. 3, 2017).

26. Cacciola v. Work N Gear, 23 F. Supp. 3d 518, 530 (E.D. Pa. 2014).

27. Most banks' procedures require any employee who either witnesses or is the victim of misconduct to immediately report the misconduct. Employees are usually told to report misconduct to human resources, but many policies include either alternatives or "bypasses" (i.e., in case the employee believes a member of human resources is engaged in misconduct), such as reporting misconduct to in-house counsel. Most banks—unlike many other employers—have both a human resources department and an in-house counsel.

28. Harris v. Julia, 2018 WL 5316352, at *4 (E.D. Pa. Oct. 25, 2018). *See also* Barber v. CSX Distrib. Servs., 68 F.3d 694, 701 (3d Cir. 1995).

29. *See, e.g.*, Wilkerson v. New Media Tech. Charter Sch. Inc., 522 F.3d 315, 322 (3d Cir. 2008); Reynolds v. Belmont Behavioral Health, 2019 WL 318258, at *2 (E.D. Pa. Jan. 24, 2019).

reasonable, does not suffice.[30] Because the complaint must involve conduct that would violate the applicable statute, a "general complaint of unfair treatment is insufficient to establish protected activity."[31] Similarly, a vague allegation of a civil rights violation does not constitute protected activity.[32]

The "adverse action" must be "materially adverse," meaning it "well might have dissuaded a reasonable worker from making or supporting a charge of discrimination."[33] But it does not necessarily have to be an adverse *employment* action; a retaliation claim can be asserted on any materially adverse action by the employer.[34]

As for the "causal connection," to decide if there is a causal connection, courts look to "temporal proximity, intervening antagonism or retaliatory animus, inconsistencies in the employer's articulated reasons for terminating the employee, or any other evidence sufficient to support the inference of retaliatory animus."[35] Temporal proximity requires facts that "are unusually suggestive of retaliatory motive" to support an inference of causation.[36] Courts have found that fairly short gaps (i.e., less than three weeks) between the protected activity and the adverse employment action defeat a suggestion of retaliatory motive.[37] "With respect to the causation prong, the court considers whether a reasonable jury could link the employer's conduct to retaliatory animus."[38] Lisa therefore makes a note to push Tom to remember the exact chronology of events, and whether there were

---

30. *See, e.g., Wilkerson*, 522 F.3d at 322; Curay-Cramer v. Ursuline Acad. of Wilmington, Del., 450 F.3d 130, 135 (3d Cir. 2006).

31. *Curay-Cramer*, 450 F.3d at 135. *See also* Smith v. Int'l Paper Co., 523 F.3d 845, 849–50 (8th Cir. 2008); Kodl v. Bd. of Educ. Dist. 45, Villa Park, 490 F.3d 558, 562–63 (7th Cir. 2007); *Barber*, 68 F.3d at 701–02.

32. *See* Slagle v. Cty. of Clarion, 435 F.3d 262, 268 (3d Cir. 2006).

33. Moore v. City of Phila., 461 F.3d 331, 341 (3d Cir. 2006), as amended (Sept. 13, 2006).

34. *See* Burlington N. & Santa Fe Railway Co. v. White, 548 U.S. 53 (2006).

35. Gavurnik v. Home Properties, L.P., 227 F. Supp. 3d 410, 420–21 (E.D. Pa. 2017), aff'd, 712 F. App'x 170 (3d Cir. 2017) (citations omitted).

36. *See Escanio*, 538 F. App'x at 200.

37. *See, e.g.*, Lichtenstein v. Univ. of Pittsburgh Med. Ctr., 691 F.3d 294, 307 (3d Cir. 2012); Thomas v. Town of Hammonton, 351 F.3d 108, 114 (3d Cir. 2003); Williams v. Philadelphia Housing Auth., 380 F.3d 751, 760 n.4 (3d Cir. 2004), superseded by statute in nonrelevant part Robinson v. First State, 920 F.3d 182, 187–89 & n.30 (3d Cir. 2019).

38. Ward v. MBNA America, 962 F. Supp. 2d 680, 687 (D. Del. 2013), aff'd, 570 F. App'x 143 (3d Cir. 2014).

other intervening acts between what he thinks constitutes a complaint and what he thinks was an adverse action taken against him.

B. Title VII

Title VII prohibits discrimination[39] based on a plaintiff's race, color, religion, sex, or national origin.[40] It is important to note that "sex discrimination" need not be sexual,[41] and the victim and the harasser may be any sex (and may also be the same sex).[42] Title VII claims (as well as Section 1981 claims and many state law antidiscrimination claims, which will be discussed later) are governed by the three-step burden-shifting framework in *McDonnell Douglas Corp. v. Green.*[43] Under *McDonnell Douglas*, a plaintiff must first establish a prima facie case.[44] If the plaintiff does so, the defendant must "articulate a legitimate, nonretaliatory or nondiscriminatory reason for its action."[45] If the defendant does so, "the burden then shifts back to the plaintiff to prove that the employer's nonretaliatory or nondiscriminatory explanation is merely a pretext for the discrimination or retaliation."[46]

39. A Title VII plaintiff must first exhaust administrative remedies by filing with the EEOC. *See* Fort Bend County, Texas v. Davis, 139 S. Ct. 1843, 1844 (2019); 42 U.S.C. § 2000e–5(b) and (e)(1); *see also* U.S. Equal Employment Opportunity Commission, *Time Limits for Filing a Charge*, https://www.eeoc.gov/time-limits-filing-charge. An EEOC charge must be filed within 180 days (or 300 days in a cofiling state) of the act giving rise to the claim. *See* 42 U.S.C. § 2000e-5(e)(1). A plaintiff must obtain a "right to sue" letter from the EEOC before filing in court. *See, e.g.*, 42 U.S.C. § 2000e–5(f)(1); U.S. Equal Employment Opportunity Commission, *After You Have Filed a Charge*, https://www.eeoc.gov/after-you-have-filed-charge. Once the right to sue letter is obtained, a plaintiff must file a lawsuit within 90 days. *See* 42 U.S.C. § 2000e-5(f)(1).

40. *See, e.g.*, 42 U.S.C. § 2000e-2(b).

41. *See, e.g.*, U.S. Equal Employment Opportunity Commission, *Sex-Based Discrimination*, https://www.eeoc.gov/sex-based-discrimination.

42. *Id.*

43. *See* 411 U.S. 792 (1973); Greer v. Mondelez Global, Inc., 590 F. App'x 170, 172 & n.4 (3d Cir. 2014); Kier v. F. Lackland & Sons LLC, 72 F. Supp. 3d 597, 607 n.1 (E.D. Pa. 2014). This burden-shifting framework does not apply when there is direct evidence of discrimination, meaning "evidence which, if believed, would prove the existence of the fact in issue without inference or presumption," but there is a "high burden" in asserting a direct evidence case. *See* Shade v. Alfa Laval, Inc., 2017 WL 839456, at *7 (M.D. Pa. Mar. 3, 2017).

44. *See, e.g.*, Tourtellote v. Eli Lilly & Co., 636 F. App'x 831, 842 (3d Cir. 2016).

45. *Id.*

46. *Id.*

A prima facie case of discrimination (again, under Title VII, Section 1981, and most state antidiscrimination laws) requires demonstrating that (1) the employee is a member of a protected class, (2) the employee is qualified for the position, (3) the employee suffered an adverse employment action, and (4) the action was taken under circumstances that give rise to an inference of unlawful discrimination.[47] In addition to arguing that they were individually harmed, a Title VII plaintiff can argue that they (and every member of their protected class) suffered a disparate impact as a result of the defendant's actions. A disparate impact claim asserts that, even though the defendant did not intend to discriminate against the plaintiff, the defendant's actions had a disproportionate impact on members of a protected class.[48] An employer can defeat a disparate impact claim by demonstrating that the challenged practice is related to the job's requirements and is consistent with business necessity.[49]

To establish pretext, a plaintiff must

> submit evidence which casts sufficient doubt upon each of the legitimate reasons proffered by the defendant so that a factfinder could reasonably conclude that each reason was a fabrication or would allow the factfinder to infer that discrimination was more likely than not a motivating or determinative cause of the adverse employment action.[50]

It is not enough to show that the employer's decision "was wrong or mistaken, since the factual dispute at issue is whether discriminatory animus motivated the employer, not whether the employer is wise, shrewd, prudent, or competent."[51] As a result, to establish pretext, a plaintiff must proffer evidence from which a factfinder could reasonably either (1) disbelieve the employer's articulated reason by showing such "weaknesses, implausibilities, inconsistencies, incoherencies, or contradictions . . . that a

47. *See, e.g.*, Sarullo v. U.S. Postal Serv., 352 F.3d 789, 797 (3d Cir. 2003); Massaro v. Wells Fargo Home Mortg., 2018 WL 4076319, at *3 (E.D. Pa. Aug. 24, 2018), appeal dismissed, 2018 WL 7890260 (3d Cir. Oct. 18, 2018); Baur v. Crum, 882 F. Supp. 2d 785, 800 (E.D. Pa. 2012), aff'd, 517 F. App'x 101 (3d Cir. 2013).

48. *See, e.g.*, 42 U.S.C. § 2000e-2(k).

49. *Id.*

50. Oguejiofo v. Bank of Tokyo, 704 F. App'x 164, 167–68 (3d Cir. 2017) (citations omitted).

51. Capilli v. Whitesell Const. Co., 271 F. App'x 261, 265–66 (3d Cir. 2008) (citations omitted). *See also* Fuentes v. Perskie, 32 F.3d 759, 765 (3d Cir. 1994).

reasonable fact finder could rationally find them unworthy of credence,"[52] or (2) believe that invidious discrimination was more likely than not the motivating or determinative cause of the employer's action.[53]

Although Lisa believes she knows the protected classes to which Tom belongs, she realizes that she has never actually asked him. Her mentor was fond of saying that "you can't (and shouldn't) judge a book by its cover," so she makes a note to start her interview by asking Tom in what classes he belongs. She can then follow up and ask what Betty Bank Manager did that could be considered to be discriminatory against someone in those classes.

C. Section 1981

Unlike Title VII claims, which can be brought by members of any race, color, religion, sex, or national origin,[54] Section 1981 claims can be brought only by a member of a race or ethnicity (not a member of a religion, sex, or nationality) that was recognized in 1866.[55]

A plaintiff must show "but for causation" to prevail on a Section 1981 claim; the motivating factor standard from Title VII does not apply. "To prevail, a plaintiff must initially plead and ultimately prove that, but for race, it would not have suffered the loss of a legally protected right."[56]

Unlike under Title VII, a Section 1981 plaintiff does not have to file with the EEOC and is not subject to the 180-day statute of limitations in which to do so.[57] Similarly, a Section 1981 plaintiff is not subject to Title VII's damages caps.[58] Lisa therefore makes a note to confirm whether Tom falls into any class protected by Section 1981, and to be sure to ask him about things that happened outside Title VII's statute of limitations (assuming, of course, Tom can avail himself of Section 1981's protections).

52. *Capilli*, 271 F. App'x at 266 (citations omitted).

53. *See* Fuentes v. Perskie, 32 F.3d 759, 764 (3d Cir. 1994).

54. *See, e.g.*, 42 U.S.C. § 2000e-2(b).

55. *See, e.g.*, St. Francis Coll. v. Al-Khazraji, 481 U.S. 604, 611–13 (1987); Torgerson v. City of Rochester, 643 F.3d 1031, 1052–53 (8th Cir. 2011).

56. Comcast Corp. v. Nat'l Ass'n of African American-Owned Media, 140 S. Ct. 1009, 1019 (2020).

57. *Compare* 42 U.S.C. §§ 2000e-5(e)(1), 12117(a) *with* Jones v. R.R. Donnelley & Sons Co., 541 U.S. 369 (2004).

58. *See, e.g.*, Williams v. ConAgra Poultry Co., 378 F.3d 790, 798 (8th Cir. 2004); 42 U.S.C. § 1981a(b)(3).

D. ADEA[59]

To establish a prima facie case of age discrimination under the ADEA, a plaintiff must allege that "(1) he is at least forty years old; (2) he suffered an adverse employment decision; (3) he was qualified for the position in question; and (4) he was ultimately replaced by another employee who was sufficiently younger so as to support an inference of a discriminatory motive."[60] Lisa realizes that she doesn't know how old Tom is. As awkward as it might be to ask, Lisa resolves to do so. She also makes a note to ask the bank who replaced Tom, and how old they were.[61]

E. FMLA

A plaintiff can assert either an interference or a retaliation claim under the FMLA. To make an interference claim under the FMLA, a plaintiff must establish that

> (1) he or she was an eligible employee under the FMLA; (2) the defendant was an employer subject to the FMLA's requirements; (3) the plaintiff was entitled to FMLA leave; (4) the plaintiff gave notice to the defendant of his or her intention to take FMLA leave; and (5) the plaintiff was denied benefits to which he or she was entitled under the FMLA.[62]

"To make a retaliation claim under the FMLA, a plaintiff must show that he invoked his right to FMLA-qualifying leave, that he suffered an adverse

59. As with Title VII and Section 1981, the elements of parallel state law claims are often the same. *See* Kelly v. Drexel Univ., 94 F.3d 102, 105 (3d Cir. 1996); *Harris*, 2018 WL 5316352, at *4.

60. Van Lieu v. Sapa Extrusions, 2019 WL 1003636, at *2 (E.D. Pa. Mar. 1, 2019); *see also* Willis v. UPMC Children's Hosp. of Pittsburgh, 808 F.3d 638, 645 (3d Cir. 2015).

61. Lisa knows that it is often difficult to determine who "replaced" a given employee. In this case, Tom was fired, and Lisa has no reason to believe that someone else was immediately moved into his job. On the contrary, she assumes that the bank simply made do with one fewer teller for a period of time, possibly with tellers from other branches providing coverage. But she decides that she still wants to ask the bank who replaced Tom, because the worst that can happens is the bank will say "no one did."

62. *Capps*, 847 F.3d at 155 (citation omitted).

employment decision, and that the adverse action was causally related to this invocation of rights."[63]

Although a qualified employee is entitled to FMLA leave, "there is no right in the FMLA to be 'left alone' and be completely absolved of responding to the employer's discrete inquiries."[64] As a result, if "the [employer's] contacts were aimed only at retaining [plaintiff] as an employee, and there is no evidence showing that [the employer] in any way hampered or discouraged [plaintiff's] exercise of her right to medical leave, or attempted to persuade her to return from her leave early," there is no claim.[65] Finally, "the FMLA does not provide employees with a right against termination for a reason other than interference with rights under the FMLA. [An employer], therefore, can defeat Plaintiff's claim if it can demonstrate that Plaintiff was terminated for reasons unrelated to his alleged exercise of rights under the FMLA."[66] As a result, if the plaintiff was terminated because of an employer's mistaken belief (for example, that the employee had exhausted all available PTO and was therefore absent without excuse), the FMLA claim will fail.[67]

Again, Lisa realizes that she doesn't know much about Tom's home situation and who he might have to care for. She therefore resolves to ask. Again, she thinks it is a long shot because employees must provide adequate notice to their employer about their need to take FMLA leave,[68] but Lisa decides there is no harm in asking Tom if he gave such notice.

F. ADA

An ADA plaintiff must prove "(1) he is a disabled person within the meaning of the ADA; (2) he is otherwise qualified to perform the essential

---

63. *Id.* at 152 n.6 (citation omitted).

64. O'Donnell v. Passport Health Commc'ns, Inc., 561 F. App'x 212, 218 (3d Cir. 2014).

65. *Id.*

66. Lassalle v. Port Auth. of N.Y. & N.J., 2013 WL 6094339, at *15 (D.N.J. Nov. 19, 2013) (citation omitted).

67. *See, e.g.*, Balding v. Sunbelt Steel Texas, Inc., 2018 WL 1281767, at *3 (10th Cir. Mar. 13, 2018); Dalpiaz v. Carbon Cty., 760 F.3d 1126, 1134 (10th Cir. 2014); Pulczinski v. Trinity Structural Towers, Inc., 691 F.3d 996 (8th Cir. 2012); Phillips v. Matthews, 547 F.3d 905, 911 (8th Cir. 2008); Kariotis v. Navistar Int'l Transp. Corp., 131 F.3d 672 (7th Cir. 1997).

68. *See Lichtenstein*, 691 F.3d at 303; 29 U.S.C. § 2612(e)(2).

functions of the job, with or without reasonable accommodation[69] by the employer; and (3) he has suffered an otherwise adverse employment decision as a result of discrimination."[70] While discrimination can include a refusal to provide a reasonable accommodation,[71] the plaintiff bears the burden of identifying a reasonable accommodation.[72] The *McDonnell Douglas* framework applies to ADA claims.[73]

It is important to remember that the plaintiff bears the burden of proving that he "is an 'otherwise qualified' individual" as defined by the ADA.[74] To determine if the plaintiff has done so, the court "must consider whether or not the individual can perform the essential functions of the position held or desired with or without reasonable accommodation."[75]

"The determination of whether an individual with a disability is qualified is made at the time of the employment decision," and the burden is on the employee to prove that he is an "otherwise qualified" individual.[76] As a result, courts have routinely held that an employee who cannot, on the date they are terminated, return to work due to a disability is not a "qualified individual" and therefore fails to state a prima facie case under the ADA.[77]

---

69. A failure-to-accommodate claim is just a different form of discrimination under the third prong of the prima facie case required for an ADA discrimination claim. *See Williams*, 380 F.3d at 761. An employee asserting a failure-to-accommodate claim must show that "(1) he was disabled and his employer knew it; (2) he requested an accommodation or assistance; (3) his employer did not make a good faith effort to assist; and (4) he could have been reasonably accommodated." *Capps*, 847 F.3d at 157 (citations omitted). A plaintiff asserting a failure-to-accommodate bears the burden of identifying a reasonable accommodation. *See Capps*, 847 F.3d at 147; *Fogleman*, 122 F. App'x at 585–86. "An employer . . . is not required to reallocate essential functions" as a reasonable accommodation. *See* Lombardo v. Air Prod. & Chemicals, Inc., 2006 WL 1892677, at *11 (E.D. Pa. July 7, 2006) (quoting ADA regulations). As a result, "a request to be exempted from an essential duty is not an accommodation designed to help plaintiff perform the job." *Lombardo*, 2006 WL 1892677, at *11 (citations omitted).

70. Taylor v. Phoenixville Sch. Dist., 184 F.3d 296, 306 (3d Cir. 1999) (citations omitted).

71. *See, e.g., Williams*, 380 F.3d at 761.

72. *See, e.g.*, Fogleman v. Greater Hazleton Health Alliance, 122 F. App'x 581, 585–86 (3d Cir. 2004).

73. *See, e.g.*, Wright v. Providence Care Ctr. LLC, 822 F. App'x 85, 90 & n.6 (3d Cir. 2020).

74. Gaul v. Lucent Techs., Inc., 134 F.3d 576, 580 (3d Cir. 1998) (citations omitted).

75. *Id.*

76. *Id.*

77. *See, e.g.*, Williams v. Pinnacle Health Family Care Middletown, 2020 WL 8991688, at *1–2 (M.D. Pa. Mar. 18, 2020), report and recommendation adopted, 2020 WL 8991685 (M.D. Pa. Aug. 4, 2020), aff'd, 2021 WL 1116390 (3d Cir. Mar. 24, 2021); Garner v. School

Although a plaintiff can bring a retaliation claim under the ADA, a retaliation claim premised on a failure to provide a requested accommodation fails as a matter of law.[78] This is because a "retaliation claim [that] is based entirely upon his failure to accommodate claim [] cannot be presented as a separate claim."[79]

Again, after thinking that Tom wouldn't qualify under the ADA, Lisa stops herself. She remembers reading that the Social Security Administration has said that approximately one-third of people born in 1997 will be disabled at some point prior to reaching their normal retirement age.[80] While the incidence of disability increases with age,[81] she resolves to ask Tom whether he considers himself disabled in any way, whether he told anyone from the bank about any sort of impairment he was suffering, and whether he requested any accommodations from the bank.

G. State Law Claims

The elements of state law discrimination claims generally parallel the federal elements, and courts often "incorporate" the federal standards (and case law) into the state statutes.[82] Why, then, would Lisa bring a state law, rather than a federal law claim? Potentially for three reasons. First, Lisa might want to be in state court. Leaving aside the question of whether she might happen to be very friendly with the local state court judge, Lisa might think

---

Dist. of Phila., 63 F. Supp. 3d 483, 489–90 (E.D. Pa. 2014), aff'd, 636 F. App'x 79 (3d Cir. 2015); Jacoby v. Bethlehem Suburban Motor Sales, 820 F. Supp. 2d 609, 622–23 (E.D. Pa. 2011).

78. *See, e.g., Garner*, 63 F. Supp. 3d at 500.

79. *Id.*; *see also* Williams v. Philadelphia Housing Auth., 230 F. Supp. 2d 631, 640 (E.D. Pa. 2002), aff'd & rev'd in nonrelevant parts, 380 F.3d 751 (3d Cir. 2004).

80. *See* Johanna Maleh and Tiffany Bosley, *Disability and Death Probability Tables for Insured Workers Born in 1997*, Social Security Administration (Oct. 2017), https://www.ssa.gov/oact/NOTES/ran6/an2017-6.pdf. *See also* Ashley Welch, *1 in 4 U.S. Adults Has a Disability, CDC Says*, CBS News (Aug. 16, 2018), https://www.cbsnews.com/news/1-in-4-u-s-adults-has-a-disability-cdc-says; The World Bank, *Disability Inclusion*, (last updated Apr. 3, 2023), https://www.worldbank.org/en/topic/disability.

81. *See, e.g.*, Ashley Welch, *1 in 4 U.S. Adults Has a Disability, CDC Says*, CBS News (Aug. 16, 2018), https://www.cbsnews.com/news/1-in-4-u-s-adults-has-a-disability-cdc-says.

82. *See, e.g.*, Kelly v. Drexel Univ., 94 F.3d 102, 105 (3d Cir. 1996); *Harris*, 2018 WL 5316352, at *4.

that a federal judge is likely to be quicker to grant a dispositive motion.[83] Second, some state law claims lack Title VII's $300,000 damages cap.[84] Third, some state laws have longer statutes of limitations.[85]

H. What Constitutes Discrimination?

After listing the elements she must prove to win a discrimination case, Lisa sits back and thinks. What is discrimination? Do microaggressions, which Lisa keeps hearing about whenever she looks at her feed, count as discrimination? Under the law, probably not. This is because courts routinely hold that the antidiscrimination laws do not amount to a "civility code,"[86] and do not require employees or supervisors to "play nice." Instead, they hold "that [plaintiff] experienced personality conflicts resulting in a less than ideal work environment is simply not actionable under Title VII."[87] To be actionable, the complained-of acts must be sufficiently "severe or pervasive" so that they alter the terms and conditions of employment.[88] Offhand comments and isolated incidents do not suffice.[89] Isolated, offhand comments do not create a hostile work environment because a comment that "falls into the category of isolated and offhand comments, and although inappropriate, cannot be considered to have altered the terms and conditions" of employment.[90] Similarly, comments that are "subject to a non-racial interpretation" and "not physically threatening or humiliating" do not create a hostile work environment.[91] Annoyances, such as unwelcome supervision or monitoring of an employee, cannot constitute an adverse employment

83. Some cynical practitioners claim to have seen a sign on the door of a rural courthouse saying "No Spittin' - No Cussin' - No Summary Judgment."

84. *Compare* 42 U.S.C. §1981a(b)(3) *with* Gagliardo v. Connaught Labs, Inc., 311 F.3d 565, 570–71 (3d Cir. 2002); *see also* Hoy v. Angelone, 691 A.2d 476, 483 (Pa. Super. 1997) (punitive damages not available under the Pennsylvania Human Relations Act).

85. *Compare* 29 U.S.C. § 626(d) and 42 U.S.C. §§ 2000e-5(e)(1) *with* 43 PA. STAT. ANN. § 962(c).

86. *See, e.g.*, Faragher v. City of Boca Raton, 524 U.S. 775, 788 (1998); Burgess v. Dollar Tree Stores, Inc., 642 F. App'x 152, 155 (3d Cir. 2016).

87. Fairclough v. Wawa, Inc., 412 F. App'x 465, 469 (3d Cir. 2010).

88. *See, e.g., Faragher*, 524 U.S. at 786.

89. *Id.*

90. *See* Huggins v. Coatesville Area Sch. Dist., 2010 WL 4273317, at *6 (E.D. Pa. Oct. 29, 2010); *see also Woodard*, 255 F. App'x at 609.

91. *See, e.g.*, Sherrod v. Phila. Gas Works, 57 F. App'x 68, 77 (3d Cir. 2003).

action if the supervision does not directly or immediately lead to a cut in job duties or pay.[92] As a result, they are not actionable. The hostility of a work environment is measured based on the totality of the circumstances, such as "the frequency of the discriminatory conduct; its severity; whether it is physically threatening or humiliating, or a mere offensive utterance; and whether it unreasonably interferes with an employee's work performance."[93] Unless extremely severe, offhand comments and isolated incidents are insufficient to sustain a hostile work environment.[94] "Every job has its frustrations, challenges, and disappointments . . . An employee is protected from a calculated effort to pressure her into resignation through the imposition of unreasonably harsh conditions . . . [the employee] is not, however, guaranteed a working environment free of stress."[95]

Indeed, courts have held that actions that go far beyond "micro" aggressions are not actionable. For example, "a paid suspension pending an investigation of an employee's alleged wrongdoing does not fall under any of the forms of adverse action mentioned by Title VII's substantive provision."[96] This is because a "suspension without pay, without more, is not an adverse employment action."[97] Lisa therefore resolves to take Tom's complaints with the proverbial grain of salt and to ask Tom to specify how Betty Branch Manager's actions changed his job duties, and how they changed his job duties in a way that is different from everyone else's job duties. After all, Lisa reminds herself, while she would make a very nice living if she could simply sue every bad boss for being a jerk, the law simply hasn't evolved that far.

III. WAGE AND HOUR CLAIMS

Wage and hour claims are usually brought under the Fair Labor Standards Act (FLSA)[98] and "parallel" state laws. The FLSA requires that all non-exempt[99] employees be paid overtime if they work more than forty hours per

92. *See, e.g., McKinnon*, 642 F. Supp. 2d at 423.

93. *Fichter*, 528 F. App'x at 230.

94. *See, e.g.*, Woodard v. PHB Die Casting, 255 F. App'x 608, 609 (3d Cir. 2007).

95. *Gray*, 957 F.2d at 1083.

96. Jones v. SEPTA, 796 F.3d 323, 326 (3d Cir. 2015).

97. *Id.*

98. 29 U.S.C. §§ 201, *et seq.*

99. *See* 29 U.S.C. § 213(a)(1); 29 C.F.R. § 541.100(a).

week.[100] Lisa remembers reading articles about an explosion of lawsuits—usually in California[101]—claiming that employees were not given uninterrupted meal or rest breaks[102] or that they were made to "work off the clock." She therefore resolves to ask Tom about how his hours were tracked and if he thinks he was paid properly. She knows that banks usually have systems for closely monitoring employees' time cards and that employees usually have to sign off on their time cards every two weeks (which makes it hard to claim that there was an underpayment, especially if substantial time has passed without protest), so a wage and hour claim would be a long shot. But as her mentor once told her, sometimes long shots pay off.

IV. WHAT CLAIMS SHOULD LISA BRING?

As she puts down her pen, Lisa realizes that she has worked through dinner. Again. The result is an impressive list of potential claims. She wonders which of them will be borne out by the facts. She also realizes that she will have to make a tactical decision: whether to bring every possible claim or whether to restrict herself to the likely winners. Lisa knows that some plaintiff's lawyers believe that the way to "buckle a defendant's knees" is to bring dozens of claims, even if many (or even most) of them are unlikely to succeed. She also knows that some judges say that the bad claims drive out the good, and that the best lawyers only plead what they can prove. She also realizes that, although she hasn't been practicing as long as her mentor, she has never seen a bank's knees buckle. Instead, in her experience, although banks usually negotiate when they think it is "just business" and there is a deal to be made, they usually dig in if they think the other side is overreaching. But, she realizes as she turns out her office lights, which claims to bring is a decision for another day, after she has interviewed Tom.

100. *See* 29 U.S.C. § 207(a)(1).

101. *See, e.g.*, Ferra v. Loews Hollywood Hotel LLC, 456 P.3d 415 (Cal. 2021).

102. *See, e.g.*, Cal. Labor Code § 512.

7

The Safe Deposit Box

Susan Verbonitz†

Many of us remember the old days when it was a big deal to go with Mom and Dad to the bank to access their safe deposit box. We would walk through the heavy, black metal gates behind the teller counters, go down the steps, and through another set of heavy black gates to enter the vault where about a hundred shiny gold boxes were stacked in rows on the wall.

I would stand in front of those boxes, thinking they contained great treasures from around the world or top-secret papers. Each box had a number on it and two keyholes. Some were bigger than others, and I imagined that the bigger ones were owned by wealthy people who had more valuable stuff to put in their boxes.

† Susan Verbonitz is a commercial litigator at Weir Greenblatt Pierce LLP. She has spent much of her thirty-five years in practice representing financial institutions in retail and commercial matters. Her representation of financial institutes covers areas of check fraud, contract disputes, commercial loan workouts, loan documentation, creditor's rights, and retail banking claims, including claims of theft of the "family jewels" from a safe deposit box. The views expressed in this section are Susan's alone and are not necessarily the views of Weir Greenblatt Pierce LLP or her financial institutional clients.

Either Mom or Dad would insert their key into one of the holes in their box as the bank manager inserted his key into the other slot. Two keys were needed to make sure the safe deposit box was extra secure. After they turned their key in unison, the long, narrow box would open and slide out. I waited in anticipation as my parents opened the lid to their box at a side table outside the vault where no one could see them, hoping to find great treasure tucked inside our little box. To my dismay, the box was just stuffed with papers, one tied with an old ribbon, and my dad's silver dollar collection, which he kept in a sock. Still, it was adventure and I hoped one day to have my own gold, shiny box in the great vault room at the bank where I would keep my treasures.

I. WHAT IS A SAFE DEPOSIT BOX?

The meaning of a safe deposit box is simple: it is an individually secure container, usually made of metal, which is often used to store important or valuable items. Its origin in the United States dates to the 1860s, when The Safe Deposit Company of New York began offering safe "boxes made of iron, each having its own combination lock. Renters of these boxes will therefore have a complete control of their individual box, and the contents can thus be kept inviolate."[1]

Today, this "secret" storage space is rented[2] at either a bank, credit union, or safe deposit box provider. Under Pennsylvania law, the relationship between a bank and the holder of a safe deposit box is that of bailee and bailor.[3] Pursuant to the terms of the rental agreement, the bank agrees to store your property in a secure container, in a secure location of the bank, for a fee.[4] Safe deposit boxes are kept in a secure vault or separate secured room at a bank. It takes two keys to open a safe deposit box—your key and a key that your bank retains.

---

1. *The Safe Deposit Company of New-York*, N.Y. Times (May 1, 1865), https://www.nytimes.com/1865/05/01/archives/the-safe-deposit-company-of-newyork.html.

2. A bank customer who rents a safe deposit box is often referred to as a "holder" or "owner," even though the customer does not own the box.

3. *See* Ellenbogen v. PNC Bank, N.A., 731 A.2d 175 (Pa. Super. 1999).

4. *See* Chris Moon, *The Average Cost of a Safety Deposit Box*, Value Penguin (Mar. 31, 2017), www.valuepenguin.com/banking/average-cost-of-safety-deposit-box, for a survey of the cost of a safe deposit box at various banks. The safe deposit box rental fee was tax-deductible until the deduction was eliminated under the Tax Cuts and Jobs Act of 2017, commonly referred to as the 2017 tax reform bill.

Safe deposit boxes come in different sizes. The fee charged for renting a safe deposit box usually depends upon the size of the box. Typically, the rental agreement with your bank will describe the fees charged for rental of a safe deposit box and when they are to be paid.

In the era of digital record-keeping and cloud storage, maintaining a safe deposit box may be considered outdated. Although a *New York Times* article[5] reported that major banks are moving away from providing safe deposit box services, an estimated 25 million boxes are still leased in the United States.[6] Due to their secure nature within a bank, safe deposit boxes are often used to store originals of key documents, such as birth certificates, real property deeds, stock certificates and U.S. savings bonds that have not been converted to electronic securities, and family keepsakes and other valuable collections, just like in the old days.

II. WHO HAS ACCESS TO A SAFE DEPOSIT BOX?

When a safe deposit box is rented, all persons authorized to access the box sign what is commonly referred to as a signature card. For the most part, no one other than the renter/owner of the safe deposit box or its pre-authorized agent can enter the safe deposit box. A bank may be liable to the renter for allowing unauthorized parties to enter a safe deposit box in violation of the rental agreement,[7] or for precluding access to a safe deposit box to one authorized to enter the box.[8]

A safe deposit box may be rented by more than one individual, and all parties to the rental agreement are considered corenters or co-owners of the safe deposit box. Corenters share equally in a safe deposit box, and either corenter will have access to the safe deposit box. However, a joint lease of a safe deposit box, without more, may not be sufficient to establish joint

---

5. Stacy Cowley, *Safe Deposit Boxes Aren't Safe*, N.Y. Times (July 19, 2019), https://www.nytimes.com/2019/07/19/business/safe-deposit-box-theft.html.

6. *See id.*

7. *See* Moen v. Norwest Bank of Minot, 647 F. Supp. 1333 (D.N.D. 1986) (bank breached its agreement that provided that the safe deposit box could only be opened in the presence of two of four named parties).

8. *See* Stevenson v. Economy Bank of Ambridge, 197 A.2d 721 (Pa. Super. 1964) (the bank was liable in conversion for precluding a surviving cotenant's access after the colessee's death).

ownership of the contents of the safe deposit box under applicable state laws.[9] Moreover, some states, such as Pennsylvania, have laws that provide that, absent a court order or indemnity bond, a bank is not required to recognize any claim to, or authority to exercise control over, a safe deposit box made by someone other than the person in whose name the box is held.[10] Pennsylvania also has laws that address a financial institution's dealing with a minor with respect to a safe deposit box and agreement.[11]

Most states have a dormancy period if the owner of a safe deposit box fails to pay the rental fee beginning on a date of the last rent payment, plus additional time to send a drill notice. If the customer does not respond to the drill notification, the bank can declare that the box has been abandoned.[12] At that time, the box will be drilled, and the contents of the safe deposit box will be inventoried and turned over to the state, which has legal procedures for handling abandoned property.

---

9. *See*, for example, in *In re Grossman's Estate*, 126 A.2d 468 (Pa. 1956), where the court held that a colease of a safe deposit box did not alone prove joint ownership of securities found in the safe deposit box that originally belonged to one of the colessees.

10. 7 PA. STAT. ANN. § 606(a) provides:

> (a) An institution shall not be required, in the absence of a court order or indemnity required by this section, to recognize any claim to, or any claim of authority to exercise control over, a deposit account or property held in safe-deposit (whether by the institution or in a safe-deposit box or other receptacle leased to a customer) made by a person or persons other than:
>
> (i) the customer in whose name the account or property is held by the institution, or
>
> (ii) an individual or group of individuals who are authorized to draw on or control the account or property pursuant to a certified corporate resolution or other written arrangement with the customer, currently on file with the institution, which:
>
> (A) has not been revoked by valid corporate action in the case of a corporation, or by a valid agreement or other valid action appropriate for the form of legal organization of any other customer, of which the institution has received notice, and
>
> (B) is not the subject of a dispute known to the institution as to its original validity.

11. *See* 7 PA. STAT. ANN. § 603(b), which permits an institution to rent a safe deposit box to a married minor and spouse, jointly. Section 603(c) provides that the agreement is binding on the minor with the same effect as though an adult.

12. Dormancy periods for unclaimed property may vary from state to state. In Pennsylvania, the dormancy period for most types of unclaimed property is three years. *See* Pennsylvania's Disposition of Abandoned and Unclaimed Property Law, 72 PA. STAT. ANN. §§ 1301.1–1301.29. Section 1301.3(4) deals with property held in a safe deposit box.

III. A BANK'S DUTY AND LIABILITY TO ITS SAFE DEPOSIT BOX CUSTOMER

Having a contract with a bank for a safe deposit box does not mean a safe deposit box or the contents therein are safe and secure. A bank that rents a safe deposit box is not the insurer of its contents. The bank is bound only to exercise ordinary care in safeguarding the contents of the safe deposit box and to return the contents to its owner on demand.[13] What constitutes ordinary care or diligence may vary with the circumstances under which the bailment is made.

When the bank's security measures are breached, the bank may be held liable for safe deposit box losses. Take for instance *Moon v. First Nat'l Bank of Benson*, 135 A. 114 (Pa. 1926), where burglars entered the bank by sawing off the iron bars, drilled an opening in the vault door, and accessed customers' safe deposit boxes. The bank's liability to its customers for the contents of their safe deposit boxes was based on negligence in failing to exercise due care and failing to provide a reasonably safe place for keeping its customers' property.

In claims against a bank for losses due to lost or stolen contents, the safe deposit box renter has a heavy burden to show that the bank permitted unauthorized access to the safe deposit box, or that the safe deposit box contained items that the renter now claims are missing or stolen, whatever the case may be, and that the loss is due to the fault of the bank. If such a showing is established, the burden shifts to the bank to show that it was authorized to provide access to the box to someone other than the renter.[14]

Some renters unfortunately discover that their boxes have been emptied since their last visit to the bank, not because of the acts of a third party, but because of the bank's lack of ordinary care in dealing with its customers' property. Take the case of Philip Poniz, who was an internationally known expert in the restoration of high-end timepieces. Mr. Poniz signed a one-page lease agreement with First Union National Bank in Highland Park, New Jersey, for a safe deposit box. Over the next few decades, the bank changed ownership many times, becoming Wells Fargo Bank. Mr. Poniz rented several other boxes. In Box 105, Mr. Poniz kept personal effects, including dozens of watches he inherited from his grandfather.

---

13. *See* Moon v. First Nat'l Bank of Benson, 135 A.114 (Pa. Super. 1926).

14. *See* Mitchell v. First Nat'l Bank of Confluence, 7 A.2d 513 (Pa. Super. 1939).

One day, Mr. Poniz went to the bank to access Box 105, opened it, and found the box was empty. Mr. Poniz pieced together that Wells Fargo, trying to evict another customer for nonpayment of the rental fee, had mistakenly drilled the lock on Mr. Poniz's Box 105 without informing him. After drilling the box open, the bank shipped its contents to a storage facility in North Carolina. When the loss was discovered after realizing there were two boxes containing the same number because of various mergers, Wells Fargo sent back what it had in storage, but Mr. Poniz claimed that items valued at more than $10 million were gone.

On January 9, 2017, Mr. Poniz sued Wells Fargo in New Jersey Superior Court[15] to recover the value of the items removed from Box 105. For nearly two years, the parties battled over Wells Fargo's request to move the case into arbitration until the judge ruled that the case should remain in court. The trial court's decision was affirmed on appeal.[16]

The trial court granted summary judgment in Mr. Poniz's favor on his negligence claim and on the issue of breach of contract, as to liability only. The court granted summary judgment in Wells Fargo's favor on all other claims. The case eventually settled.

Although it has long been held that the relationship between a renter and bank is that of bailor and bailee[17] whose relationship is defined by the safe deposit box rental agreement,[18] under circumstances such as in the *Poniz* case, courts have held that a bank or safe deposit company could be held liable under tort theories for the loss of the customer's contents from their safe deposit box.

For instance, in 2012, Lianna Saribekyan entered into a safe deposit box rental agreement with Bank of America. Ms. Saribekyan claims to have filled the safe deposit box with jewelry, gemstones, and family heirlooms. Nine months later, Ms. Saribekyan went to the bank and discovered her box was gone. Employees told her that all boxes at the branch were drilled and relocated due to the bank's permanent closure of that branch and due to Ms. Saribekyan's failure to close her safe deposit box. Ms. Saribekyan

---

15. *See* Philip Poniz v. Wells Fargo Bank, N.A., No. L-0163-17 (N.J. Super., Middlesex County Nov. 1, 2019). Poniz asserted claims against Wells Fargo for conversion, negligence, breach of contract, breach of fiduciary duty, misrepresentation, and trespass to chattel, among other claims.

16. *See* Poniz v. Wells Fargo Bank, N.A., 2019 WL 5681206 (N.J. Super. Nov. 1, 2019).

17. *See* Mitchell v. First Nat'l Bank, 7 A.2d 513 (Pa. Super. 1939).

18. *See* Ellenbogen v. PNC Bank, N.A., 731 A.2d 175 (Pa. Super. 1999) (where the agreement contained express contractual duties of the bank).

claimed she never received any notice that the branch was closing nor any notice that she should close her safe deposit box or it would be drilled and the contents removed by the bank.

When Ms. Saribekyan retrieved the items Bank of America shipped back from its storage facility, she found many items were missing. She sued the bank for, among other things, breach of contract, conversion, and negligence and sought approximately $7.3 million in damages.[19] Bank of America claimed that the rental agreement Ms. Saribekyan signed expressly incorporated rules and regulations that gave Bank of America the right to relocate a safe deposit box if the banking center is scheduled to close and Bank of America "shall not be liable for loss, damage or breakage to the contents of the Box during relocation." Bank of America's efforts to have the case dismissed were unsuccessful.

At trial, the jury awarded Ms. Saribekyan $2.5 million for the loss of her property and $2 million in punitive damages. Bank of America challenged the verdict, arguing that the damages are limited by the terms of the rental agreement, which provided, "The bank's liability for any loss in connection with the box for whatever reason shall not exceed ten (10) times the annual rent charged for the box," which was about $246 annually. The trial court agreed and reduced the verdict for lost items to $2,460 and reduced the punitive damages award to $150,000.

The appellate court reversed that decision, finding that Bank of America's dealings with the content of the plaintiff's box were inconsistent with the bank's own policies for the treatment of bailed property, demonstrated interference with its customer's possession of her property, and, therefore, constituted a conversion of property. The appellate court found the trial court's grant of nonsuit on the plaintiff's negligent claim was in error, holding an action to recover damages for loss of bailed property need not be predicated on breach of the bailment agreement and that alternative negligent claims may be pled. Finally, the appellate court found that the rental agreement's provision limiting damages was unconscionable and, therefore, unenforceable. The court noted that it was unexpected that the bank could fail to notify the plaintiff of its intent to drill the box, drill open her box without her authorization, remove its contents in violation of the bank's own procedures, lose $2.5 million of the contents, and then attempt to limit its liability to $2,460.[20]

---

19. *See* Saribekyan v. Bank of America, N.A., No. BC549374 (Cal. Super.).

20. *See* Saribekyan v. Bank of America, 2020 WL 38676 (Cal. Ct. App. Jan. 3, 2020).

In August 2016, Jennifer Williams Morsch went to open her safe deposit box at Chase. The box would not open even though she accessed her box successfully multiple times before. Ms. Morsch asked about the problem and was told the box was in another location, also with her number on it, but her key would not open that box either. Morsch discovered that the bank had leased her safe deposit box to someone else. When the box was opened, Morsch found the items inside the box were not hers.

Morsch sued J.P. Morgan for negligence, theft-conversion, specific performance, breach of contract, and negligent misrepresentation.[21] Although the case made its way to a jury, the court granted the bank's motions for judgment as a matter of law on Morsch's claims for conversion, finding there was no evidence that the bank intentionally deprived Morsch of her property, and on the negligent misrepresentation claim. Judgment was also granted in the bank's favor on the negligence and breach of contract claims because those claims arose in November 2012, when the bank leased Morsch's box to a new tenant, and, therefore, were time-barred.[22]

Third parties may gain legitimate access to a safe deposit box under other certain circumstances. For instance, a law enforcement agency may obtain a court order freezing an owner's access to a safe deposit box or forcing the box open and seizing the contents upon a showing that there is probable cause to suspect that the box's owner is hiding something illegal in the box, such as illegal drugs or stolen property.[23] In noncriminal cases such as tax matters, the IRS can freeze a taxpayer's assets, including a safe deposit box.[24] The contents of a safe deposit box may be subject to garnishment by a creditor who has a judgment against the holder of a safe deposit box the same way that a bank account is subject to garnishment.[25]

---

21. *See* Morsch v. J.P. Morgan Chase Bank, N.A., No. 6:18-cv-148-Orl-DCI (M.D. Fla. Nov. 7, 2018).

22. *See id.*

23. *See* U.S. v. Henkel, 451 F.2d 777 (3d Cir. 1971) (issuance of a search warrant based on probable cause that proceeds of a bank robbery were in the box did not render a search in violation of the Fourth Amendment); U.S. v. Phan, 628 F. Supp. 2d 562 (M.D. Pa. 2009) (seizure of a safe deposit box key was warranted under the plain view doctrine where the government had probable cause to believe the box contained evidence and the key was in plain view).

24. *See* U.S. v. Mellon Bank, N.A., 521 F.2d 708 (3d Cir. 1975) (an order seeking to open a safe deposit box to enforce the government's jeopardy assessment under 26 U.S.C. § 6861 against a third-party bank was necessary and appropriate).

25. *See* Pa. R. Civ. P. 3110.

IV. ACCESSING A SAFE DEPOSIT BOX UPON THE DEATH OF THE OWNER

Most state laws address who can access and when a safe deposit box can be accessed upon the death of the owner of the safe deposit box. The purpose of these laws is to prevent the contents of the safe deposit box from escaping inheritance or estate taxing authorities. In Pennsylvania, restrictions on access apply to a safe deposit box held in the decedent's name alone, jointly in the name of the decedent and one or more others, or in the name of an entity where the decedent has access to the safe deposit box. The restrictions imposed by law do not apply to a safe deposit box held in the name of the decedent and the decedent's spouse. The decedent's surviving spouse may enter the safe deposit box and remove anything from it without restrictions.

Pennsylvania law provides that no person having knowledge of the death of a decedent shall enter a safe deposit box of the decedent.[26] One exception is that the bank may permit entry into a safe deposit box of a decedent for the sole purpose of removing the decedent's will or deed to a burial lot.[27] The search for the decedent's will or cemetery deed must be conducted in the presence of a bank employee. Once the will or cemetery deed is removed, the bank cannot permit access to the safe deposit box until the contents are inventoried in accordance with Pennsylvania law and the Pennsylvania Department of Revenue's procedures.[28]

Banks are often sued for refusing to permit access to safe deposit boxes upon the death of a decedent. In *Stevenson v. Economy Bank of Ambridge*, 413 Pa. 442 (1964), the plaintiff sued Economy Bank for conversion of the contents of a safe deposit box leased to the plaintiff's brother-in-law, claiming the plaintiff was entitled to the contents of the box under the lease agreement. The plaintiff, along with the decedent, signed the lease agreement, which stated, "either of them shall have access" and further declared

---

26. *See* 72 Pa. Stat. Ann. § 9191.

27. *See id.* § 9192(e).

28. *See* Pennsylvania's procedures for inventorying and closing a decedent's safe deposit box, which changed on May 11, 2011. The Pennsylvania Department of Revenue no longer requires a department representative, bank employee, lawyer, or accountant to be present at the inventory conducted of the safe deposit box. Instead, a decedent's safe deposit box may be entered upon notice of the date of entry mailed to the department and the bank where the box is located within seven days of the date proposed for entry. Note that entry to a decedent's safe deposit box may vary from state to state.

that "each of them has such interest in the entire contents of said box as to entitle him or her to the possession thereof." Notwithstanding this language, the bank denied the plaintiff access to the safe deposit box after the decedent died until a qualified executor was appointed.

The plaintiff sued the bank for conversion for denying her access to the safe deposit box. The court held that the plaintiff had a contractual right of access to and entry into the box, and the bank was without authority or justification to preclude her access. The bank's interference with the plaintiff's right to possession of the contents of the box constituted a conversion. The court found, however, that "the technical and temporary interference" with the plaintiff's right of access to the safe deposit box would be vindicated by an award of nominal damages only.[29]

V. LAWS TYPICALLY DO NOT GOVERN WHAT CAN BE PUT IN A SAFE DEPOSIT BOX

There are no federal or state laws concerning what can be stored in a safe deposit box. Instead, banks often put restrictions on what can be put in a safe deposit box in the rental agreement. Explosives, firearms, illegal substances, hazardous materials, liquids, cremations, and things considered to be dangerous are among the items banks prohibit from being kept in a safe deposit box. Some banks limit the number of items you can keep in a safe deposit box. A rental agreement with a bank may include a provision that, if the bank has reason to believe the contents of a safe deposit box are dangerous or illegal, the bank can drill open the safe deposit box and dispose of such items.

A safe deposit box is not insured by the Federal Deposit Insurance Corporation (FDIC) or financial institutions, so its contents, including cash, are not insured by FDIC deposit insurance if lost, damaged, or stolen. Banks typically disclaim liability for theft or damage to the contents of a safe deposit box. If you want to insure your property in a safe deposit box, coverage can be obtained through a homeowner's policy or another private safe deposit box special agent.[30]

---

29. *See* Stevenson v. Economy Bank of Ambridge, 413 Pa. 442 (1964).

30. *See, e.g.*, Federal Deposit Insurance Corporation, *Five Things to Know About Safe Deposit Boxes, Home Safes and Your Valuables*, FDIC Consumer News (Winter 2018), fdic.gov/consumers/consumer/news/cnwin18/fivethings.html.

VI. A BANK'S MONITORING OF A SAFE DEPOSIT BOX IS LIMITED

Monitoring a safe deposit box can be difficult because a safe deposit box is accessible only to the renter and access is in person. Typical systems used by banks to detect fraud and suspicious activity in connection with retail bank transactions, such as check cashing, deposits, or collection, are of no use in the case of safe deposit boxes. In monitoring a safe deposit box, banks rely on information received from the customer when a safe deposit box is rented.

Despite the absence of or inability to monitor safe deposit box access, thefts from safe deposit boxes are not typical. A *New York Times* article revealed that of the 19,000 bank robberies reported to the FBI in the five years preceding the article, only forty-four involved safe deposit boxes.[31]

VII. RENTING A SAFE DEPOSIT BOX IS A MATTER OF CHOICE

A safe deposit box, while intended to be a safe, secure container for your property, is not without risk. As seen above, there is the risk that a safe deposit box may be relocated or misplaced, or its contents mistakenly removed, as happened to Philip Poniz. Safe deposit boxes may not be fireproof and waterproof, as we saw with the virtual destruction of items in safe deposit boxes in a branch bank in 5 World Trade Center after the events of September 11.[32] However, for many, a safe deposit box at a bank provides an added measure of security beyond what they may have at home and is a logical consumer choice for safekeeping of items.

---

31. *See* Stacy Cowley, *Safe Deposit Boxes Aren't Safe*, N.Y. TIMES (July 19, 2019), https://www.nytimes.com/2019/07/19/business/safe-deposit-box-theft.html.

32. Pamela Sebastian Ridge, *People Retrieve Charred Memories from World Trade Center Vault*, WALL ST. J., (Jan. 18, 2002), https://www.wsj.com/articles/SB1011305764356207080.

8

Fiduciary Claims Against Banks

Thomas Wiegand and Benjamin Woodring†

Cindy Client comes to Lisa Lawyer's office and says she wants to sue her bank because it broke a promise to her. Lisa thinks, "Is this a simple contract case or something else?" and asks for more information. Cindy explains further: "The bank said it would take my money and invest it for me in good low-risk investments, but I found out later it just put my money into a bunch of risky bets that the bank had their own investments in. And they never told me about how they were involved in the things they invested in; I found that out through a friend." A light bulb goes off in Lisa's head. This is not about (or only about) a contract as she first suspected, but it is a potential fiduciary duty breach case.

An important context in which banks can face liability is in the realm of fiduciary duties. A fiduciary duty is, in

† Thomas Wiegand is a partner at MoloLamken LLP. He is a trial lawyer and mediator who represents clients across the country in complex business litigation, class actions, personal and family trust disputes, antitrust matters, and state and federal government investigations. He serves as cochair of the CPLR Committee for the New York State Bar Association and is the outgoing president of the Seventh Circuit Bar Association. He can be reached at (312) 450-6703 or twiegand@mololamken.com.

essence, a requirement to act in the best interests of another (a client, a beneficiary, etc.). "Though difficult to define in precise terms, a fiduciary relationship is generally described as arising when there has been a special confidence reposed in one who in equity and good conscience is bound to act in good faith and with due regard to the interests of the one reposing confidence."[1]

This chapter discusses various roles and situations in which banks may owe fiduciary duties—whether to a customer, a beneficiary, a corporation, a borrower, or an ERISA investment plan. In each, the fundamental components of the duty are care and loyalty. While each context has its own applied meanings of those concepts, "care" consistently means carrying out tasks with an expected level of skill and diligence (as opposed to negligently). "Loyalty" means avoiding self-dealing and conflicts of interest and operating transparently. Where a bank breaches a fiduciary duty, it can be liable for damages where it has harmed a client or beneficiary. To establish a breach of fiduciary duty, a plaintiff must prove that (1) the defendant owed the plaintiff a fiduciary duty, (2) that duty was breached, (3) the plaintiff suffered damages, and (4) the breach caused those damages.

This chapter covers fiduciary issues and expectations in the following roles assumed by banks:

- banks as investment advisers
- banks as lenders/creditors
- banks as trustees
- banks as ERISA trustees
- banks in other fiduciary roles (transfer agents, registrars, executors)

I. BANKS AS INVESTMENT ADVISERS

Banks serving as or employing registered investment advisers have recognized fiduciary responsibilities to clients. The Investment Advisers Act of 1940 (IAA), 15 U.S.C. §§ 80b–1 to b–21, makes it unlawful for an investment adviser

---

Benjamin Woodring is a partner at Kirkland & Ellis LLP. His practice focuses on complex commercial disputes, including fiduciary, securities, and qui tam litigation. He serves on the Council for the ABA Litigation Section and as the ABA Young Lawyers Division liaison to the ABA Litigation Section. He can be reached at (312) 862-0540 or benjamin .woodring@kirkland.com.

The views expressed in this chapter are those of the authors, do not constitute legal advice, and are not necessarily the views of MoloLamken LLP or Kirkland & Ellis LLP.

1. Dallaire v. Bank of America, N.A., 367 N.C. 363 (N.C. 2014).

> (1) to employ any device, scheme, or artifice to defraud any client or prospective client; (2) to engage in any transaction, practice, or course of business which operates as a fraud or deceit upon any client or prospective client; (3) acting as principal for his own account, knowingly to sell any security to or purchase any security from a client, or acting as broker for a person other than such client, knowingly to effect any sale or purchase of any security for the account of such client, without disclosing to such client in writing before the completion of such transaction the capacity in which he is acting and obtaining the consent of the client to such transaction . . . [and] (4) to engage in any act, practice, or course of business which is fraudulent, deceptive, or manipulative.[2]

In *SEC v. Capital Gains Research Bureau, Inc.*, 375 U.S. 180 (1963), the U.S. Supreme Court interpreted the antifraud provision of the Advisers Act as Congress's recognition that an investment adviser is a fiduciary with a duty of "utmost good faith, and full and fair disclosure of all material facts, as well as an affirmative obligation to avoid misleading his clients."[3] It held that an investment adviser who purchases a security for its own account and then recommends the same security to its client without disclosing its own ownership violates the antifraud provision of the IAA and breaches its fiduciary duty.[4] Subsequent Supreme Court elaborations of *Capital Gains Research* confirmed the case as the federal fiduciary standard for investment advisers.[5]

Investment advisers' duties of care and loyalty include a duty to recommend suitable investments, a duty to inform, a duty to act promptly, a duty to act with authorization, a duty to refrain from self-dealing, and a duty to avoid conflicts of interest. Regarding duty of care, an investment adviser's negligence can lead to a breach of fiduciary duty. Advisers are

---

2. Investment Advisers Act of 1940, 15 U.S.C. § 80b-6.

3. SEC v. Capital Gains Research Bureau, Inc., 375 U.S. 180, 194 (1963); *see also id.* at 191 (discussing Congressional recognition of "the delicate fiduciary nature of an investment advisory relationship").

4. *See id.* at 201.

5. *See* Santa Fe Indus., Inc. v. Green, 430 U.S. 462, 472 n.11 (1977) (*Capital Gains Research*'s "references to fraud in the 'equitable' sense" are "recognition that Congress intended the Investment Advisers Act to establish federal fiduciary standards for investment advisers"); Transam. Morg. Advisors (TAMA) v. Lewis, 444 U.S. 11, 17 (1979) ("the [Advisers] Act's legislative history leaves no doubt that Congress intended to impose enforceable fiduciary obligations").

expected to use their specialized skill and expertise for the benefit of the client. Failing to do so or doing so at a substandard level can breach one's fiduciary duty.

Regarding the duty of loyalty, examples of potential investment adviser breaches of self-dealing or conflict of interest include churning, misrepresentations, unauthorized trading, and other types of securities fraud that benefit the adviser (or someone else) at the expense of the client. The federal fiduciary standard requires an investment adviser to act in the "best interest" of its client.[6] Through this "best interest" lens, an adviser may benefit from a transaction recommended to a client only if the benefit and any related information are fully disclosed.[7]

The SEC released further guidance on fiduciary duties of investment advisers under the IAA in 2019 (2019 Release).[8] It reiterated that the IAA's fiduciary duties are based on common law principles of a client-adviser relationship founded on "trust and confidence." It stated that the duty of care requires the provision of advice in the client's best interest and based on the client's objectives. The duty of loyalty requires full disclosure of any conflicts so that a client can give informed consent concerning any potential conflict. The 2019 Release also states that the duties apply regardless of the wealth or sophistication of the client, but that context should be considered to allow for different types of adviser relationships in terms of scope and objectives. Fiduciary duties may be narrowed in some agreed situations, but they can never be fully waived. More recent guidance from the SEC addressing investment advisers of private funds (but applicable more widely) has emphasized that so-called "hedge clauses"—clauses that purport to waive the fiduciary's duties in some form or another or can mislead a client into thinking so—likely violate Section 206 of the IAA.[9]

---

6. *See, e.g.*, SEC v. Tambone, 550 F.3d 106, 146 (1st Cir. 2008) ("[15 U.S.C. § 80b-6] imposes a fiduciary duty on investment advisers to act at all times in the best interest of the fund and its investors.").

7. *See Capital Gains Research*, 375 U.S. at 191–92 (IAA designed to "eliminate, or at least to expose, all conflicts of interest which might incline an investment adviser—consciously or unconsciously—to render advice which was not disinterested").

8. Securities and Exchange Commission, *Release IA-5248*, 17 C.F.R. Part 276 (June 5, 2019), www.sec.gov/rules/interp/2019/ia-5248.pdf.

9. *See* SEC Division of Examinations Risk Alert, *Observations from Examinations of Private Fund Advisers*, (Jan. 27, 2022), www.sec.gov/files/private-fund-risk-alert-pt-2.pdf.

The IAA does not grant a private right to bring a claim in federal court for a breach of fiduciary duty. IAA breach claims are pursued through federal prosecutions (for instance, the Securities and Exchange Commission regulates investment advisers). But this does not mean that a private individual alleging a bank's fiduciary breach has no legal recourse. Fiduciary duty claims often relate to allegations of manipulative and deceptive practices relating to the purchase or sale of a security, and accordingly can be pursued through a Rule 10b-5 claim under the Securities Exchange Act of 1934 (which does allow private actions).[10] Additionally, fiduciary breach allegations will sometimes overlap with negligence allegations (through what a duty of care requires) and can thus be potentially pursued through a negligence claim.[11]

Often, however, states provide a remedy for breach of fiduciary duty. To prevail on a breach of fiduciary claim under various state laws, a plaintiff usually must prove (1) the existence of a fiduciary duty, (2) breach of that duty, and (3) damages proximately caused by that breach.[12] Plaintiffs often seek equitable compensation to be "made whole" or put back in the same position they were in before the alleged breach of fiduciary duty. This might include costs suffered by the client as well as forgone market gains or lost profits.

A registered investment adviser is not automatically a fiduciary under all state common law, but can become one if the advisee places trust and confidence in the adviser such that the adviser assumes influence over the advisee and/or places the adviser on unequal (superior) footing vis-à-vis the advisee.[13] For instance, plaintiffs who "entrusted [registered investment advisers] with approximately $500,000 of their personal funds and placed their confidence in defendants' ability to invest those funds to yield returns" prevailed on common law fiduciary claims where it was shown those advisers concealed information about the real estate projects they advised plaintiffs to invest in.[14]

10. *See* Note, *Fiduciary Suits Under Rule 10b-5*, 1968 Duke L.J. 791–815 (1968).

11. *See, e.g.*, Brown v. Roth, 514 S.E.2d 294 (N.C. App. 1999) ("fiduciary duty" used to describe duty to exercise care).

12. *See, e.g.*, Neade v. Portes, 193 Ill. 2d 433, 444 (Ill. 2000); Basile v. H & R Block, Inc., 563 Pa. 359 (Pa. 2000).

13. *See, e.g.*, Hollerich v. Acri, 259 F. Supp. 3d 806 (N.D. Ill. 2017) (applying Illinois law); Belmont v. MB Inv. Partners, Inc., 708 F.3d 470, 500–07 (3d Cir. 2013) (applying Pennsylvania law).

14. *See Hollerich*, 259 F. Supp. 3d at 814 (applying Illinois law).

Banks serving as advisers to mutual funds or investment companies also have fiduciary duties to their advisees, in this context specifically under the Investment Company Act of 1940 (ICA), 15 U.S.C. § 80a. For mutual funds, investment advisers will often help establish the fund, choose its directors, and then manage the fund's investments and provide ongoing advisory support. Unlike the IAA, the ICA does grant a private right of action for breach of fiduciary duty, specifically to mutual fund shareholders against advisers for excessive compensation (but not for other types of breaches).[15] In *Jones v. Harris Assocs. L.P.*, 559 U.S. 335 (2010), the U.S. Supreme Court established the standard for mutual fund shareholders bringing a fiduciary duty breach claim under the ICA. Adopting the Second Circuit's test in *Gartenberg v. Merrill Lynch Asset Mgmt. Inc.*, 694 F.2d 923 (2d Cir. 1982), the Court held that "to face liability [for breach of fiduciary duty] under [the ICA], an investment adviser must charge a fee that is so disproportionately large that it bears no reasonable relationship to the services rendered and could not have been the product of arm's length bargaining."[16]

Fiduciary duties do not generally extend to other categories of financial personnel such as financial planners or broker-dealers, but the inquiry is fact-driven and depends on the extent to which a client has reposed trust and confidence in the financial professional and whether an unequal relationship has been created.[17]

While some courts have held that broker-dealers are, as a matter of course, in a fiduciary relationship with their clients,[18] more commonly courts have not acknowledged a full fiduciary relationship[19] unless specific circumstances make the broker-dealer more of an adviser figure, a scenario discussed more generally immediately below.

15. *See* 15 U.S.C. § 80a-35(b)(1)(2).

16. Jones v. Harris Assocs. L.P., 559 U.S. 335, 335 (2010).

17. *See, e.g.*, Diest v. Wachholz, 208 Mont. 207 (Mont. 1984) (fiduciary duty found where widow relied exclusively on bank's advice in financial matters for twenty years); *Basile*, 563 Pa. at 359 (fiduciary duties accrue where "one person has reposed a special confidence in another to the extent that the parties do not deal with each other on equal terms").

18. *See* Marchese v. Shearson Hayden Stone, Inc., 734 F.2d 414, 418 (9th Cir. 1984).

19. *See, e.g.*, Kronfeld v. First Jersey Nat'l Bank, 638 F. Supp. 1454, 1467 (D.N.J. 1986) (a "stockbroker may have a quasi-fiduciary duty toward his customer").

II. BANKS AS LENDERS: EXCESSIVE CONTROL OF BORROWER/LENDER AS ADVISER

It is well established that banks normally do not have a fiduciary responsibility when they serve as a lender.[20] This is instead a creditor-debtor relationship.[21]

Under certain special circumstances, however, courts have imposed fiduciary duties on a lender bank where it assumes excessive control or influence over a borrower. Although the jurisprudence varies across states, certain patterns emerge. To the extent courts find special relationships among lenders and borrowers warranting imposition of fiduciary duties, the lender has typically either (1) transformed into an investment adviser, causing the borrower to repose trust and faith in the lender's judgment, and/or (2) the lender has derived some uneven advantage or control in its dealings with the borrower, either through ability to apply financial pressure or through superior information.

For example, in *Barnett Bank v. Hooper*, 498 So. 2d 923 (Fla. 1986), the Supreme Court of Florida imposed fiduciary duties on a bank lender where it had a long relationship with the borrower and made representations through its employees concerning the soundness of a proposed investment with an independent tax shelter adviser. Affirmations from the bank persuaded the borrower to borrow money from the bank to invest with the tax shelter adviser. Shortly after, the bank began to suspect the adviser, also a customer, of running a check-kiting scheme and stopped cashing his checks. It nevertheless allowed the borrower to borrow additional funds to invest with the suspectedly fraudulent adviser, without informing the borrower of the information it acquired in its own investigation. It was in the bank's interest to allow the borrower's infusion of funds to replenish the check-kiter's account. After the borrower received no returns from the

20. In the rare event where a court finds a fiduciary or quasi-fiduciary duty in the standard lender-borrower context, it is narrowly confined to the duty to handle properly confidential borrower information. *See, e.g.*, Djowharzadeh v. City Nat'l Bank & Tr. Co. of Norman, 646 P.2d 616 (Okla. App. 1982) (bank has implicit duty to keep loan application information confidential and can be held accountable for negligence).

21. *See, e.g.*, Continental Bank NA v. Everett, 964 F.2d 701 (7th Cir. 1992); Black Canyon Racquetball Club, Inc. v. Idaho First Nat'l Bank, 804 P.2d 900, 905 (Ida. 1991); Power Equip. Co. v. First Alabama Bank, 585 So. 2d 1291 (Ala. 1991); McCoy v. First Citizens Bank, 148 P.3d 677 (Mont. 2006); Union State Bank v. Woell, 434 N.W.2d 712, 721 (N.D. 1989); Sec. Nat'l Bank of Greensboro v. Educators Mut. Life Ins. Co., 143 S.E.2d 270, 276 (N.C. 1965).

adviser, it brought suit, including against the bank. The court found that "where a bank becomes involved in a transaction with a customer with whom it has established a relationship of trust and confidence, and it is a transaction from which the bank is likely to benefit at the customer's expense, the bank may be found to have assumed a duty to disclose facts material to the transaction, peculiarly within its knowledge, and not otherwise available to the customer."[22] A similar conclusion occurred in *American Bank Ctr. v. Wiest*, where the North Dakota Supreme Court affirmed a finding that a bank owed fiduciary duties to a borrower where a loan officer told the borrower he "was taking care" of him while telling the borrower to keep making payments on obligations that would benefit the bank but not the borrower.[23]

Fiduciary duties have also been recognized in the lender-borrower context where a bank makes gratuitous promises, gives additional affirmations, or takes on other guidance roles that increase repose of trust and confidence. For instance, in *Lowery v. Guaranty Bank & Trust Co.*, 592 So. 2d 79 (Miss. 1991), the Mississippi Supreme Court affirmed a fiduciary duty where plaintiffs consistently dealt with one bank officer who gave the impression he would bend the rules or make exceptions according to their circumstances. On the other hand, a loan officer's assertion to borrowers that they "could obtain a first priority lien mortgage loan" was not enough to create a fiduciary relationship.[24] Giving advice to a borrower does not automatically transform the relationship into a fiduciary one.[25] Advice from a bank will not transform the relationship when it is not relied upon by the borrower, or if a borrower had additional sources of advice (such as legal counsel).[26] Some courts have found that mortgage servicers, where they engage extensively with a borrower and encourage and guide a

22. Barnett Bank v. Hooper, 498 So. 2d 923, 925 (Fla. 1986).

23. *See* American Bank Ctr. v. Wiest, 2010 N.D. 251 (N.D. 2010). *See also* Central States Stamping Co. v. Terminal Equip. Co., Inc., 727 F.2d 1405 (6th Cir. 1984) (bank treated as fiduciary where it represented financial soundness in a customer to induce investment in a (foundering) agricultural business that would be beneficial to itself—reducing debt owed by another customer—and detrimental to the plaintiff); Frydman & Co. v. Credit Suisse First Boston Corp., 708 N.Y.S.2d 77 (N.Y. App. Div. 2000) (financier defendant had fiduciary responsibility to borrower where it gave investment banking advice and conducted negotiations on borrower's behalf).

24. *See Dallaire*, 367 N.C. at 363.

25. *See Woell*, 434 N.W.2d at 721.

26. *See* Simmons Oil Corp. v. Holly Corp., 852 P.2d 523, 526 (Mont. 1993).

borrower to seek a loan modification, take on a fiduciary role distinct from the traditional "silent lender."[27]

Another situation in which courts recognize a fiduciary duty in the lender-borrower or creditor-debtor relationship is where the lender exercises excessive control over the borrower or debtor. For example, a Texas court stated a fiduciary relationship might obtain between lender and borrower where a bank was alleged to have (1) stacked the borrower's board with its own officers and directors, (2) installed one of the bank's directors as CEO of the borrower, and (3) facilitated the stripping of borrower assets to make unnecessary prepayments on the loan.[28] Courts require a high standard of interference or influence to find a fiduciary relationship on this basis. "[A]ctual day-to-day involvement in management and operations of the borrower or the ability to compel the borrower to engage in unusual transactions is required for the purposes of showing that a lending institution had control over a borrower."[29]

Finally, a bank, like any other person or entity, will assume fiduciary duties if it agrees to serve as an agent for a borrower or becomes a partner with the borrower. Agency can occur in contexts such as where the bank acts as a borrower's closing agent or escrow agent related to a transaction. Another way banks can go beyond traditional creditor-debtor relationships is through participating in an investment. For example, if a bank exchanges its rights to foreclose on a loan for a percentage share of profits, a joint venture is established entailing fiduciary responsibilities between partners.

---

27. *See, e.g.*, Crilley v. Bank of Am., N.A., 2012 U.S. Dist. LEXIS 58469, at *27–29 (D. Haw. Apr. 26, 2012).

28. State Nat'l Bank of El Paso v. Farah Mfg. Co., Inc., 678 S.W.2d 661 (Tex. App. El Paso 1984). Note, however, that in this case the plaintiff did not actually bring a breach of fiduciary claim. *See also* Johnson v. First Nat'l Bank of Shreveport, 792 So. 2d 33 (La. App. Ct. 3 Cir. 2001) (fiduciary relationship established where bank officer pressured borrower to make drastic changes in his cattle operation to receive financing and saddled borrower with unnecessary fees and transactions to gain further leverage over him).

29. St. Matthew's Baptist Church v. Wachovia Bank Nat'l Ass'n, Civ. No. 04-4540, 18-19 (D.N.J. May. 18, 2005); *see also* Flying J Fish Farm v. Peoples Bank of Greensboro, 12 So. 3d 1185 (Ala. 2008) (finding no fiduciary relationship "even where the bank has taken an active role in attempting to improve a debtor company's financial position," including "caus[ing] various documents to be prepared, ma[king] additional secured loans, and ke[eping] close tabs on the Company's operation").

III. BANKS AS TRUSTEES

Banks often serve as trustees, and accordingly assume long-recognized fiduciary duties undertaken in the trust context. As a trustee of a revocable trust, banks will owe duties to the settlor of the trust. As trustee of an irrevocable trust, banks will owe duties to the trust's beneficiaries and to the settlor. States follow the Uniform Trust Code (2000) to differing extents (if at all), but across all jurisdictions run the common law trustee fiduciary duties of prudence and loyalty.

As trustees, banks must also administer the trust faithful to the trust's purpose and terms. These will be set out in a trust instrument and/or certain other documents. It also must render personal attention to the trust, as a trustee's exercise of discretion is not fundamentally delegable (though circumscribed delegations with periodic review are often permitted).

A prudent trustee is one who invests trust assets in a manner consonant with the duty of care the financial community recognizes in a prudent investor. The trustee should make investments at a level of risk calibrated to the terms and purpose of the trust. Courts evaluate a trustee's investment decisions based on the context of the time the decision was made, not how an investment ultimately fared. The prudence and wisdom of investment decisions should be evaluated in light of an entire investment portfolio.

With respect to prudence, a bank serving as trustee must administer a trust with reasonable skill and diligence. It must preserve and protect the trust corpus and make the trust's assets productive. For example, in *Namik v. Wachovia Bank*, 612 S.E.2d 270 (Ga. 2005), Georgia's Supreme Court affirmed a finding by the trial court that a bank breached its fiduciary duty as a trustee by failing to follow instructions of the settlor (set forth in a memorandum documenting discussion with the settlor upon formation of the trust). The memo stated that all funds were to be invested in U.S. government issues. The funds were placed in a money market fund, and when the settlor died, the estate paid millions in taxes it would not otherwise have had to if it had invested in certain tax-free investments of U.S. government issues available to the settlor (a non-U.S. citizen). Although the trust documentation did not specify the precise investment vehicles to use, the court affirmed the trial court's ruling that a prudent person in the capacity of a trustee at the time would have been aware of the comparative tax consequences of its investment decisions and have followed the memo.

Regarding loyalty, the trustee is forbidden from self-dealing. "A trustee is held to something stricter than the morals of the market place. Not honesty alone, but the punctilio of an honor the most sensitive, is then the standard of behavior. As to this there has developed a tradition that is unbending and inveterate."[30] A trustee should "derive[] no unfair advantage from [its] fiduciary relation."[31]

> The law does not permit a person in a fiduciary capacity to handle the beneficiary's property so as to further his own ends . . . As soon as a corporate fiduciary places itself in a position where its interest may conflict with that of the beneficiary, it has violated the trust, regardless of whether or not the transaction seemed at the time to be fair or unfair.[32]

The comment to Uniform Trust Code 1003(a) (2010) makes clear that any profit by a trustee outside of its standard compensation breaches its fiduciary duty, regardless of whether there was a breach of trust.[33] If the terms of a trust authorize a type of transaction that would otherwise be understood as self-dealing by the trustee, that is a defense available to challenge liability.

A straightforward example of a bank breaching its fiduciary duty of loyalty occurred in *In re Estate of Binder*, 137 Ohio St. 26 (Ohio 1940). Trustee Guardian Trust Co. used Binder trust assets to purchase land trust certificates representing interests in a theater building site. But it had first purchased the assets in its own capacity, then transferred them into a joint syndicate account, then onto a larger banking group, then to a selling syndicate, ultimately profiting from these transactions before placing the land trust certificates in the Binder trust. Guardian argued that the profit was "compensation for services in making such certificates available as forms of investment for its trusts." The court disagreed: "Clearly this transaction

30. Meinhard v. Salmon, 249 N.Y. 458, 464 (N.Y. 1928).

31. Vinlis Constr. Co. v. Roreck, 30 A.D.2d 668, 668 (N.Y. App. 2d Dept 1968); *see also* Barker v. First Nat'l Bank of Birmingham, 20 F. Supp. 185, 187 (N.D. Ala. 1937) ("the relation between a trustee and its cestui is the most intense fiduciary relation in our law . . . All personal or selfish interests and all consideration of the interests of third parties must be excluded. His must be an undivided loyalty.").

32. Hutchings v. Louisville Trust Co., 276 S.W.2d 461, 464 (Ky. Ct. App. 1955).

33. *See also* CAL. PROB. CODE § 16004(a) (fiduciary duty breach presumed where trustee profits aside from routine compensation).

was tainted with the vice of self-dealing, profit-taking, underwriting and syndicate participation before the trust certificates in question came into the Binder trust."[34] The beneficiaries were entitled to rescind the transactions, and the bank was liable for surcharge of the amounts invested.

A trustee also has a duty to keep beneficiaries reasonably informed about the administration of a trust, including material facts related to their interest. "[I]t is the trustee's duty to disclose to the beneficiary fully, frankly, and without reservation all facts pertaining to the trust."[35] In *Miller v. Bank of America*, 326 P.3d 20 (N.M. Ct. App. 2014), the bank trustee was found liable for breach of fiduciary duty because it did not inform the beneficiary of its internal assessment of the state of the trust's main asset (a derelict building that was a drain on resources) and instead pursued an aggressive and risky rehabilitation program for the building, again keeping the beneficiary in the dark as to important details regarding the precise amount of trust expenditure. Even though the beneficiary had consented to the building renovations, it did not have critical pieces of information, and thus the defense of consent was rejected.

The trustee also has a duty to keep and render written accounts of the trust's administration. Most states require that the trustee of an irrevocable trust provide to all beneficiaries a periodic accounting of trust assets, market value, and other information required by state statute or common law. For instance, under New York law, a trustee has the duty of showing that the transactions in an accounting that it provides were "correct, just, and necessary."[36] Records should document not just the transactional details of the trust's activity but information sufficient to keep a beneficiary informed of the administration of the trust and material facts related to the beneficiary's interest. In *Matter of Shulsky*, 34 A.D.2d 545 (N.Y. App. 2d Dept 1970), the court determined that although the proposed accounting detailed tax and penalty amounts, the executor failed to account where it had no contemporaneous records of why it paid estate taxes late and incurred penalties, explaining that "[t]he burden was upon the fiduciary to show that the delays were justified."[37] A trustee's failure to account is typically considered a breach of fiduciary duty.

34. In re Estate of Binder, 137 Ohio St. 26, 45 (Ohio 1940).

35. In re Enger's Will, 225 Minn. 229, 239 (Minn. 1948).

36. White v. Rankin, 18 A.D. 293, 294–95 (N.Y. App. 2d Dept 1897), aff'd, 162 N.Y. 622 (N.Y. 1900).

37. Matter of Shulsky, 34 A.D.2d 545, 546 (N.Y. App. 2d Dept 1970).

IV. BANKS AS ERISA TRUSTEES

Banks routinely serve as sponsors or advisers for tax-qualified retirement investing plans under ERISA. The fundamental fiduciary duties of care and loyalty adhere to these roles just as they do in the contexts described above.[38] ERISA layers on additional fiduciary responsibilities, recognized by statute or case law. The trustee of an ERISA plan breaches its fiduciary duties to a plan participant when it commits serious procedural irregularities (e.g., making arbitrary decisions or singling out claims for additional required documentation) in evaluating a claim for benefits.[39] This can go both ways—not just for arbitrary rigor but arbitrary laxity. A plan administrator under ERISA has fiduciary duties that extend to everyone under the plan. Therefore, failing to adequately investigate a claim of an unqualified claimant potentially breaches its fiduciary duty to all bona fide plan beneficiaries.[40]

Banks also often serve as trustees for collective investment trusts (CITs) or collective investment funds (CIFs), trusts made for pooled investments from ERISA-qualified plans. The bank typically becomes an ERISA fiduciary for the CIT itself and owes fiduciary duties to the individual plan administrators (and their beneficiaries) to whom it provides investment management services. If the bank itself administers one of the ERISA plans under a CIT for which it also serves as trustee, the layers of fiduciary duties can become complex and elaborate.

V. OTHER FIDUCIARY ROLES

In addition to the contexts discussed above, banks will also have fiduciary duties—or be potentially liable with respect to other fiduciaries—in a variety of other situations. If a bank serves as an executor of an estate, it will—like any other executor—have duties of loyalty and care. So too if a bank is entrusted with funds to carry out bill-paying services: it cannot use them for its own benefit. A bank as executor of an estate must further avoid asset decay (e.g., waiting too long to sell a marketable asset).

38. *See, e.g.*, Barnhart v. Unum Life Ins. Co. of America, 179 F.3d 583 (8th Cir. 1999) (addressing conflicts of interest as fiduciary breach in the ERISA context).

39. *See* Morgan v. Contractors, Laborers, Teamsters & Engineers Pension Plan, 287 F.3d 716, 724 (8th Cir. 2002).

40. *See* Tillery v. Hoffman Enclosures, Inc., 280 F.3d 1192, 1197 (8th Cir. 2002).

Some transactional roles a bank commonly plays can also entail limited fiduciary duties or make the bank potentially liable for aiding and abetting a fiduciary breach. Banks may serve as transfer agents, a corporate assignee charged with maintaining investor financial and account balance records, and with handling and recording certificate transactions. Accordingly, a transfer agent helps a company with its own fiduciary responsibilities to its shareholders. A transfer agent, when registering transfers of stock, is to exercise the care of a fiduciary in protecting persons having legal or equitable interests in the stock.[41] The Second Circuit also recently described alleged actions of a transfer agent charging excessive and misleading fees (some of which involved kickbacks to an affiliate) as those of a "faithless fiduciary."[42] The transfer agent role should thus not be used for self-dealing or self-serving purposes.

Outside of fiduciary duties inhering in the transfer agent itself, it can aid or abet fiduciary breaches if it knowingly facilitates another party's breach. For a transfer agent to be liable for aiding and abetting a breach of fiduciary duty, (1) there must be a fiduciary relationship between the two parties, (2) the fiduciary breached that relationship, (3) the transfer agent knowingly and substantially participated in the breach, and (4) the plaintiff suffered damages as a result of the breach.

Banks also commonly serve as registrars, a keeper of records for bond- and shareholders after an issuance to the public, and an entity that assists in the preparation of dividend and bond interest payments. Similar to the transfer agent role, the registrar assists a company in carrying out its fiduciary duty to shareholders and bondholders. The role should not be abused or put toward self-dealing purposes. And a bank as registrar can be liable for aiding or abetting a breach of fiduciary duty if the same four elements noted above for transfer agents are present.[43]

---

41. *See* West v. American Tel. & Tel. Co., 108 F.2d 347 (6th Cir. 1939).

42. Operating Local 649 Annuity v. Smith Barney Fund, 595 F.3d 86 (2d Cir. 2010).

43. Directors and officers of publicly traded banks have additional fiduciary duties to shareholders like those of any other corporation—duties of care, loyalty, and good faith. Litigation involving alleged breaches of those duties is common (though sometimes preempted by the Securities Litigation Uniform Standards Act [SLUSA]). As these fiduciary duties are obligations of corporations generally, however, and not banks specifically, they are not explored further in this chapter.

VI. CONCLUSION

In today's sophisticated financial world, banks can come to wear many different hats. Some of these roles stay completely in the realm of arms-length commercial transactions. Others, however, entail fiduciary responsibilities by the bank because of a special relationship of trust or dependence. Having a firm grasp on when and how such duties arise will be critical in Lisa Lawyer's evaluation of Cindy Client's case and would similarly be helpful to the defendant bank to understand the full scope of its obligations.

Third-Party Discovery of Banks

9

Lori Goldman and Megan Iannacone†

Whether you are representing someone that is a customer of a bank, or you are handling a matter that somehow requires you to obtain information from a bank, it is helpful for you to understand the parameters within which banks operate and the requirements that impact how they will process and respond to third-party discovery requests.

In this chapter, we will explain why a bank cannot and should not respond to a discovery request unless legally obligated to do so, and why the bank, when responding, must do so in a narrowly tailored fashion. We will also discuss service of process requirements, the methods by which banks will accept service of process, and the different standards that may apply to various discovery requests. Finally,

† Megan Iannacone is senior vice president and general counsel of WSFS Financial Corporation and WSFS Bank, a diversified financial institution holding company and bank in Delaware and the greater Philadelphia region. Megan has been practicing law for fourteen years and serving banking institutions as in-house counsel for the greater part of a decade. Having started as associate counsel and later senior counsel at the Bryn Mawr Trust Company, she has amassed a wealth of experience on all things banking.

we will provide insight into the pitfalls that many lawyers face when wording their third-party discovery requests, and we will make suggestions for how to avoid these pitfalls.

I. RIGHT TO FINANCIAL PRIVACY

Banks are subject to a myriad of regulations and are examined for compliance with those regulations on a regular basis. One of the regulations that drives bank policy when it comes to providing customer information is the 1978 Right to Financial Privacy Act. This act provides specific procedures that federal governmental authorities must follow to obtain information about a customer's financial records, including that they notify the customer of the request (unless an exception applies) and provide the customer with the opportunity to object. For a bank to be authorized to provide a governmental authority with a customer's records, the bank must receive one of the following: (1) a judicial subpoena, (2) a search warrant, (3) an administrative subpoena or summons, (4) a signed and dated authorization from the customer, or (5) a formal written request by the governmental agency.

In certain circumstances, banks may release customer records without notifying the customer. Among others, these circumstances include situations where the information is:

Lori Goldman is the founder and managing member of Goldman Oak Law, PLLC, providing external general counsel services to businesses of all sizes and stages, and estate planning services to families and individuals. Prior to founding Goldman Oak Law, Lori was executive vice president and general counsel of Bryn Mawr Bank Corporation and the Bryn Mawr Trust Company, and later executive vice president–legal and head of vendor management of WSFS Financial Corporation and WSFS Bank. Her practice began nearly two decades ago in the corporate, M&A, and securities areas at Kaye Scholer, LLP (now Arnold Porter Kaye Scholer, LLP), followed by Stradley Ronon Stevens & Young, LLP.

In their spare time, Megan and Lori are both moms to young children and often can be found playing bus driver to their many soccer, football, baseball, and basketball games. They enjoy it most when their children's teams overlap and they get to attend games together.

This chapter should not be construed as giving legal advice. If you would like to receive legal advice, contact Lori Goldman. Lori can be reached at (610) 295-5002 or lgoldman@goldmanoak.com. The views expressed in this chapter are the views of Megan Iannacone and Lori Goldman alone, and are not necessarily the views of any company, firm, or other person.

- requested by the Government Accountability Office for an authorized proceeding, investigation, examination, or audit directed at a federal agency;
- subject to a subpoena issued in conjunction with proceedings before a grand jury (with the exception of cost reimbursement and the restricted use of grand jury information);
- requested by a government authority subject to a lawsuit involving the bank customer;
- not individually identifiable with respect to a particular customer;
- requested pursuant to the Internal Revenue Code, or required to be reported in accordance with any other applicable federal or state statute, such as the Bank Secrecy Act;
- required to be provided by the bank in order to perfect a security interest, file a proof of claim for bankruptcy, or collect a debt for itself or a fiduciary;
- required to be provided by the bank in response to a regulatory examination request or customer complaint; and/or
- required to be provided by the bank to notify law enforcement officials of information relevant to a violation of the law.

Generally, within the communication that a governmental agency sends to the bank, the governmental agency will indicate their compliance with the various requirements under the Right to Financial Privacy Act. Each bank will have its own policies and practices when it comes to releasing customer records, and we will provide tips later in this chapter for contacting a bank to understand its requirements.

II. OTHER PRIVACY LAWS

In addition to the Right to Financial Privacy Act, banks are required to comply with a variety of other laws and regulations governing the privacy of customer information. These may include, without limitation, the Gramm–Leach–Bliley Act (GLBA), the California Consumer Privacy Act, the California Privacy Rights Act, and the General Data Protection Regulation. While not all of these regulations may apply in each circumstance (though some, like GLBA, do), bank policy is often informed by its terms in order to ensure compliance in all situations. This may mean that bank policy is more stringent or rigid than one would typically expect. That being the case, when seeking information from banks in third-party discovery situations, patience and communication are key. If you have an urgent need, be sure to communicate that with the team that handles third-party discovery requests at the bank.

III. NOTICE TO BANK CUSTOMER

The rules of civil procedure in many jurisdictions require that the counterparty to litigation be notified prior to service of a third-party subpoena. Where third-party discovery is served on a bank seeking customer or account information, the bank will review the docket for the matter to understand whether appropriate notice has been given. Banks will not typically respond to subpoenas where this step has not been taken. Attorneys should comply with the notice requirements applicable to their litigation to ensure timely processing of their third-party discovery requests.

IV. PERFECTING SERVICE OF PROCESS

Due to all the regulations imposed upon banks, banks will generally comply with third-party discovery requests only when service of process has been perfected. How one perfects service of process generally depends on state law and the rules of civil procedure, and may be impacted by the method of service, the type of document being served, the type of discovery request, and any domestication requirements.

V. METHODS AND STANDARDS OF SERVICE

The methods of service of process that banks will accept vary based on several factors, including, but not limited to, statute and jurisdiction. The most common methods of service include personal service on a branch or other bank location, certified mail, and nationally recognized courier services. Attorneys serving third-party discovery on banks should check the applicable rules of civil procedure to ensure proper service methods are used.

Additionally, some banks will accept service of process via email or facsimile, but this is bank-specific, and the bank may require additional processes. To determine whether a bank will accept service via email, you should contact the bank's legal documents processing team.

VI. HOW TO ASK A BANK TO ACCEPT SERVICE OF PROCESS

Every bank is different and there are a variety of departments or sub-departments that could handle legal documents processing. That being the case, if you do not already know the best address/department or where to serve process, it is best to contact the bank's customer service department. Banks' customer service representatives are generally trained on where to direct service of process questions (e.g., to the legal department or other legal documents processing units) and often will be able to direct you as to where legal documents can be served.

If the bank's customer service representatives are unable to answer your questions about service of process (e.g., whether they will accept service via email), you should ask to speak with someone from the legal department or legal documents processing team. Some questions go beyond the customer service department's responsibilities, but the representative should be able to direct you and possibly connect you with the right people.

Where possible, avoid serving process at a teller window or branch of a bank unless it is the registered office location on file with the Secretary of State. While serving on a branch or teller window is permitted and may seem more accessible, branch staff are often not well trained on how to send or input the served paperwork to the legal department or legal documents processing unit. It is not uncommon for documents served on a branch to be routed and rerouted to the wrong places within the bank. They either never show up on the legal documents processing docket or show up weeks or even months after they were served. While this should not be the case, and certainly does not excuse any noncompliance with required time frames and deliverables, it is a practical reality. Therefore, it is best to either serve process at the registered office location or contact the bank's customer service department for more information.

VII. AVOIDING POTENTIAL ISSUES WHEN SERVING SUBPOENAS

Often, when a subpoena gets rejected, waylaid in a bank's processing department, or is not otherwise responsive to what you intended, it may be for one of the following reasons:

- **Too Broad/Vague.** It can be problematic when a subpoena is drafted in the "kitchen sink" style and lacks specificity or clarity. At best, this is a burdensome task that may require a significant extension to the response time for the bank to gather the large volume of responsive documents. At worst, the request may be so vague that the bank is unable to determine what, if any, documents may be responsive, in which case the bank will either reject the subpoena or reach out to gain more clarity on the request. When looking for specific information, it is better and more efficient to draft the subpoena in a precise manner.

- **Lack of Understanding of Target Structure.** In some instances, the client/customer account at a bank may be structured with complexity, including multiple accounts, subaccounts, related/affiliated accounts, etc. In this instance, the subpoena may be either too broad or too narrow to obtain the desired information. To the extent that you are aware of affiliates or other reasons that an account structure/client relationship may be complicated, you should take that knowledge into account when drafting your subpoena. Bear in mind that banks are not freely allowed to provide customer/client information, and likely will not be able to advise on the complexity of the account structures that could be applicable to your request.
- **Typos or Errors.** Typos or errors often cause subpoena problems. For example, if you provide the routing number instead of the account number in the subpoena, it will not yield the desired information. Additionally, if you are seeking information on an individual who may have the same name as another customer, then you should add additional identifying information (e.g., address, date of birth, or Jr./Sr. suffix, etc.) to avoid a delay when the bank is processing the subpoena.
- **Wrong Entity Listed.** Many banks have affiliates and subsidiaries within their structures that service clients/customers. If your subpoena is addressed solely to the bank, but the client account is located within a subsidiary, the subpoena response will likely not provide you with the desired information. In most cases, the bank will contact you and request that you send a revised subpoena, but that may delay the response. To the extent that you know the entity that holds the requested information, you should be sure to address the subpoena accordingly.

VIII. INTERSTATE DISCOVERY

The Uniform Interstate Deposits and Discovery Act (UIDDA), which has been adopted in some form by most states, governs the process for seeking out-of-state discovery in a state court proceeding. As counsel, it is important that you check the requirements of both the state and local courts where your case is venued, as well as those of the state and locale where you seek to conduct discovery, because some states have adopted slight variations of the Model UIDDA. If the states applicable to your case have adopted the UIDDA, the process for interstate discovery should be streamlined. If the UIDDA is not applicable to your case, then any state subpoena you are looking to serve over state lines will need to be domesticated in that state's courts.

In either event, depending on the resources and level of sophistication of the bank and its legal documents processing system, the documents processing team at the bank may need additional time to review a request from a jurisdiction that is not familiar to them. You should allow ample time and keep the lines of communication open with the bank's team.

IX. EXPECTATIONS REGARDING INFORMATION

A. What Types of Information Can You Expect a Bank to Have?

This depends on the relationship the bank has with the "target," and the variety (or lack thereof) of products and services that are offered by the bank. Many banks provide a variety of financial services in addition to deposit accounts and loans, such as services related to trusts, custodianship, investments, insurance, etc. If the relationship is solely depositary in nature, information will be largely limited to account/transactional data and the basic information gathered at account opening. If there is a loan relationship, or a loan has been applied for, the bank will likely have more fulsome information, such as financial/income data, credit information, business information if it is a business, etc., as well as the loan documents and transactional information. If the relationship relates to wealth management or trust services, there could be a host of information, such as financial position, investments, beneficiary designations, etc.[1]

If you are seeking information regarding an account or loan that was originally made with a predecessor bank (e.g., a bank that was acquired by or merged into the current bank), you should understand that while the bank should have a document retention policy, at times, data, documents, and information can be lost or land in not-easily-accessible archives due to conversion of systems and/or bank acquisition.

B. What About Joint Accounts?

If you issue a subpoena for one individual but the accounts (and loans, etc.) are held jointly with a second individual (whether they are married or not), what does the bank do? Typically, the bank will focus its response on information solely pertaining to the individual who is the target of the subpoena. If the target has a joint account with another individual who is not named in the subpoena, due to privacy and ownership laws, the bank may not provide information—or may limit the information provided—regarding the joint account. For example, if you issue a subpoena for a husband but there are accounts (and loans, etc.) that are held jointly with his wife, while the bank may note their existence, it might exclude other information related to those accounts when producing responsive documents.

X. CONCLUSION

Every bank is different, but every bank will have a dedicated person or team that is responsible for responding to third-party discovery requests. If you need help or anticipate any issues, you should not hesitate to reach out to any contact you have at the bank, or through the customer service line. They should be able to direct you to the appropriate department or individual.

---

1. *See also* the sections on "Lack of Understanding of Target Structure" and "Wrong Entity Listed" in this chapter.

Class Actions

10

Mitchell R. Edwards and Katherine B. Savage†

Lisa Lawyer is sitting in her Boston office when she gets a call from her client, Bob Boston. Bob is having a very bad day. That morning, he purchased a $7 pumpkin spice latte from his favorite coffee shop, something he treats himself to only once a week. After he ran his card for the latte purchase, he noticed the freshly baked muffins and decided to buy one of those too, running his card again for the additional $3 charge. Bob sat down to enjoy his drink and grabbed his phone to take a picture of the particularly spectacular latte art so he could send it to his friend, when he noticed that his bank had charged him two separate $30 overdraft fees for insufficient funds. Bob doesn't understand how this can be, when his account shows an actual

† Mitchell R. Edwards is a partner at Hinckley Allen & Snyder LLP and is chair of the firm's Complex Commercial Litigation Group. His practice includes complex commercial cases and product liability matters, with experience representing clients in class action lawsuits. Katherine B. Savage is an associate at Hinckley Allen & Snyder LLP. Her practice focuses on general commercial litigation and energy and environmental law, and includes experience representing clients in class action lawsuits.

balance of $25.97 before the coffee shop charges, which should have left him with a balance of $15.97.[1]

Bob thinks it is unfair that the bank would charge him two overdraft fees when his account had enough money to cover the charges. Bob comes from a litigious family, and his immediate reaction is to ask Lisa whether he can sue the bank. Lisa thinks for a minute and then asks Bob to come to her office and bring with him a copy of the customer agreement he signed when he opened his checking account. When she hangs up the phone, Lisa takes out her notepad and starts brainstorming.

Lisa knows that Bob has suffered a concrete harm—$60 of allegedly improper fees—so she is confident that he will have standing to bring a claim. She also remembers that the Electronic Funds Transfer Act (EFTA) did away with the practice of automatic enrollment of customers in overdraft coverage, and now requires banks to get affirmative consent from customers for overdraft services.[2] Therefore, Bob's bank should have some contract language addressing his enrollment (or lack thereof) in its overdraft program. She thinks Bob could have a federal statutory claim under the EFTA as well as a state law contract claim, depending on how the facts shake out. As with all contract-based claims, however, Lisa knows that Bob's success will depend heavily on the specific language of the agreement, so she makes a note to go through the contract and all its addendums with a fine-toothed comb. Lisa also recalls that chapter 93A of the Massachusetts General Laws prohibits unfair or deceptive business practices. She writes herself a note to look up the elements of this and any other state law statutory claims and reminds herself to confirm that Bob's bank operates in the Commonwealth.[3]

As Lisa is taking notes, she realizes that this is going to be a very expensive suit to litigate—tens of thousands of dollars at least—to recover $60 in fees. With a quick internet search, Lisa learns that the bank has

---

1. Bank customers have filed numerous class actions stemming from this same conduct: a bank charging an allegedly unlawful overdraft fee when the actual balance of the customer's account showed enough money to cover the transaction. *See, e.g.*, Bettencourt v. Jeanne D'Arc Credit Union, 370 F. Supp. 3d 258 (D. Mass. 2019); Salls v. Digital Fed. Credit Union, 349 F. Supp. 3d 81 (D. Mass. 2018); Walbridge v. Ne. Credit Union, 299 F. Supp. 3d 338 (D.N.H. 2018); Pinkston-Poling v. Advia Credit Union, 227 F. Supp. 3d 848 (W.D. Mich. 2016).

2. *See* Tims v. LGE Cmty. Credit Union, 935 F.3d 1228, 1234 (11th Cir. 2019).

3. *See* Mass. Gen. L. ch. 93A § 2(a) (forbidding "unfair or deceptive acts or practices in the conduct of any trade or commerce").

more than 100,000 customers. If all those customers have been wrongly charged fees as Bob has, then the economies of scale might make a lawsuit worthwhile. And if the possible damages suffered by all those customers is $6 million (i.e., $60 in overdraft fees for each), then the case would exceed the $5 million minimum threshold set forth in the Class Action Fairness Act (CAFA), and Lisa could potentially file the suit in federal court.[4]

When Bob arrives at Lisa's office, she tells him that he might have a claim but that it may be expensive. Lisa quickly adds that this case might be a good candidate for a class action lawsuit.

Class action lawsuits are a form of representative litigation where one or more people (the class representatives) litigate on behalf of many other people (the class members) who have all suffered the same type of harm. When the lawsuit ends, all the class members are bound by the outcome of the case.

Technically speaking, a class action is a procedural mechanism by which a large group of similarly situated plaintiffs (or, less commonly, defendants) try to prosecute (or defend) a lawsuit based on common claims that they share as a class, instead of bringing many individual cases. Under certain circumstances, the class action device can simplify litigation involving large numbers of individuals with similar claims, and it encourages a uniform decision for the claims.

When it comes to banks and financial services companies, consumers or shareholders bring most class actions. The alleged amount of damage is often small, but the number of class members can be large. For plaintiffs, a class action lawsuit can be a very favorable mechanism to litigate claims. For the banks and other financial services institutions, however, defending a class action lawsuit can be frustrating because, regardless of how meritorious or frivolous the plaintiffs' claims are, defending a class action lawsuit is usually a very expensive proposition. As a result, many companies try to settle the case early—even if they believe they have done nothing wrong.[5]

---

4. *See* 28 U.S.C. § 1332(d)(2).

5. *See* Messner v. Northshore Univ. HealthSystem, 669 F.3d 802, 825 (7th Cir. 2012) ("Even if a class's claim is weak, the sheer number of class members and the potential payout that could be required if all members prove liability might force a defendant to settle a meritless claim in order to avoid breaking the company.").

I. INITIATING A CLASS ACTION LAWSUIT

A. Class Action Requirements

Initiating a class action begins like any other lawsuit, with the filing of a complaint. The class action complaint must plead that the putative class satisfies the following conditions: (1) numerosity, (2) commonality, (3) typicality, and (4) adequacy of representation.[6]

Lisa tells Bob that they first need to demonstrate numerosity—i.e., that there are too many individual plaintiffs to name them all in the case. Numerosity is satisfied when the class is "so numerous that joinder of all members is impracticable[.]"[7] For purposes of the rule, impracticable does not mean impossible, but rather "that it is extremely difficult or inconvenient to join all the members of the class."[8] Unfortunately, when Bob asks Lisa just how many potential class members are required to meet the numerosity requirement, she cannot give him a number certain. This is because the text of Rule 23(a) fails to affirmatively establish a threshold number to satisfy numerosity, but Lisa knows that courts generally will find that a class of forty or more individuals establishes numerosity[9] and that, absent extraordinary circumstances, a class of fewer than twenty members does not.[10] Lisa determines that the bank has around 100,000 customers, so numerosity is easily met.

Lisa next tells Bob that the factual or legal questions in the complaint must be common to the class.[11] She explains that a question is common

---

6. *See* Fed. R. Civ. P. 23(a). ("One or more members of a class may sue or be sued as representative parties on behalf of all members only if: (1) the class is so numerous that joinder of all members is impracticable; (2) there are questions of law or fact common to the class; (3) the claims or defenses of the representative parties are typical of the claims or defenses of the class; and (4) the representative parties will fairly and adequately protect the interests of the class.").

7. *See* Fed. R. Civ. P. 23(a)(1).

8. Anderson v. Weinert Enter., Inc., 986 F.3d 773, 777 (7th Cir. 2021) (quoting 7A Charles Alan Wright & Arthur R. Miller, Federal Practice & Procedure § 1762 (3d ed. 2008)).

9. *See, e.g.*, Mielo v. Steak 'n Shake Operations, Inc., 897 F.3d 467, 486 (3d Cir. 2018) (recognizing that a plaintiff can generally satisfy numerosity by establishing that the number of potential plaintiffs exceeds forty).

10 *See* Cox v. American Cast Iron Pipe Co., 784 F.2d 1546, 1553 (11th Cir. 1986) (recognizing that although the numerosity requirement is not fixed at a certain number, "generally less than twenty-one is inadequate").

11. *See* Fed. R. Civ. P. 23(a)(2).

if the putative class members "have suffered the same injury and have claims that depend on a common contention capable of class-wide resolution."[12] If all the class members had the same contracts with the bank and were all charged the same types of allegedly improper fees, then the court may find that the bank's overdraft program violated federal and/or state laws, which might resolve all the claims.[13] Lisa makes a note to check whether the bank has recently or repeatedly revised its customer contracts, because the claims she would be advancing in the lawsuit are inextricably tied to each customer's individual contract. Bob asks whether it matters that he was charged two overdraft fees, totaling $60, while other customers may have been charged only a single overdraft fee of $30. Lisa explains that commonality pertains to the merits of the dispute, not the damages awarded,[14] so the commonality requirement can be met even if different plaintiffs may require different damages calculations.

Next, they must demonstrate that "each class member's claim arises from the same course of events and each class member makes similar legal arguments to prove the defendant's liability."[15] Bob thinks that the commonality and typicality requirements seem very similar.[16] Lisa knows that Bob is an avid football fan (a few years ago, he tried to retain her to trademark his fantasy football team name, Boston TD Party), so she asks Bob to imagine a proposed class of retired professional football players who are suing the National Football League (NFL) for the league's alleged failure to inform and protect the players from the risks of concussion in football.[17] She explains the retired players would satisfy the commonality requirement

12. Willis v. City of Seattle, 943 F.3d 882, 885 (9th Cir. 2019).

13. *See* Wal-Mart Stores, Inc. v. Dukes, 564 U.S. 338, 350 (noting that a common contention is capable of class-wide resolution when the "determination of its truth or falsity will resolve an issue that is central to the validity of each one of the claims in one stroke").

14. *See* In re Whirlpool Corp. Front-Loading Washer Prod. Liab. Litig., 722 F.3d 838, 854 (6th Cir. 2013) (quoting Sterling v. Velsicol Chem. Corp., 855 F.2d 1188, 1197 (6th Cir. 1988) ("'No matter how individualized the issue of damages may be,' determination of damages 'may be reserved for individual treatment with the question of liability tried as a class action[.]'").

15. Robidoux v. Celani, 987 F.2d 931, 936 (2d Cir. 1993).

16. *See* Hassine v. Jeffes, 846 F.2d 169, 176 n.4 (3d Cir. 1988) (recognizing that typicality and commonality are separate and distinct requirements under Rule 23(a) but are often discussed together due to the overlapping analyses).

17. *See* In re Nat'l Football League Players Concussion Injury Litig., 821 F.3d 410, 421, 426, 428 (3d Cir. 2016) (NFL Concussion Litigation).

of Rule 23(a) because the negligence and fraud claims advanced by each player all depended on the same questions regarding the NFL's conduct, including when the league knew there were risks of concussion and what it did to protect the players from that risk.[18] In contrast, the typicality requirement would go further and focus on whether the interests of the class members are so closely aligned that pursuit of each member's individual interest will also promote the interests of the class.[19] In the case of the retired professional football players, it would not matter whether each claimant played in the league for different amounts of time and suffered different injuries, because the class as a whole sought recovery under the same legal theory: that the NFL fraudulently concealed the risk of head injuries.[20]

Finally, Lisa explains that she must show she is competent to be class counsel and that Bob, as the putative class representative, is "'willing' and 'able' to 'take an active role in and control the litigation and to protect the interests of absentees.'"[21] Lisa explains that Bob could serve as the class representative if his situation is very similar to that of other customers of the bank. Although Bob's involvement would be very public and he would be named as a plaintiff on all the court filings, Lisa explains to him that named plaintiffs usually get a "service fee" award—an extra $2,500 or $5,000 in addition to their prorated payout—for taking a leading role in the case.[22]

B. State or Federal Court?

Once Bob has left Lisa's office, she begins to think about where she should file the class action. Many class action lawsuits can be brought in federal

---

18. *See NFL Concussion Litigation*, 821 F.3d at 427.

19. *See* In re American Med. Sys., Inc., 75 F.3d 1069, 1082 (6th Cir. 1996).

20. *See NFL Concussion Litigation*, 821 F.3d at 427.

21. *See* Berger v. Compaq Comput. Corp., 257 F.3d 475, 479 (5th Cir. 2001) (quoting Horton v. Goose Creek Indep. Sch. Dist., 690 F.2d 470, 484 (5th Cir. 1982)).

22. *See* Rodriguez v. West Publ'g Corp., 563 F.3d 948, 958–59 (9th Cir. 2009) (noting that representative service awards "are fairly typical in class action cases" and "are intended to compensate class representatives for work done on behalf of the class, to make up for financial or reputational risk undertaken in bringing the action, and, sometimes, to recognize their willingness to act as a private attorney general").

court.[23] CAFA also makes it easier for defendants to remove a class action to federal court, provided there are at least 100 putative class members.[24]

Lisa ultimately proceeds with filing a class action complaint in the United States District Court, alleging violation of the EFTA, breach of contract, breach of the implied covenant of good faith and fair dealing, unjust enrichment, conversion, and violation of Massachusetts state consumer protection laws.[25] The crux of the complaint is that the bank represented to its customers that it would impose an overdraft fee only when the member's *actual* account balance is insufficient to pay for the charge, but that the bank really uses the customer's *available* balance.[26] The actual balance is "the standing balance of the member's account less any payments that have actually been processed[,]" while the available balance is an internal figure calculated by the bank that subtracts anticipated future debts from the actual balance.[27] Therefore, the available balance can, at times, be lower than the actual balance and result in overdraft fees even if the customer's account shows sufficient funds to cover the transaction.[28]

II. ANSWERING OR RESPONDING TO A CLASS ACTION COMPLAINT

A. Litigation Hold

Bill Banker is just about to pack up his briefcase and depart for the evening when he receives the class action complaint filed by Lisa. Bill does what any defendant bank or financial institution should do upon receiving a class

23. CAFA significantly expands the jurisdiction of the federal courts by decreasing the amount-in-controversy requirement to more than $5 million, when aggregating all claims of all the plaintiffs, and by allowing the court to exercise diversity jurisdiction when there is only "minimal diversity"—that is, where any class member resides in a different state from any defendant. *See* 28 U.S.C. § 1332(d)(2)(A).

24. *See* Tanoh v. Dow Chem. Co., 561 F.3d 945, 952 (9th Cir. 2009).

25. The claims advanced by a particular class action lawsuit will vary depending on the specific facts of the case and the jurisdiction in which it is brought. Moreover, it bears mentioning that there are several exceptions to CAFA, and a federal court has discretion to decline to exercise diversity jurisdiction. However, for purposes of this chapter, we assume that the federal court would have jurisdiction over the lawsuit.

26. *See Salls*, 349 F. Supp. 3d 81, 85 (D. Mass. 2018).

27. *See Bettencourt*, 370 F. Supp. 3d 258, 261 (D. Mass. 2019).

28. *See id.*

action complaint: he immediately contacts the bank's attorney, Laura Lawyer, to issue a litigation hold to the relevant bank employees.[29] Laura will send a letter or other communication to the bank, explaining the duty of all personnel to suspend the bank's typical document retention/destruction policy and preserve all unique, relevant evidence that might be useful to the class action plaintiffs. With the revolution of technology, the preservation of electronically stored information is critical.[30] At a recent conference, Bill learned that "[o]ne of the primary reasons that electronic data is lost is ineffective communication with information technology personnel."[31] Since then, Bill has taken the time to fully understand the bank's document retention policies, including system-wide backup procedures and the bank's recycling policy.[32] He has also made a company-wide effort to educate all employees about how electronically stored information should be managed.[33]

The failure to preserve evidence—known as spoliation of evidence—can lead to severe sanctions. If the court finds that the destroying party had control over documents related to the litigation, was obligated to preserve those documents at the time they were destroyed, and proceeded to destroy the documents with a culpable state of mind, then the court may issue an adverse inference instruction allowing the jury to assume that the destroyed evidence would have been unfavorable to the destroying party.[34] Thus, it is imperative that a lawyer representing a bank or other financial institution advise their client promptly of its obligation to preserve evidence.

Of course, the scope and timing of a specific litigation hold will depend on the facts and circumstances of each case, including the nature of the claims alleged and the identity of the parties. Accordingly, counsel for the defendant bank/financial institution must think carefully about the universe of potentially relevant documents and scrutinize the complaint before instructing their client about what it is obligated to preserve.

---

29. *See* Borum v. Brentwood Vill., LLC, 332 F.R.D. 38, 45 (D.D.C. 2019) (discussing that when a party reasonably anticipates litigation, it must put in place a "litigation hold" to preserve relevant documents).

30. *See* Zubulake v. UBS Warburg LLC, 229 F.R.D. 422, 432 (S.D.N.Y. 2004).

31. *See id.* at 434.

32. *See id.* at 432.

33. *See id.* (some people may create separate computer files containing discoverable information, while others may print relevant emails and retain in hard copy only).

34. *See* Chin v. Port Auth. of New York & New Jersey, 685 F.3d 135, 162 (2d Cir. 2012).

B. Answers, Motions to Dismiss, and Early Settlement Discussions

After notifying the bank about the need to preserve evidence, Laura contacts Bill Banker to discuss how to respond to the class action complaint. Bill Banker is presented with three options: (1) file an answer, (2) file a motion to dismiss, or (3) reach out to Lisa to discuss an early settlement. The bank's choice among these three options is based on the same factors that guide any party facing litigation, including the strength of the plaintiffs' claims and the bank's aversion to risk.

Filing an answer in a class action is no different from any other case—the defendant must be sure to admit or deny each allegation in the complaint, lest the court infer an admission.[35] The defendant must be sure to also set forth all its affirmative defenses and counterclaims, or it will lose the right to argue those issues in the future.[36]

If the bank believes that it can prove that no law supports the plaintiffs' claims, it may file a motion to dismiss in lieu of an answer.[37]

Finally, the bank may choose to settle the class action. The mechanics of a class action settlement are further discussed *infra*, but at this early stage of the litigation, the bank, in consultation with its attorneys and advisers, must make a business decision about whether settlement makes sense. Considerations should include, among other things, the likelihood of class certification, the potential size of a judgment (on a per-plaintiff and a class-wide basis), and the costs of litigating the case.

C. Damages[38]

Bill is a numbers man, so he calls Laura the following week to get a rundown about the estimated potential liability the bank is facing. The EFTA entitles a class action claimant to recover any actual damages sustained

---

35. *See* Fed. R. Civ. P. 8(b).

36. *See id.* 12(b).

37. *See id.* 12(b)(6).

38. Although we use the EFTA for a framework by which to discuss the potential universe of damages a bank or financial institution may face when sued in a class action, the available damages and the burden to prove those damages will vary from claim to claim. For example, under the Fair Credit Reporting Act, recovery for a negligent violation of the act is limited to actual damages, attorneys' fees, and costs. *See* 15 U.S.C. § 1681o. However, if the breach is willful, the plaintiff is entitled to recover actual damages of not less than $100

by the consumer but, in the case of a class action, limits the total recovery of the class to not more than the lesser of $500,000 or 1 percent of the defendant's net worth.[39] Bill knows that the bank's net worth is less than $50 million, and therefore, the class recovery under the EFTA would be capped at $500,000.

Much to Bill's discomfort, Laura does not stop at actual damages. She tells Bill that the EFTA might entitle the plaintiffs to punitive damages.[40] That means a consumer might obtain treble damages if the court finds that the defendant bank/financial institution "(1) fails to comply with certain investigation requirements before declining to provisionally credit the consumer with the disputed funds, or (2) otherwise acts unreasonably in determining whether account charges were in error."[41] While Bill is always wary of the possibility of punitive damages, he holds out hope that the plaintiffs did not report the unauthorized overdraft fees soon enough to trigger the EFTA's investigation and provisional credit requirements, and/or that the bank performed a thorough and reasonable investigation of the disputed charges.[42]

The last class of damages the bank's attorney discusses is costs. The EFTA specifically allows successful plaintiffs to recover costs and reasonable attorneys' fees.[43] Costs may include, without limitation, court costs, expert witness costs, transcript fees, printing fees, and filing fees.[44] Attorneys' fees include the time that the plaintiffs' attorneys spent working on the case. These fees must be reasonable both in amount of time worked and the hourly rates charged. An award of attorneys' fees can be part of the settlement negotiations, so that whatever fees the plaintiffs' attorneys

---

and not more than $1,000, in addition to attorneys' fees and costs. *See* 15 U.S.C. § 1681n. A willful violation may also incur punitive damages. *See id.*

39. *See* 15 U.S.C. § 1693m(a)(2)(B).

40. *See id.* § 1693f(e).

41. Rusthoven v. TCF Nat'l Bank, No. CIV 07-3154 JRTJJK, 2009 WL 2171105, at *4 (D. Minn. July 20, 2009).

42. *See Rusthoven*, 2009 WL 2171105, at *4.

43. *See* 15 U.S.C. § 1693m(a)(3).

44. *See* Moore v. Southtrust Corp., 392 F. Supp. 2d 724 (E.D. Va. 2005) (holding that bank was entitled to recover both taxable and reimbursable costs in the amount of $6,680.55 as the defendant in bank account holder's action under the Electronic Funds Transfer Act (EFTA), which was brought in bad faith, where costs included photocopy fees, process server fees, long-distance telephone charges, legal research charges, airfare and lodging to attend depositions, transcription fees, and private investigator fees to locate account holder's wife, and costs were reasonably incurred in defending account holder's claim).

receive are deducted from the defendant bank's payout to putative class members.[45]

And, of course, Laura reminds Bill that he cannot forget about the state law claims, including the alleged violation of the state consumer protection act. Although Bill's last encounter with federalism was in a high school history class, it seems odd to him that the plaintiffs can potentially recover under the EFTA *and* a state law that covers the same conduct. Laura informs him that Congress specifically provided in the EFTA that if a state consumer protection law provides the consumer greater protections, then the state law is not preempted by the EFTA.[46]

D. Motion to Dismiss/Shareholder Litigation

As expected, Lisa receives a motion to dismiss all putative class action claims. The motion to dismiss attacks two things: the class requirements and the substantive law. First, the motion argues that the class action does not meet the requirements of Rule 23(a) because the class is not so numerous that joinder of all members is impracticable, and there are no questions of law or fact common to the class Bob seeks to represent. Second, the motion argues that the substantive claims of the class fail because the bank is insulated from liability by the safe harbor provision,[47] and the bank did not breach the terms of the account agreement or the opt-in agreement.

Although Lisa is eager to start drafting her opposition to the motion to dismiss, she has lunch plans with a colleague, Lana. Over lunch, Lisa reveals that she is working on an action against the bank. She is surprised

45. *See* Cox v. Clarus Mktg. Grp., LLC, 291 F.R.D. 473, 482 (S.D. Cal. 2013).

46. *See* 15 U.S.C. § 1693q. Unlike the EFTA, the Truth-in-Lending Act, 15 U.S.C. §§ 1601 *et seq.*, contains an express preemption provision whereby the state laws that are inconsistent with the provisions of TILA are preempted by the act. 15 U.S.C. § 1610(a)(1). The plaintiff in any class action must be certain to bring all available state and federal law claims, lest they risk being precluded from doing so in a separate action. *See* Houston Pro. Towing Ass'n v. City of Houston, 812 F.3d 443, 447 (5th Cir. 2016) (discussing the principle of res judicata, which prohibits a party, in certain situations, from litigating a claim that should have been raised in an earlier suit).

47. Some of the federal statutes banks and financial institutions may be sued under contain safe harbor provisions. For example, under the EFTA, a defendant is shielded from liability if it acted in good faith to comply with the opt-in provisions of the act, and under the Truth in Lending Act, a creditor may suspend an account or lower the credit limit when the value of the home securing any unpaid balance drops significantly below its original appraisal value.

to learn that Lana is defending a different local bank in a shareholder class action alleging that the bank and its directors and officers made misrepresentations and omissions about core elements of the bank's business, thereby artificially inflating the bank's stock price. The bank was allegedly opening new accounts and issuing debt or credit cards without customer knowledge. Lana describes that there are two other pending actions relating to the same operative set of facts: a shareholder derivative action filed on behalf of the bank alleging that the bank's officers and directors decided to pursue a course of conduct that was unlawful and/or remained consciously inactive despite actual knowledge of the wrongdoing at the bank,[48] and a consumer class action in which the bank's customers allege that the bank opened accounts in the customers' names without their knowledge or consent. Lana is close to reaching a settlement agreement with the shareholders, but she plans to make it clear that the bank denies the claims and allegations in the class action, admits no wrongdoing, and is entering into the settlement agreement to avoid further litigation costs and other business disruptions.

III. LITIGATION

Bill Banker is disappointed to learn that the court denied the bank's motion to dismiss and instead certified the class to allow it to proceed as a class action. Although the parties agreed to stay discovery on the merits during the class certification proceedings, the court has now lifted the stay. Lisa, as the appointed class counsel, has given "the best notice that is practicable under the circumstances" to the class members, "including individual notice to all members who can be identified through reasonable effort."[49] The bank, in consultation with its attorneys and advisers, decides not to appeal the court's order granting class certification because the appellate

48. It is important to distinguish a shareholder class action from a shareholder derivative action. In a derivative action, the shareholder sues on behalf of the bank and, therefore, represents the interests of the corporation. A derivative action is governed by Rule 23.1 and, although the two types of suits may appear to proceed with procedural similarities, they are distinct actions. When considering whether a suit is properly classified as a class action or a derivative suit, one should consider "[w]ho suffered the alleged harm—the corporation or the suing stockholder individually—and who would receive the benefit of the recovery or other remedy?" Tooley v. Donaldson, Lufkin & Jenrette, Inc., 845 A.2d 1031, 1035 (Del. 2004).

49. Fed R. Civ. P. 23(c)(2)(B).

court would have absolute discretion in whether to permit the appeal, and in any event, the appeal would not automatically stay the district court proceedings.[50]

The bank has received some adverse discovery rulings and decides to double down on settlement efforts.[51] Bill knows that taking a class action to trial is uncommon, and he is hopeful that the bank can resolve the class action on the most favorable terms possible.[52] The bank's attorney informs Bill that if there is a trial, it will likely be bifurcated, meaning that the trial will be split into a liability phase and a damages phase.[53] That way, the common question of the bank's liability can be determined first, and, if the bank is found liable, then each class member's individualized damages will be later determined.

IV. ALTERNATIVE DISPUTE RESOLUTION AND SETTLEMENT

A. Arbitration

In some circumstances, banks can avoid litigation if the customer's contract requires the parties to arbitrate the dispute. For example, let us imagine that Bob's contract with the bank contained the following clause:

> **Arbitration of Disputes/Waiver of Jury Trial and Participation in Class Actions.** If you have a dispute with the bank, you and the

---

50. *See id.* 23(f).

51. While the bank is certainly entitled to discovery to help develop the facts of the case and mount a defense to the class claims, if those facts reside with absent class members, the bank may not be able to propound discovery upon those members. Courts have generally developed a balancing test under which the defendant must (1) demonstrate that the discovery request is appropriate and does not seek information already known by the proponent, (2) establish that the discovery request is not designed to take undue advantage of class members or reduce the size of the class, and (3) prove that responding to the discovery requests would not require the assistance of counsel. *See* Clark v. Universal Builders, Inc., 501 F.2d 324, 340–42 (7th Cir. 1974).

52. Because bringing a class action to trial is rare, we do not devote an entire section of this chapter to discussing trial.

53. *See* Crutchfield v. Sewerage & Water Bd. of New Orleans, 829 F.3d 370, 378 (5th Cir. 2016) (recognizing that "damages are often an individualized determination," and so in class action cases, courts often "provide for bifurcated damages trials after a classwide trial on other issues").

> bank agree that it shall be resolved by arbitration. The arbitration will be brought individually and not as part of a class action. **YOU UNDERSTAND AND KNOWINGLY AND VOLUNTARILY AGREE THAT YOU AND WE ARE WAIVING THE RIGHT TO A TRIAL BY JURY AND THE RIGHT TO PARTICIPATE OR BE REPRESENTED IN ANY CLASS ACTION LAWSUIT.**

In this circumstance, the bank would likely move to dismiss Bob's class action and compel arbitration, and Bob would assert that the arbitration clause is invalid based on contract defenses such as unconscionability or illusory agreements.

A contract is illusory when it gives one party the power to change or terminate the contract at its own option. As long as the customer agreement requires the bank to give the customer notice prior to making any changes to the agreement, a reviewing court will likely find that the agreement is not illusory.[54] As to unconscionability, a reviewing court will assess two elements: (1) how the contract was negotiated and whether the customer lacked a meaningful choice as to the terms of the agreement in light of the facts and circumstances, and (2) whether those terms are overly harsh or one-sided.[55] Because contract defenses are creatures of state law, whether they apply will turn on the law of the particular state and on the other provisions contained within the particular contract.

B. Mediation-Assisted Settlement

Lisa and Laura decide to try mediating the class action. The bank is walking a fine line as it manages this class action. It does not want to pay for meritless claims, but it wants to maintain a relationship with its customers. In light of this, the bank thinks that mediation could be a helpful tool because mediation is a nonbinding dispute resolution process that allows the parties to engage with "a neutral third party who tries to help the disputing parties reach a mutually agreeable solution."[56] Having a successful mediation depends on many things, including proper selection of a mediator, adequate preparation, and a good-faith attitude.

---

54. *See* Larsen v. Citibank FSB, 871 F.3d 1295, 1321 (11th Cir. 2017).

55. *See* Ragone v. Atlantic Video at Manhattan Ctr., 595 F.3d 115, 121 (2d Cir. 2010) (applying New York law).

56. *Mediation*, Black's Law Dictionary (11th ed. 2019).

Lisa and Laura know that an unwilling participant will rarely settle during a mediation, and so before setting up the mediation, they confer to ensure that both the bank and the class are open to mediation and willing to fully engage and participate in the process.[57] The lawyers next turn to selecting the mediator. At a minimum, the mediator should be qualified, competent, and have experience handling class action banking mediations, and the parties should closely inquire about the mediator's style to ensure that it will be conducive to the parties' needs.[58] After agreeing on a mediator, each party must diligently prepare for the mediation. The mediator will likely request briefs from the parties to familiarize themselves with the case. Under the Uniform Mediation Act, these briefs are designated a privileged communication not subject to discovery and are inadmissible evidence, though state law may vary.[59]

Preparing for mediation is a joint effort between a client and their attorney. The attorney should determine what the client's goals are in settling the dispute, and the attorney should advise the client about the strength and weaknesses of their position.[60] Lisa and Bob need to go into the mediation with a bottom-line settlement figure, just as Laura and the bank should go into the mediation with a maximum settlement authority amount.[61] With diligent preparation, mediation can be a powerful tool to help the parties resolve their disputes.[62]

C. Class Action Settlement

Lisa and Laura have finally reached a settlement agreement. Unlike settlement in a typical civil case where the parties' settlement agreement is a new

57. *See* Gail M. Valentine-Rutledge, *Mediation as a Trial Alternative: Effective Use of the ADR Rules*, 57 Am. Jur. Trials 555 § 17 (Originally published 1995) (a party unwilling to make concessions or who has unreasonable expectations will lead to an unsuccessful mediation).

58. *See* Robert M. Smith, *Alternative Dispute Resolution for Banks and Other Financial Institutions*, 46 Am. Jur. Trials 231 § 26 (Originally published 1993).

59. *See* Unif. Mediation Act § 2(2) (Unif. Law Comm'n, amended 2003).

60. *See* Robert M. Smith, *Alternative Dispute Resolution for Banks and Other Financial Institutions*, 46 Am. Jur. Trials 231§ 30 (Originally published 1993).

61. *See id.* (setting a bottom-line position in advance).

62. *See* Advanced Bodycare Sols., LLC v. Thione Int'l, Inc., 524 F.3d 1235, 1240 (11th Cir. 2008) ("Simply stated, mediation does not resolve a dispute, it merely helps the parties to do so.").

contract and the plaintiff dismisses their case with prejudice under Rule 41(a), settlement in a class action is carefully supervised and reviewed by the court. This makes sense because the class members who are the beneficiaries of the settlement agreement, and who are thereby bound by its terms, are not actually involved in the negotiations. Accordingly, the class members need to be given notice and an opportunity to object.

Lisa and Laura begin drafting the settlement agreement. In the agreement, they include all the usual terms of settlement, along with draft notice forms. These notice forms are sent to the class after a court preliminarily approves the proposed settlement.[63] In her culminating act as class counsel, Lisa must prove to the court that the proposed settlement is fair, adequate, and reasonable.[64] Lisa knows that her conduct will be scrutinized by the court "to ensure that the settlement resulted from an arm's-length, good faith negotiation between experienced and skilled litigators."[65] Because the settlement was reached after class certification, the court will not apply a higher standard of fairness.[66] Lisa knows that the court cannot modify the settlement agreement, so she must ensure that every provision therein will gain the court's approval.[67]

At the fairness hearing, Lisa describes to the court that she has already been litigating the case for two years, and recovery by any means other than settlement would require many more years of litigation.[68] She also described to the court the bank's various defenses to the class claims, the merits of those defenses, and the risk of little to no class recovery if the bank were successful on them. A particularly irksome issue for Lisa throughout the litigation is that approximately three-fourths of the bank's overdraft fee revenues were generated from only 7 percent of its customers,

---

63. At this point, the court is simply looking to see whether there are any glaring omissions with the settlement or whether it appears to be the product of uninformed or collusive negotiations. *See* Rhodes v. Olson Ass'n, P.C., 308 F.R.D. 664, 666 (D. Colo. 2015).

64. *See* Fed. R. Civ. P. 23(e)(2).

65. *See* Charron v. Wiener, 731 F.3d 241, 247 (2d Cir. 2013)

66. *See* Roes, 1-2 v. SFBSC Mgmt., LLC, 944 F.3d 1035, 1043 (9th Cir. 2019) (reviewing court must apply an even higher level of scrutiny to detect evidence of collusion of other conflicts of interest when a settlement is proposed prior to class certification).

67. *See* Klier v. Elf Atochem North America, Inc., 658 F.3d 468, 475 (5th Cir. 2011). While the court cannot redline the settlement agreement, it can advise the parties that it will not approve the settlement unless certain provisions are modified.

68. *See* Reed v. Gen. Motors Corp., 703 F.2d 170, 172 (5th Cir. 1983) (recognizing that the very purpose of a class action settlement is to avoid the delay and expense of trial).

who overdrafted six or more times a month.[69] The bank has asserted the voluntary payment doctrine, which provides that unless there is fraud or duress, money voluntarily paid under a claim of right cannot be recovered on the ground that the claim was illegal.[70] The bank argues that the customers who overdrafted more than six times in a month had actual or constructive knowledge of the bank's practice of calculating insufficient funds from using the available balance.[71] If she were to lose on this point, the value of the class claim would fall over 70 percent—thus jeopardizing the federal court's ability to exercise subject matter jurisdiction under the CAFA.[72]

Lisa rebuts this contention by explaining to the court that the value of the settlement to the class members does not just lie in the compensation they will receive. In the proposed settlement, the bank has agreed to stop calculating the availability of funds from the available balance. Accordingly, the class members who continue to be customers of the bank will see a reduced number of overdraft fees in the future. Lisa retained an expert to estimate the value of this relief, which is projected to be a savings of over $100 million over the next ten years.

Much to Lisa's delight, the court granted final approval of the settlement. After many months and countless hours of work, the class action she brought on behalf of Bob and similarly situated bank customers results in an outcome acceptable to both the bank and its customers.

69. *See* Schulte v. Fifth Third Bank, 805 F. Supp. 2d 560, 582 (N.D. Ill. 2011).

70. *See* Spivey v. Adaptive Mktg. LLC, 622 F.3d 816, 822 (7th Cir. 2010).

71. *See Schulte*, 805 F. Supp. 2d at 582.

72. *See id.*

Index

D

E

F

L

M

N

O